Exchange Rate Policy and Modelling in India

Exchange Rate Policy and Modelling in India

PAMI DUA
RAJIV RANJAN

OXFORD
UNIVERSITY PRESS

OXFORD
UNIVERSITY PRESS

Oxford University Press is a department of the University of Oxford.
It furthers the University's objective of excellence in research, scholarship,
and education by publishing worldwide. Oxford is a registered trademark of
Oxford University Press in the UK and in certain other countries

Published in India by
Oxford University Press
YMCA Library Building, 1 Jai Singh Road, New Delhi 110001, India

ISBN-13: 978-0-19-807720-6
ISBN-10: 0-19-807720-3

Typeset in 10.5/13 Minion Pro
by Excellent Laser Typesetters, Pitampura, Delhi 110 034

Contents

Tables and Figures

FIGURES

BOXES

Foreword

I am delighted to have the opportunity to write a foreword to this book for several reasons. I have professional regard and personal respect for Professor Pami Dua and Dr Rajiv Ranjan. Professor Dua has been associated with the Reserve Bank of India (RBI) where I was Deputy Governor, and later Governor, for several years. Her association was in connection with studies under the Development Research Group series, and we benefited from the valuable research. Dr Rajiv Ranjan has been working closely with me, and has assisted me in preparing several speeches, and accompanied me for lectures in Basel, Zurich, Geneva, and New York on a range of subjects.

The book displays a unique combination of strong scholarship and deep insights into policies. Such a holistic view is of particular relevance to countries like India, which are undergoing significant structural transformation. The subject matter of the book, namely, exchange rate is of great contemporary interest, especially in the light of the experience with the global financial crisis. Currently, there is a substantial rethinking on a range of macroeconomic policies, and the issues of exchange rate regimes, and policies are being viewed in the context of emphasis on the policy goals relating to financial stability. The book is thus timely and could help better informed debate on the subject of vital policy significance.

I hope that the book will contribute to removing some misunderstandings and misconceptions on the subject in India. For example, some academics mistakenly describe the exchange rate regime as fixed or pegged to the US dollar. Some of them wrongly hold that the objective of managing capital account is to arrest any appreciation of rupee. There is a psychological fixation with the US dollar among both market-players and academics, whenever assessments of movements in the value of rupee are made. The popular impression is that exchange rate is of primary concern to exporters, while in reality, with liberalization of trade the exchange rate has an impact on a large part of domestic industry. Further, while financial analysts consider almost exclusively balance sheet effects, sentiments, market noises, and global liquidity conditions, macro-economists tend to look significantly at domestic economy, its fundamentals and impact on trends in balance of payments, growth, and inflation. It is heartening to note that many of these biases and wrong notions are on the decline and a book like this should expedite the process of improved understanding and informed debate in India.

This book is, in many ways, a comprehensive account of a journey of India's public policy from managing crisis due to scarcity to building strengths and, resolving dilemmas of plenty in foreign exchange. The journey is marked by some exciting moments, many of which could not be, by their very nature, captured fully in the narration in the book. Yes, there were moments of high drama and tough political sensitivities even as cumbersome details had to be mastered, and judgements made on how burdens of adjustments had to be shared among several sections of population through crisis-management, global uncertainties, and domestic reforms.

When the Gulf crisis struck in 1990–1, decisive steps had to be taken for severe import-compression and use of gold held with the government, and some gold which was part of reserves with the Reserve Bank of India. No restructuring or roll-over of debt was even seriously discussed. Depreciation, in two quick steps, introduction of dual exchange rate followed by a single rate and convertibility on current account were certainly not gradual or incremental steps. Where decisive actions had to be taken on the issues relating to exchange rate, there was no hesitation, contrary to general impression of excessive caution, while gradualism was adopted as befitting progress in reform in other sectors.

Academic and policy studies globally have started appreciating the significance of India's unique policy framework in the external sector that served us very well. In fact, the policies adopted by India in the two decades since the Gulf crisis which were outliers when they were initiated, have become mainstream after the experience with two crises—Asian and Global. The parameters for managing capital account, effective direct and indirect intervention in forex markets to moderate excess volatility, building adequate forex reserves, and managing impossible trinity are some of the original contributions of Governors, Dr C. Rangarajan and Dr Bimal Jalan. I hope the economists recognize the lasting value of their thoughts and actions which lie behind the detailed presentations in this book. At the same time, India may be currently missing a full understanding of developments in the global economy and, in particular, in the recent thinking on macroeconomic policies. In fact, the book's value lies in taking an overall and not a narrow view of the exchange rate policies and analysing exchange rate policies in the context of broader economic policies. It tries to draw on the experience with regard to exchange rate policies in the context of the global financial crisis. While in many studies, there is often a tendency to focus on the relationship between the exchange rate in the economy through current account transactions of the balance of payments, the book rightly stresses the importance of capital flows in the context of exchange rate policies. The book also makes heroic, but worthwhile, attempts at modelling and forecasting of exchange rates. In brief, here is a grand story on India's exchange rate policies over two decades that I have been personally associated with, in some capacity or the other, and I find the narration informative, comprehensive, objective, well-researched, and above all, stimulating.

DR Y.V. REDDY
Former Governor,
Reserve Bank of India

Acknowledgements

This book is an expanded version of the study undertaken under the aegis of the Reserve Bank of India. The authors are thankful to the Reserve Bank of India for allowing the study to be published in book form. Of course, several new chapters have been added to bring it to its present form. We gratefully acknowledge and appreciate invaluable help and support received from the Development Research Group team in completing the study with the Reserve Bank of India.

The authors also gratefully acknowledge insightful inputs and suggestions from Sangita Misra, Harendra Behera, Binod B. Bhoi, Vijay Raina, Somnath Sharma, and Arvind Jha of the Reserve Bank of India. Special thanks are also due to Ganesh Manjhi, Chhanda Mandal, and Reetika Garg for competent research assistance. The authors are also grateful to two anonymous referees for constructive suggestions and comments.

The views expressed in the book are those of the authors and do not necessarily represent those of the institutions they represent. Finally, we acknowledge that we are solely responsible for errors, if any.

Abbreviations

AD	Authorized Dealer
ADF	Augmented Dickey-Fuller
ADR	American Depository Receipt
ANN	Artificial Neural Networks
ARCH	Autoregressive Conditional Heteroskedasticity
ARIMA	Autoregressive Integrated Moving Average
AREAER	Annual Report on Exchange Arrangements and Exchange Restrictions
ASEAN	Association of Southeast Asian Nations
BIS	Bank for International Settlements
BPLR	Benchmark Prime Lending Rate
BPO	Business Process Outsourcing
BVAR	Bayesian Vector Autoregressive
CAC	Capital Account Convertibility
CAL	Capital Account Liberalization
CCIRS	Cross Currency Interest Rate Swap
CD	Certificates of Deposits
CFA	Communauté Financiére Africaine (Financial Community of Africa)
CCIL	Clearing Corporation of India Limited
CMIM	Chiang Mai Initiative Multilateralization
CRR	Cash Reserve Ratio
DF-GLS	Dickey Fuller Generalized Least Squares
ECB	External Commercial Borrowings
ECD	Exchange Control Department
EEC	European Economic Community

EEFC	Exchange Earners Foreign Currency
EFSF	European Financial Stability Facility
EME	Emerging Market Economy
EMS	European Monetary System
EMU	Economic and Monetary Union
ERM	Exchange Rate Mechanism
ESM	European Stabilization Mechanism
EU	European Union
EXIM	Export Import
FCA	Foreign Currency Assets
FCAC	Fuller Capital Account Convertibility
FCCB	Foreign Currency Convertible Bonds
FCNR	Foreign Currency Non-Resident
FDI	Foreign Direct Investment
FED	Foreign Exchange Department
FEDAI	Foreign Exchange Dealers' Association of India
FEMA	Foreign Exchange Management Act
FERA	Foreign Exchange Regulations Act
FFMC	Full Fledged Money Changers
FI	Financial Institution
FIIs	Foreign Institutional Investors
FIPB	Foreign Investment Promotion Board
FIPC	Foreign Investment Promotion Council
FSA	Financial Services Authority
FX	Foreign Exchange
GATT	General Agreement on Tariffs and Trade
GDP	Gross Domestic Product
GDR	Global Depository Receipt
HFC	Housing Finance Company
IBRD	International Bank for Reconstruction and Development
IDB	India Development Bonds
IDR	Indian Depository Receipts
IMD	India Millennium Deposit
IMF	International Monetary Fund
IOC	Indian Oil Corporation
IOF	Imposto sobre Operações Financeiras
IT	Information Technology

ITES	Information Technology-Enabled Services
KCIF	Korea Centre for International Finance
KPSS	Kwiatkowski-Phillips-Schmidt-Skin
KYC	Know-Your-Customer
LAF	Liquidity Adjustment Facility
LERMS	Liberalized Exchange Rate Management System
LIBOR	London Inter Bank Offer Rate
MAP	Mutual Assessment Process
MCX-SX	Multi Commodity Exchange—Stock Exchange
MDB	Multilateral Development Banks
MF	Mutual Fund
MMMF	Money Market Mutual Fund
MSE	Mean Square Error
MSIH	Markov Switching Intercept Heteroscedastic
MSS	Market Stabilization Scheme
NABARD	National Bank for Agriculture and Rural Development
NBFC	Non Banking Financial Company
NCD	Non-Convertible Debenture
NDF	Non Deliverable Forward
NDTL	Net Demand and Time Liabilities
NHB	National Housing Bank
NOP	Net Open Position
NRE(R)A	Non-Resident External (Rupee) Accounts
NRI	Non-Resident Indian
NR(NR)RD	Non-Resident (Non-Repatriable) Rupee Deposits
OCA	Optimum Currency Area
OCB	Overseas Corporate Body
OECD	Organization for Economic Co-operation and Development
OMC	Oil Marketing Company
OMO	Open Market Operations
OTC	Over-the-Counter
PBC	People's Bank of China
PBM	Portfolio Balance Model
PE	Private Equity
PIIGS	Portugal, Ireland, Italy, Greece, Spain
PPP	Purchasing Power Parity

RBI	Reserve Bank of India
RCA	Regional Currency Area
REER	Real Effective Exchange Rate
RIB	Resurgent India Bonds
RMDS	Reuters Market Data System
RMSE	Root Mean Square Error
RRB	Regional Rural Banks
SBI	Bank Indonesia Certificates
SDR	Special Drawing Rights
SEBI	Securities and Exchange Board of India
SLAF	Second LAF
SLR	Statutory Liquidity Ratio
SMO	Special Market Operations
TARP	Troubled Asset Relief Program
UK	United Kingdom
URR	Unremunerated Reserve Requirement
US	United States
VAR	Vector Autoregressive
WPI	Wholesale Price Index
WTO	World Trade Organization
VECM	Vector Error Correction Model

Introduction

The exchange rate is a key financial variable that affects decisions made by foreign exchange investors, exporters, importers, bankers, businesses, financial institutions, policymakers, and tourists in the developed as well as the developing world. Exchange rate fluctuations affect the value of international investment portfolios, competitiveness of exports and imports, value of international reserves, currency value of debt payments, and the cost to tourists in terms of the value of their currency. Movements in exchange rates, thus, have important implications for the economy's business cycle, trade, and capital flows, and are, therefore, crucial for understanding financial developments and changes in economic policy. Timely forecasts of exchange rates can provide valuable information to decision makers and participants in the spheres of international finance, trade, and policymaking.

The book covers four main topics: first, various facets of economic policy with respect to the exchange rate; second, the recent global financial crisis and the role of exchange rates therein; third, the pattern of capital flows and capital account liberalization; and fourth, modelling and forecasting exchange rates. Accordingly, the book analyses India's exchange rate story and discusses the structure of the foreign exchange market in India in terms of participants, instruments, and the trading platform, as also turnover in the Indian foreign exchange market and forward premium. The Indian foreign exchange market has evolved over time as a deep, liquid, and efficient market as against a highly regulated market prior to the 1990s. The market participants have become sophisticated, the range of instruments available for trading have increased, the turnover has also increased, while the bid-ask spreads have declined. This book also covers the exchange rate policy of India in the background of large capital flows. While the main focus of the book is on the exchange rate, an attempt has been made to cover several aspects that affect exchange rate behaviour. Some of these features are capital flows and capital account liberalization. A chapter on global financial crisis has also been included as the financial markets were adversely affected during the crisis. The book also attempts to develop a model for the rupee—dollar exchange rate, taking into account variables from the monetary and micro structure models as well as other variables, including intervention by the central bank. The focus is on the exchange rate of the Indian rupee vis-à-vis the US dollar, that is, the Re/$ rate. To model the exchange rate, the monetary model has been expanded to include variables that may have been important in determining exchange rate movements in India such as forward premiums, capital flows, order flows, and central bank intervention.

In Chapter 1, a description of different exchange rate regimes is given. The choice of an appropriate exchange rate regime is one of the most debated issues in international economics. There is no consensus regarding an ideal exchange rate regime. The choice of the optimal exchange rate regime varies across countries, and through time, depending upon circumstances. An optimal exchange rate system evolves over a period of time after experimenting with different regimes. Further, the optimal system may be imposed by exogenous developments such as the increased financial integration of the 1990s. Thus, the challenge confronting the policymakers is to pre-empt changes in the economic environment, and to adjust the exchange rate and other policies consistently.

This book analyses India's exchange rate story with particular focus on the policy responses during difficult times and the reforms undertaken to develop the rupee exchange market during relatively stable times. A broad description of developments on the exchange rate front, since 1993–4, is undertaken in Chapter 2. India has been operating on a managed flexible exchange rate regime from March 1993, marking the start of an era of a market determined exchange rate regime of the rupee with provision for timely intervention by the central bank.[1] India's exchange rate policy has evolved over time in line with the global situation and as a consequence of domestic developments. The year 1991–2 represents a major break in policy when India harped on reform measures following the balance of payments crisis and shifted to a market determined exchange rate system. As has been the experience with exchange rate regimes the world over, the Reserve Bank as the central bank of the country has been actively participating in the market with a view to signalling its stance and maintaining orderly conditions in the foreign exchange market. The broad principles that have guided India's exchange rate management have been periodically articulated in the various Monetary Policy statements. These include careful monitoring and management of exchange rates with flexibility, no fixed target or a pre-announced target or a band and ability to intervene, if and when necessary. Based on the preparedness of the foreign exchange market and India's position on the external front (in terms of reserves, debt, current account deficit, and so on), reform measures have been progressively undertaken to have a liberalized exchange and payments system for the current and capital account transactions and, further, to develop the foreign exchange market.

The structure of the foreign exchange market in India in terms of participants, instruments, and the trading platform, as also turnover in the Indian foreign exchange market is discussed in Chapter 3. The Indian foreign exchange market has evolved over time as a deep, liquid, and efficient market, as against a highly regulated market prior to the 1990s. The market participants have become sophisticated, the range of instruments available for trading has increased, and the turnover has also increased, while the bid-ask spreads have declined.

[1] The exchange rate regime up to 1990 was an adjustable nominal peg to a basket of currencies of major trading partners with a band. In the early 1990s, India was faced with a severe balance of payment crisis due to the significant rise in oil prices, the suspension of remittances from the Gulf region, and several other exogenous developments. Amongst the several measures taken to tide over the crisis was a devaluation of the rupee in July 1991 to maintain the competitiveness of Indian exports. This initiated the move towards greater exchange rate flexibility. After a transitional 11-month period of dual exchange rates, a market determined exchange rate was established in March 1993. The current exchange rate policy relies on the underlying demand and supply factors to determine the exchange rate with continuous monitoring and management by the central bank.

Trading volumes in the Indian foreign exchange market have grown significantly over the last few years. The daily average turnover has seen almost a 10-fold rise during the 10-year period from 1997–8 to 2007–8 from US $ 5 billion to US $ 48 billion. However, it displayed a declining trend during the crisis period 2008–9 and 2009–10.

In Chapter 4, a study of the recent global financial crisis, in terms of its genesis and manifestation, is undertaken. From the perspective of the emerging market economies (EMEs) including India, a major lesson from this crisis is that with increasing globalization of trade, finance, and labour, these economies are more closely integrated with advanced economies than ever before. Consequently, any crisis that affects a major country or group of countries in the global economy, or the financial system will have implications for EMEs as well, sooner or later, depending on the nature and magnitude of the crisis. Thus, policymakers need to enhance their capacity to pre-empt the potential of such global shocks while formulating their policies. EMEs need to carry out their own due diligence to ensure that systemic risks are monitored within their countries. Large and volatile capital inflows are considered to be one of the key contributing factors in many financial crises that have hit EMEs in the past. The recent experience of EMEs with capital flows seems to point towards the potential role for prudential measures to reduce systemic risk associated with large capital inflows. Recent experience suggests a cautious approach to the pace and scope of capital account liberalization as there is a strong linkage among capital account liberalization, domestic financial sector reform, and the design of monetary and exchange rate policy.

Liberalization of the capital account and capital flows has an important bearing on the exchange rate. In subsequent Chapters 5 and 6, these two aspects are dealt with in detail. In Chapter 5, country experience with liberalization of capital account, the Indian approach, and also the future of capital account liberalization in India is discussed. India's approach towards liberalizing the capital account has been one of gradualism, treating the liberalization as a continuous process rather than a single event. Lessons from the East Asian and other financial crises of the 1990s have brought about a marked shift in the approach towards capital account liberalization, particularly among developing countries. The opening up of the capital account in India was an integral part of the well sequenced economic reforms programme initiated in 1991. Recognizing the macroeconomic implications of volatility and possibility of reversals associated with capital inflows, as experienced by many EMEs, India has adopted a policy of managing the capital account with a preference for non-debt flows, de-emphasis on short-term debt flows, and adequate foreign exchange reserves, which has ensured the sustainability of capital flows and minimized contagion that could have arisen from financial crises elsewhere. In retrospect, this calibrated approach has paid India rich dividends. India plans to continue its gradualist approach as it enables harmonization and synchronization with reforms in other sectors of the economy.

In the recent period up to 2007–8, external sector developments in India have been marked by strong capital inflows. Capital flows to India, which were earlier mainly confined to small official concessional finance, gained momentum from the 1990s after the initiation of economic reforms. Chapter 6 discusses the exchange rate policy of India in the background of large capital flows, in terms of their magnitude, composition, and management. The impact of the recent crisis on capital flows and, also, how capital flows are managed in India are described in the chapter. The experience with managing large capital flows in recent years, prior to 2008–9, suggests that apart from allowing for some degree of appreciation in the exchange rate, the excess liquidity generated in the system due to regular intervention by the RBI was managed through a mix of instruments, namely, increase in Cash Reserve Ratio (CRR), auctions under the day-to-day Liquidity Adjustment Facility (LAF), open market operations (OMO), the Market Stabilization Scheme (MSS), building up of surplus balances of the Government with the Reserve Bank, foreign exchange swaps, relaxations with respect to capital outflows, and modulating debt creating flows, depending on the financing needs of the corporate sector. Given the availability of multiple instruments at its command, the Reserve Bank has the flexibility to use these instruments and modulate the liquidity and interest rate conditions amidst large capital flows during 2009–10. The use of specific instrument is contextual, and would depend not only on the nature and size of flows but also on domestic considerations.

Further, this book also attempts to gauge the ability of economic models to forecast exchange rates in the context of a developing country that follows a managed floating (as opposed to flexible) exchange rate regime (Chapter 7). Starting from the naïve model, this chapter examines the forecasting performance of the monetary model and various extensions of it in the vector autoregressive (VAR) and Bayesian vector autoregressive (BVAR) framework. Extensions of the monetary model considered in this book include variables such as forward premium, capital inflows, volatility of capital flows, order flows, and central bank intervention. The chapter, therefore, first examines whether the monetary model can beat a random walk. Second, it investigates if the forecasting performance of the monetary model can be improved by extending it. Third, the chapter evaluates the forecasting performance of a VAR model versus a BVAR model. Lastly, it considers if information on intervention by the central bank can improve forecast accuracy.

This book concentrates on the post-March 1993 period and provides insights into forecasting exchange rates for developing countries where the central bank intervenes periodically in the foreign exchange market. The alternative forecasting models are estimated using monthly data from July 1996[2] to December 2006 while out-of-sample forecasting performance is evaluated from January 2007 to June 2008. This book negates the finding of the seminal book by Meese and Rogoff (1983) that models, based on economic fundamentals, cannot outperform a naive random walk model.

---

[2] The starting period is based on availability of data for all series.

1

Exchange Rate Regimes

The conduct of exchange rate policy in an open economy framework has become increasingly complex, especially in the presence of increased volatility in international capital flows that has resulted from the integration of global financial markets. In the past decade, emerging market economies (EMEs) have been characterized by major features such as increased capital mobility, greater exposure to exchange rate risk, increased openness to international trade, and shift in the composition of exports from primary products towards manufactures and services. Moreover, rapid advances in telecommunication and information technology have dramatically lowered transaction costs and reaction times for market participants and have contributed to sharp increases in the volume and mobility of capital flows. Taking into account all the external factors described above, the choice of an appropriate exchange rate regime has been a challenging task.

The history of the international monetary system can be broadly divided into four regimes: (i) the Gold Standard (1870–1914), (ii) the Interwar Period and the Gold Exchange Standard (1919–39), (iii) the Bretton Woods System (1944–73), and (iv) Breakdown of the Bretton Woods system and the Flexible Exchange Rate Regime.

The exchange rate during the classical period of the Gold Standard system was fixed and domestic currency had parity with gold. Under this system, deficits were adjusted with internal deflation and surpluses were removed by internal inflation. Therefore, external disequilibrium was to be corrected by domestic inflation and unemployment. Thus, the focus was on the external balance. The system worked well with flourishing trade and finance as there was no uncertainty about exchange rate movements.

After World War I, the gold standard was abandoned. The inter-war period was characterized by chaotic conditions with respect to exchange rates. Most countries let their exchange rates to fluctuate in response to market forces. The importance shifted from external to internal balance. Trade and tariff restrictions began to expand and the British Pound Sterling lost its international status. The gold standard regained importance from 1927. For management of foreign exchange reserves, interest bearing foreign exchange securities, as an alternative to gold, were used to manage the fixed parity domestic currency with gold.

The period 1944–71 can be considered as a period of fixed exchange rates. With the creation of the Bretton Woods System in 1944, the fixed exchange rate system became an officially declared one. The Bretton Woods system sought to secure the advantages of the gold standard without its disadvantages. Thus, a compromise was sought between the polar alternatives of either freely floating or irrevocably fixed rates—an arrangement that sought to gain the advantages of both without suffering the disadvantages of either—while retaining the right to revise currency values on various occasions as circumstances warranted.

Under the Fixed Exchange Rate system, fixed parity of the US dollar with gold was US$ 35 per ounce and the domestic currency was determined against the US dollar using this parity. The outstanding features of the Bretton Woods system were an obligation for each country to adopt a monetary policy that maintained the exchange rate of its currency within a fixed range in terms of gold and the ability of the International Monetary Fund (IMF) to bridge temporary imbalances of payments. In the face of increasing financial strain, the system collapsed in 1971 after the United States unilaterally terminated convertibility of the dollar to gold. This action caused considerable financial stress in the world economy and created the unique situation whereby the US dollar became the reserve currency for the states that signed the agreement.

Since the creation of the IMF at Bretton Woods,[1] the international exchange rate regime has undergone very substantial changes which

---

[1] The United Nations Monetary and Financial Conference, commonly known as the Bretton Woods conference, was a gathering of 730 delegates from all 44

may be broken down into four main phases. The first was a phase of reconstruction and gradual reduction in inconvertibility of current account transactions under the aegis of the Marshall Plan and the European Payments Union, culminating in the return to current account convertibility by most industrial countries in 1958. The second phase corresponds to the Bretton Woods system, which was characterized by fixed, though adjustable, exchange rates, the partial removal of restrictions on capital account transactions in the industrial countries, a gold–dollar standard centred on the United States and its currency, and a periphery of developing country currencies that remained largely inconvertible. The third phase started after the collapse of Bretton Woods System in 1971. During the third phase, the US dollar remained firmly at the centre of the system. The 1980s saw the gradual emergence of a European currency area, however, coupled with increasing capital market integration, and the 1990s witnessed the progressive drawing into an increasingly globalized economy of the developing countries. The exchange rate regime in the third phase was a mixed one, with independently floating currencies of major industrial countries. At the same time, there were repeated attempts to limit exchange rate variability among various European Union countries which culminated in the Exchange Rate Mechanism (ERM) of the European Monetary System (EMS) and ultimately in the creation of the Euro. The US dollar, however, remained by far the major international currency in both goods and asset trade. For developing and (later) transition countries, a mixture of exchange rate regimes prevailed, with a growing trend toward the adoption of more flexible exchange rate arrangements. The birth of the Euro at the beginning of 1999 may mark the fourth phase in the evolution of the post war exchange rate system, a phase characterized by a high degree of capital mobility and a variety of exchange rate practices across countries.

Allied nations at the Mount Washington Hotel, situated in Bretton Woods, New Hampshire, to regulate the international monetary and financial order after the conclusion of World War II. The conference was held from 1–22 July 1944, when the agreements were signed to set up the International Bank for Reconstruction and Development (IBRD), the General Agreement on Tariffs and Trade (GATT), and the IMF.

Table 1.1 presents the four main phases of the international exchange rate regime, in context to the sacrifice each one entails from the perspective of the macroeconomic trilemma (of choice between autonomous monetary policy, free capital mobility, and fixed exchange rate regime). Obstfeld and Taylor (2004) have pointed out that the Great Depression represents a watershed, in the sense that it was a result of the imprudent primacy accorded to the gold standard (or the exchange rate constraint) over the autonomy of monetary policy. This, according to them, led to the subsequent evolution of alternative approaches to deal with the trilemma.

In recent years, fixed or pegged exchange rates have been a factor in every major emerging market financial crisis—Mexico at the end of 1994; Thailand, Indonesia, and Korea in 1997; Russia and Brazil in 1998; Argentina and Turkey in 2000; and Turkey, again, in 2001. Emerging market countries without pegged rates—including South Africa, Israel, Mexico, and Turkey in 1998—have been able to avoid such crises.

The regulatory framework for the functioning of the foreign exchange market and the operational freedom to the market participants often get influenced by the exchange rate regimes followed by the economies, thus, enunciating the need to have a glimpse of the exchange rate regimes that various countries have adopted. In an integrated environment, the experience with capital flows has had important lessons for the choice of the exchange rate regime for the EMEs.

Table 1.1   Resolving the Impossible Trinity

Era		Sacrifice		
Exchange Rate Regime	Activist Monetary Policy	Capital Mobility	Fixed Exchange Rate	Notes
Gold Standard	Most	Few	Few	Broad Consensus
Interwar period (when of gold)	Few	Several	Most	Capital controls especially in Central Europe and Latin America
Bretton Woods	Few	Most	Few	Broad consensus
Float	Few	Few	Many	Some consensus except for hard pegs (currency boards, dollarization, etc.)

Source: Obstfeld and Taylor (2004: 40).

The advocacy for corner solutions—a fixed peg, a la the currency board, without monetary policy independence or a freely floating exchange rate retaining discretionary conduct of monetary policy—is distinctly on the decline. The weight of experience seems to be clearly in favour of intermediate regimes with country specific features and no targets for the level of the exchange rate. With this background, it is important to understand different classifications of exchange rate regimes and the criteria to choose an exchange rate system suitable for a particular country.

CLASSIFICATION OF EXCHANGE RATE REGIMES

The choice of an appropriate exchange rate regime is one of the most debated issues in international economics. There is no consensus regarding an ideal exchange rate regime. The choice of the optimal exchange rate regime varies across countries and through time, depending upon circumstances. There is a tendency among countries to switch regimes after eruption of a crisis, which makes their existing regime ineffective, in ensuring economic stability and growth. Fixed versus floating is a simple approach to analyse an exchange rate regime. However, between the two poles exists a string of inter-mediate arrangements forming a continuum. Broadly, the spectrum for exchange rate arrangements can be reduced to the three central options of hard pegs, intermediate regimes, and floating exchange rate regimes, though the IMF's *Annual Report on Exchange Arrangements and Exchange Restrictions*[2] (AREAER) classifies exchange rate arrangements maintained by IMF members into eight categories: (1) Hard pegs comprising (a) Exchange arrangements with no separate legal tender; and (b) Currency board arrangements; (2) Soft pegs consisting of (a) Conventional pegged arrangements; (b) Stabilized arrangement; (c) Crawling pegs; (d) Crawl-like arrangement; (e) Pegged exchange rates within horizontal bands; and (f) Other managed arrangement; and (3) Floating regimes characterized as (a) Floating; and (b) Free

---

[2] IMF (2010). *The Annual Report on Exchange Arrangements and Exchange Restrictions* draws together information available to the IMF from a number of sources, including during official IMF staff visits to member countries. There is a separate chapter for each of the 187 countries included, and these are presented in a clear, easy-to-read tabular format.

floating. These categories are based on flexibility of the arrangement and how they operate in practice, that is, the de facto regime is
described, rather than the de jure or official description of the arrangement. The various exchange rate arrangements are described below:

Exchange Arrangements with No Separate Legal Tender

The country has legislatively surrendered sole control over domestic
monetary policy. Two types of arrangements fall under this category.
Another currency as legal tender, in which the country has adopted a
foreign currency as the sole legal tender (it may issue subsidiary units
[coins], so long as they are at par), and currency union, in which the
country is a member of a currency union with banknotes being issued
by and the exchange rate policy determined by a multinational central
bank in which the country has representation.

Currency Board Arrangements

The country has an explicit legislative commitment to exchange
domestic currency for a specified foreign currency at a specified rate,
combined with restrictions on the activities of the issuing authority
to ensure the fulfilment of the legal obligation, including a backing
requirement and restrictions on some typical central bank activities.

Conventional Pegged Arrangements

The country fixes its exchange rate to an anchor currency or basket
within margins of less than ±1 per cent. There need not be a
commitment to maintain the peg irrevocably. The peg may be formal
and explicit or de facto. In the latter case, the country must actively
maintain the peg for at least six months.

Stabilized Arrangement

The classification does not imply a policy commitment on the part
of the country authorities. Classification as stabilized arrangement
entails a spot market exchange rate that remains with a margin of 2

per cent for six months or more (with the exception of a specified number of outliers or step adjustments) and is not floating. The required margin of stability can be met either with respect to a single currency or a basket of currencies, where the anchor currency or the basket is ascertained or confirmed using statistical techniques. Classification as a stabilized arrangement requires that the statistical criteria are met and that the exchange rate remains stable as a result of official action (including structural market rigidities).

Crawling Peg

The country adjusts the exchange rate periodically or frequently in small amounts in response to changes in quantitative indicators or in order to effect a gradual devaluation or revaluation against a single currency or a basket. As in the case of a conventional peg, the exchange rate remains within a margin of less than ±1 per cent around a central rate.

Crawl-like Arrangement

The exchange rate must remain within a narrow margin of 2 per cent relative to a statistically identified trend for six months or more (with the exception of a specified number of outliers), and the exchange rate arrangement cannot be considered as floating. Usually, a minimum rate of change greater than allowed under a stabilized (peg-like) arrangement is required; however, an arrangement is considered crawl-like with an annualized rate of change of at least 1 per cent provided the exchange rate appreciates or depreciates in a sufficiently monotonic and continuous manner.

Pegged Exchange Rate within Horizontal Bands

As in the case of a conventional peg, the value of the currency is maintained within a band, but the range was at least 2 per cent (or ±1 per cent around a central rate). Countries under the ERM and ERM II are included in this category unless the country explicitly maintains narrower margins.

Other Managed Arrangement

This category is a residual one and is used when the exchange rate arrangement does not meet the criteria for any other categories. Arrangements characterized by frequent shifts in policies may fall into this category.

Floating

A floating exchange rate is largely market determined, without an ascertainable or predictable path for the rate. Foreign exchange market intervention may be either direct or indirect and serves to moderate the rate of change and prevent undue fluctuations in the exchange rate, but policies targeting a specific level of the exchange rate are incompatible with floating. Indicators for managing the rate are broadly judgmental (for example, balance of payments position, international reserves, parallel market developments). Floating arrangements may exhibit more or less exchange rate volatility, depending on the size of the shocks affecting the economy.

Free Floating

A floating exchange rate can be classified as free floating if intervention occurs only exceptionally and aims to address disorderly market conditions and if the authorities have provided information or data confirming that intervention has been limited to at most three instances in the previous six months, each lasting no more than three business days. If the information or data required are not available to the IMF staff, the arrangement is classified as floating

CHOICE OF EXCHANGE RATE REGIME: EVOLUTION

There is no consensus regarding an ideal exchange rate regime. The early literature on the choice of exchange rate regime took the view that the fixed exchange rate regime would serve better the smaller and more open economies (higher ratio of external trade to GDP). Given the sacrifice of monetary freedom, the protagonists of the fixed exchange rate regime favoured this system for two main reasons:

(i) absence of unpredictable volatility, both from the perspective of short-term and long-term

(ii) help in restraining domestic inflation pressure by pegging to a low inflation currency and providing a guide for private sector inflation expectations.

According to its supporters, the most extreme forms of fixed exchange rate regimes, known as super fixed or hard pegs, provide credibility, transparency, very low inflation, and financial stability to the economy concerned. By reducing speculation and devaluation risk, hard pegs are believed to keep the interest rates lower and more stable compared to any other alternative regime. Currency board, dollarization, and monetary union are some of the examples of super fixed exchange rate regime.

A later approach to the choice of exchange rate regime looks at the effects of the various random disturbances on the domestic economy. In this framework, the best regime is one that has a stabilizing impact on various macroeconomic indicators like output, prices, consumption, and so on. In this approach, ranking of fixed and flexible regimes depends on the nature and sources of shocks to the economy, policy-makers' preferences, and the structural characteristics of the economy. This approach was further extended to choice, not only between purely fixed exchange rate regime and fully flexible exchange rate regime but a range of possibilities in-between with varying degree of flexibility.

Friedman (1953), while making a case for flexible exchange rate argued:

> ... instability of exchange rates is a symptom of instability in the underlying economic structure. A flexible exchange rate need not be an unstable exchange rate. If it is, it is primarily because there is underlying instability in the economic conditions ....

According to Friedman, the floating system has the advantage of monetary independence, insulation from real shocks, and a less disruptive adjustment mechanism in the face of nominal rigidities than in the case of pegged exchange rates.

Mundell (1963) extended Friedman's analysis to a world of capital mobility. According to his analysis (and that of Fleming 1962), the choice between fixed and floating depended on the sources of shock, whether real or nominal, and the degree of capital mobility.

According to them, in general, a fixed exchange rate (or a greater degree of fixity) is preferable if the disturbances impinging on the economy are predominantly monetary, such as changes in demand for money and, thus, affect the general level of prices. Thus, when inflation is high, a relatively fixed exchange rate regime could be a more preferred choice. A fixed exchange rate requires that monetary policy be directed ultimately (and in case of perfect capital mobility, exclusively) to the task of defending the chosen exchange rate. On the other hand, classic arguments in favour of floating exchange rate is that it permits monetary policy to be directed instead to the need of domestic stabilization. A flexible rate (or a greater degree of flexibility) is preferable if disturbances are predominantly real, such as changes in taste or technology that affects the relative prices of domestic goods—or originate abroad (Caramazza and Aziz 1998). Advocates of flexible exchange rates argue that free markets tend to allocate resources efficiently, which leads to stability and policy independence. Again, in order to cope up with large capital inflows, greater degree of flexibility could be required to help relieve pressures and to signal the possible need of adjustments to contain an external imbalance.

International experience reveals that apart from the G-3 countries,[3] a number of medium-sized industrial countries, namely, Canada, Switzerland, Australia, New Zealand, Sweden, and the United Kingdom (UK) have also maintained floating exchange rate regimes. The main disadvantage of a free float is a tendency towards volatility that is not always due to macroeconomic fundamentals. This is especially so in emerging markets where the foreign exchange markets are relatively thin and dominated by a small number of players. In addition, financial markets may not be deep or broad enough to allow hedging at a reasonable cost.

---

[3] The G-3 is a free trade agreement between Colombia, Mexico, and Venezuela that came into effect on 1 January 1995, which created an extended market of 149 million consumers with a combined GDP of US$ 486.5 billion. The agreement states a 10 per cent tariff reduction over 10 years (starting in 1995) for the trade of goods and services among its members. The agreement is a third generation one, not limited to liberalizing trade, but includes issues such as investment, services, government purchases, regulations to fight unfair competition, and intellectual property rights.

In the last decade, there has been a general shift away from intermediate exchange rate regimes (or soft pegs) towards either an independent float or very hard pegs. This has been described as the hollowing out of the middle or the bipolar view. After the experience with the currency crises of the 1990s, a consensus seemed to be emerging among economists that corner solutions, that is, either freely floating or hard pegs, were the only viable regimes for countries with open capital markets and intermediate regimes were seen as being unsustainable. The view of corner solutions or vanishing intermediate regime was originally discussed by Eichengreen (1994). Support to this corner hypothesis has come forth from other high profile writings including Fischer (2001), Frankel (1999b), and Summers (2000). However, the Argentinean crises gave a severe jolt to the theory of hollowing of the middle. Even currency board type of arrangement of a fixed peg was found to be unviable. There are a number of difficulties associated with super fixed systems including complete loss of monetary control on the part of central bank (Edwards 2002).

In the recent period, growing dominance of intermediate regimes seriously challenged the new paradigm on two corner exchange rate regimes. Calvo and Reinhart (2000) and Levy-Yeyati and Sturzenegger (2000) have shown that many of those countries, which had declared themselves as independent floaters, in the IMF statistics were indeed heavily intervening in foreign exchange markets. Thus, in most cases floating means managed floating. Studies by the IMF and several experts also show that, by far, the most common exchange rate regime adopted by countries, including industrial countries, is not a free float. Most countries have adopted intermediate regimes of various types such as managed floats with no preannounced path and independent floats with foreign exchange intervention moderating the rate of change and preventing undue fluctuations. This has also been true of industrial countries. The proportion of countries that have an intermediate regime de facto is nearly 40 per cent. Additionally, experience has shown that both extreme regimes have their shortcomings. The preconditions for maintaining a credible hard peg have proved to be difficult to meet and some countries with independent float have experienced large depreciation raising concerns about their ability to finance foreign currency debt. As countries develop economically and institutionally, there appear to be considerable benefits to more flexible regimes (Rogoff et al. 2003). However, the Argentine and Turkish experiences provide a useful reminder that pegging the exchange rate in disinflation programme is not a magic bullet if insufficient attention is paid to accompanying fiscal and structural reforms. At the same time, Bulgaria's experience highlights that a carefully implemented exchange rate based stabilization can achieve durable disinflation.

Table 1.2   Evolution of Exchange Regimes

Type of Regime	Number of Countries							
	1996	2001	2004	2005	2006	2007	2008	2009
Hard pegs	30	47	48	48	48	23	23	23
No separate legal tender	24	40	41	41	41	10	10	10
Currency board arrangements	6	7	7	7	7	13	13	13
Soft pegs	94	58	59	61	60	82	81	65
Conventional pegged Arrangements	50	42	48	49	49	70	68	55
Pegs to single currency	36	32	40	32	44	49	56	33
Pegs to composite	14	10	8	5	5	7	7	4
Stabilized arrangement								13
Other						14	5	5
Intermediate pegs	44	16	11	12	11	12	13	10
Pegged exchange rates within horizontal bands	18	5	5	6	6	5	3	4
Crawling pegs	14	6	6	6	5	6	8	5
Crawling bands	12	5	0	0	0	1	2	1
Floating regimes	60	81	80	78	79	83	84	46
Managed floating	37	43	49	52	53	48	44	13
Independently floating	23	38	31	26	26	35	40	33

Source: IMF (2010).

The recent information from IMF's AREAER shows that most of the countries were either in floating regime or had conventional pegged arrangement during 2009. Further, the number of countries in currency board arrangements increased by almost double during last three years. Classification of exchage rate arrangements as per the recent AREAER (2010) is given in Table 1.3.

ALTERNATIVE REGIMES AND THEIR CHARACTERISTICS

Studies by IMF indicate that success or failure of an exchange rate regime depends on a number of critical factors and there is no one

Table 1.3   Exchange Rate Arrangements (Position as of 31 December 2009)

Arrangements	Total Number of Member Countries with this Feature
Hard pegs	**25**
No separate legal tender	12
Currency board arrangements	13
Soft pegs	**96**
Conventional peg	44
Stabilized arrangement	24
Crawling peg	3
Crawl-like arrangement	2
Pegged exchange rates within horizontal bands	2
Other managed arrangement	21
Floating regimes	**68**
Floating	38
Free floating	30

Source: IMF (2010).

size fits all while choosing the appropriate exchange rate regime. Some of the important factors include:

- Credibility of economic policy making in the country, aimed at building strong macroeconomic fundamentals and ensuring healthy economic governance.
- The country's trade policy and degree of financial integration.
- The country's capacity to commit convincingly to a sound fiscal and monetary policy (that is, the country's ability to have a credible nominal anchor).
- The soundness and resilience of the banking sector (that is, the capacity of banks to withstand shocks).
- Robustness of the risk management systems amongst the country's corporates and the extent of unhedged exposures.
- The size of the pass-through coefficient from depreciation to inflation (extent of increase/decrease in inflation brought about by depreciation/appreciation of local currency) and the extent of other nominal rigidities (especially in wages).

There are no clear-cut answers as to when should a country switch between regimes. Countries like Argentina resorted to a currency board in 1991 after a series of stabilization programmes had failed to curb inflation. Mexico, in 1994, and Brazil, in 1998, adopted a free float after a peg led to an overvalued currency and associated Balance of Payments crisis. After the 1997 South-East Asian crisis, Malaysia moved towards less flexibility while Korea, Indonesia, Philippines, and Thailand moved towards greater flexibility.

Independent Float

The independent float has its pros and cons. On the one hand, a flexible exchange rate can speed adjustment to changing conditions. It can also insulate the economy from temporary external shocks such as commodity price swings and changes in sentiment in the international capital market. Floating exchange rates in commodity exporting countries tend to reduce the local currency volatility of export prices. Additionally, exchange rate movements can provide an effective signal that macroeconomic policies need to change. On the other hand, a rigid link to a credible currency can anchor inflation and inflationary expectations. Additionally, with free capital flows, floating exchange rates in emerging economies can be very volatile. To reduce this risk, Asian countries have tended to combine the move towards an independent float with a substantial build-up of foreign exchange reserves. EMEs like South Africa, Brazil, and Turkey, which have floating exchange rates, have faced depreciation in exchange rates in the past, more because of external events rather than weaknesses in economic fundamentals. Floating exchange rates seem to have worked well in the case of EMEs like Chile and Mexico which could manage to control inflation in the past despite a depreciating exchange rate. In general, it seems that floating exchange rate regime works better in larger economies, perhaps because they are less open and have deeper financial markets. Based on the experiences of countries like Chile, Israel, and Mexico, the IMF has noted the following four factors (particularly relevant for emerging markets) which determined the success and failure of free float:

1. The behaviour of the pass-through coefficient
2. The behaviour of inflation (a low and decreasing inflation rate reduces the incentives to target the nominal exchange rate)
3. The response of the private sector to foreign borrowing (are private agents responding with greater or lesser caution when handling exchange rate risk?), and,

4. Whether volatility in the financial market is increasing significantly.

If the above-mentioned factors behave favourably, the central bank is likely to refrain from intervening in the foreign exchange market.

Intermediate Regime

For any small open economy, exchange rates are universally regarded as the key relative price to determining its macroeconomic configuration. However, a question as to what constitutes the appropriate or optimal exchange rate regime for developing countries and EMEs has long been in the domain of intense debates among academics and policymakers alike. The choice of the exchange rate regime is complicated because the exchange rate policy affects both external balance and internal balance in terms of macroeconomic adjustment as a stabilization instrument as well as an expenditure-switching policy instrument. In turn, as expenditure-switching policy, the exchange rate policy influences not only net external trade balances through the competitiveness of tradable goods but also the internal resource allocation between tradables and non-tradables through changes in the real exchange rates.

Some countries maintain a managed float or another type of intermediate regime, for example, Israel and, until recently, Chile and Poland. Their experience suggests that mixed systems work for a while but are costly, since quasi fiscal deficits due to sterilized intervention rise rapidly. Also, surges in capital inflows and increased financial integration often force authorities to abandon the exchange rate target to avoid higher inflation. However, experiences of South-East Asian countries such as Korea, Indonesia, Philippines, and Thailand, suggests that under some conditions (such as after a crisis, or while rebuilding the country's fundamentals, or when the country's fundamentals are not very strong, and when the preconditions for corner solution regimes are not fully satisfied) the intermediate regimes can work efficiently. In recent years, many studies have detected the growing dominance of intermediate regimes which seriously challenges the new paradigm on two corner exchange rate regimes.

Dr Bimal Jalan, former Governor, RBI, in his speech at the 14th National Assembly of Forex Association of India has strongly advocated the intermediate exchange rate regime. According to Dr Jalan, in the aftermath of various currency crises in the recent period there is a shift in this paradigm. The possibility of having a viable fixed rate mechanism, which entails loss of monetary control on the part of central bank, has been generally discarded and the dominant view, now, is that for most countries floating or flexible rates are the only sustainable way of having a less crisis-prone exchange rate regime. Dr Jalan is of the opinion that with regard to the desirable degree of flexibility in exchange rates, opinions and practices vary. According to Dr Jalan, a completely free float, without intervention, is not a favoured alternative except perhaps in respect of a few global or reserve currencies. In respect of these currencies also (say the Euro and the US dollar) concerns are expressed at the highest levels if the movement is sharp in either direction. Studies by the IMF and several experts also show that by far the most common exchange rate regime adopted by countries, including industrial countries, is not a free float. Most of the countries have adopted intermediate regimes of various types such as managed floats, with no pre-announced path, and independent floats, with foreign exchange intervention, moderating the rate of change and preventing undue fluctuations. By and large, with a few exceptions, countries have managed floats i.e. central banks intervene periodically. This has also been true of industrial countries. In the past, the US, the EU and the UK have also intervened at one time or another. Thus, irrespective of the purely theoretical position in favour of a free float, the external value of the currency continues to be a matter of concern to most countries as well as central banks. The Indian experience of ensuring development of the forex market and maintaining orderly conditions therein and escaping the contagion effect of most of the currency crises in the 1990s corroborates the success of the managed float exchange rate regime.

In a similar vein, succinct observations made by Mohan (2007) on the exchange rate regime are noteworthy:

> The experience with capital flows has important lessons for the choice of the exchange rate regime. The advocacy for corner solutions—a fixed peg a la the currency board without monetary policy independence or a freely floating exchange rate retaining discretionary conduct of monetary policy—is distinctly on the decline. The weight of

experience seems to clearly be in favour of intermediate regimes with country-specific features, no targets for the level of the exchange rate, exchange market interventions to ensure orderly rate movements, and a combination of interest rates and exchange rate interventions to fight extreme market turbulence. In general, EMEs have accumulated massive foreign exchange reserves as a circuit-breaker for situations where unidirectional expectations become self-fulfilling. It is a combination of these strategies which will guide monetary authorities through the impossible trinity of a fixed exchange rate, open capital account and an independent monetary policy.

Currency Boards and Dollarization

Currency Board is a monetary institution that only issues domestic currency that is fully backed by foreign assets. The domestic currency is convertible into a foreign anchor currency at a fixed rate and on demand. Currency boards are appropriate in countries where national currency has not performed as well in the long-term as major internationally traded currencies. Dollarization occurs when residents of a country extensively use a foreign currency alongside or instead of the domestic currency. Official dollarization occurs when the government adopts the foreign currency as a legal tender. There have been many evidences when the authorities in a small country unilaterally decide to use the currency of a larger country, usually the US dollar or the Euro, which is called dollarization. This is done mainly because there is lack of confidence in the domestic currency of these small countries. It is not merely the high degree of openness of these small economies which acts as an impetus for abandoning of local currency. More often the credibility of monetary policy making which is called into question which makes dollarization an attractive alternative to restore investor confidence. However, dollarization is not a panacea. If the initial conversion rate turns out to have been inappropriate or if the unit labour cost increases run ahead of those in the country whose currency is adopted, the economy may suffer. Again, if the loss of monetary and exchange rate policy as an instrument is not compensated by greater flexibility elsewhere and if access to foreign credit is limited, the risk of default is high. In some countries, lack of confidence in the domestic currency has led to an unofficial dollarization. Monetary control by local central banks is likely to be weaker in heavily dollarized economies. Successful macroeconomic stabilization might be expected to lead to a decline in unofficial dollarization but regaining credibility may be a protracted process as in the case of Peru.

The emerging market crises of the 1990s, viz., Mexico in 1994–5, the Asian crisis, in 1997–8, and Brazil, in 1999, forced many emerging economies to abandon soft pegs. Some countries introduced currency boards or even abandoned a national currency altogether. Some of the conditions required for a hard peg to work, as noted by the IMF, based on experiences of countries operating a currency board such as Argentina, Estonia, and Hong Kong, would include a relatively flexible labour market, a large trade sector, a large stock of foreign exchange reserves, strong financial institutions, and a robust fiscal position. These conditions were satisfied in the case of Hong Kong and, to a lesser extent, Estonia, but not in the case of Argentina.

The underlying logic of a currency board is that all the currencies are automatically guaranteed to be fully backed by a reserve currency at a fixed rate and the monetary authorities are obliged to redeem their liabilities at that rate. For this, it is important that the currency reserves are very large and foreign currency liabilities small as in the case of Hong Kong. The Argentine experience has shown that the preconditions for a successful currency board are more stringent than initially assumed. In particular, a lack of fiscal discipline and increasing foreign debt can progressively erode confidence. Wage and price flexibility is also needed to maintain external competitiveness when the anchor currency appreciates against third party currencies and to ease the adjustment in terms of trade shocks. Another risk related to operation of currency boards is complacency about currency mismatches.

Again, abandoning of the domestic currency in times of crisis (hyperinflation, default on external debt, precariously low forex reserves, etc, leading to lack of confidence in domestic currency) even in the case of a medium-sized economy is possible. This has happened in the case of El Salvador and Ecuador, and was given serious consideration for a country like Argentina.

Regional Currency Areas

The adoption of a common currency has mostly resulted from political objectives of greater cooperation and integration. The most prominent regional currency area (RCA) is the euro area. Joining an RCA means creating a regional institution, which adheres to a common monetary policy? One of the major factors in RCA is the extent of internal trade among the countries. Another factor determining the suitability of RCA is vulnerability to terms of trade shocks. Two countries, for example, USA and Canada although having a high degree of bilateral trade remain vulnerable to divergent terms of trade shifts that would affect their equilibrium exchange rates in different ways. The regional central bank should be independent, which requires that any financing of fiscal deficits must be limited. The criteria set for joining or remaining in a RCA could facilitate faster economic reforms. Regional surveillance procedures may apply peer pressure on governments to adopt needed structural policies in areas where interest groups otherwise resist changes which are generally unpalatable to them.

However, there are drawbacks associated with RCAs. There is a risk that unilaterally adopting another currency is seen as an alternative to harder but more beneficial reforms. A general risk is that countries may become complacent about the external constraints. The time necessary for a successful currency union is also likely to be underestimated (over half a century of effort in the case of EU).

There is a debate regarding which fiscal constraints are required in an RCA. Some argue that the prohibition of monetization of a deficit is the only form of fiscal discipline that is needed. However, some feel that it may not work and, in fact, a lack of fiscal discipline in any one country may harm other members. Moreover, large deficits and debt servicing burdens could put pressure on the central bank to lower interest rates and, thus, reduce the resistance to inflation.

Other rules relate to macroeconomic performance. For instance, countries are often required to meet convergence criteria as an initial qualification for joining. The ability to satisfy convergence criteria is an indication that the political commitment to RCA will be durable. Additionally, the more similar the countries' initial macroeconomic situations, the less likely are their interests to diverge subsequently.

The rules also cover inflation, which entails keeping long-term bond yields and exchange rates within specified margins.

A new common currency can either float or be fixed against a major international currency. At present the euro is the only floating regional currency issued by a supranational central bank. The advantage of a floating currency is that it allows a degree of flexibility in dealing with cyclical divergence between a RCA and the rest of the world. With floating, an alternative domestic policy anchor like inflation is required. Choosing an inflation target is better if the RCA members are at similar stages of development have well developed financial markets and have harmonized inflation indices.

If the decision is made to fix the new currency, then an anchor currency or basket of currencies must be selected. It is logical to choose a basket of currencies as it could help in stabilizing the nominal exchange rate. In practice, the choice of an anchor currency, depended in part on trade flows, has been influenced by the current dominance of the dollar in international trade, in finance, and in the pricing of commodities. One of the ways in which a regional monetary authority can maintain a fixed link is by way of governments giving it the mandate (and the reserves) to do so. The problem is that the link may be subject to speculative attacks in the presence of high capital mobility. To address this, the regional monetary authority in the eastern Caribbean operates like a currency board.

Regional Exchange Rate Arrangements

The degree of economic integration among countries has important implications for the exchange rate regime they choose. Countries that are highly integrated with each other with respect to trade and other economic and political relations, and have high labour mobility, symmetric shocks, and high income correlation are likely to constitute an optimum currency area (OCA). It is beneficial for these countries to establish regional cooperation on exchange rate policy. Small countries are better off pegging their currencies to a large neighbour's or adopt a neighbour's currency as their own because integration substantially reduces the benefits of their own monetary policy. These arrangements would reduce transaction costs and interest rates, eliminate exchange risks, and encourage further integration and growth. In countries satisfying OCA conditions, but where a regional common currency is not politically feasible, for example, in East Asia, McKinnon (1999) advises establishing efficient common monetary rules to stabilize their exchange rates to avoid competitive devaluation under a common dollar peg. There are three main approaches to regional exchange rate cooperation.

One approach is a mutual exchange rate pegging arrangement. In this arrangement, members of the group agree to limit fluctuations of their exchange rates to within agreed bands around prescribed central parities. They also agree to coordinate economic policies to react collectively when the exchange rates near the edges of the bands. The ERM of the EMS is a good example. The ERM was established in 1979 by 11 of the 12 member countries to eliminate intra-European exchange rate volatility along the lines of the Bretton Woods System. As the effective capital market integration increased in Europe, the ERM became increasingly vulnerable to speculative attacks in 1992–3, after which the bands were widened. In 1999, the system evolved into Europe's Economic and Monetary Union (EMU) with its current single currency, the Euro.

The second approach is to create a regional currency union. This is a more ambitious approach because it may involve giving up national currencies, building regional monetary institutions, and coordinating macroeconomic policy. The largest currency union is the EMU. Other examples include, Communauté Financiére Africaine Franc Zone (CFA Franc Zone), the East Caribbean dollar area, and the Common Monetary Area. The CFA franc zone consists of two separate monetary unions of sub-Saharan African countries and the Comoros. The first union includes eight members and the second group consists of six members. Both groups have their own central banks to conduct the common monetary policy for the groups. Each group maintains a separate currency, but these currencies are pegged at the same fixed rate against the French Franc (and the Euro) with financial support from the French Treasury. The East Caribbean dollar area includes eight members. The East Caribbean Central Bank conducts a common monetary policy. The common currency, the Eastern Caribbean dollar, has been pegged to the US dollar since 1976. The Common Monetary Area includes four south African countries: South Africa, Lesotho, Namibia, and Swaziland. The South African rand circulates freely in Lesotho, Namibia, and Swaziland along with their own currencies.

A third approach is common links to an outside currency or a basket of currencies as the monetary standard for the regional group. This approach avoids the need to create complex intra-regional institutions such as a central bank, but requires very close policy coordination among the members of the group. This may be an option in the longer term for Association of Southeast Asian Nations (ASEAN) and Mercosur. For these groups, a currency union does not seem to be feasible at this time because intra-regional trade links, while important, are significantly less than in Europe, and countries in these groups seem to be subject to much greater asymmetry of shocks.

FUTURE OF RESERVE CURRENCY

The US dollar has been enjoying the status of an international reserve currency for the last about 65 years by virtue of the size of the US economy, which accounts for 22 per cent of world GDP during the 2000s, so far, and the importance of the economy in international trade (its share being 13 per cent of world trade during 2000–9), the size, depth, and openness of its financial markets, the convertibility of the currency, and its ability to generate sufficient amount of high quality liabilities to meet the international assets denominated in dollars (Triffin Dilemma)[4] for which the US dollar is widely held and transacted than any other currency in the world. As a result, a comparison of share of major currencies in total identified official holdings of foreign exchange, as released by IMF, shows that the share of the US dollar, on an average, stood at 68.6 per cent in 1980, contracted to 59.0 per cent during 1990s before retrieving its position again to 66.9 per cent during 2000–7. In other words, the US dollar has been holding its ground rather stable during 1980–2008 despite a rapid growth of reserves and exports. Bulk of the foreign exchange transactions, about as high as 90 per cent, are also conducted in US dollars. Also, according to IMF (2008a), the US dollar is linked to the

---

[4] Robert Triffin (1961) indicated that in order to meet the global demand for an adequate amount of US dollar, USA must run persistent current account deficits. Otherwise, there would be shortage of liquidity and the global economy would contract.

exchange rates of as many as 66 countries among its 186 members as against 27 countries to the Euro. Further, recently Goldberg and Tille (2008) examined 23 advanced and emerging economies in Asia and Europe and found that these economies settled a greater proportion of their trade in dollars than their trade with USA. The divergence was particularly stark for emerging Asia, where trade with USA accounted for only 20 per cent of their trade and yet a bulk of their total trade was settled in dollars. All these show the pre-eminence of the US dollar as the international reserve currency.

Under these circumstances, it is natural that the international reserve currency country runs the risk of persisting with an unsustainable current account deficit over a longer period without any short-term punitive consequences that may also cause global imbalances. In fact, the US dollar appreciated at the height of the crises in USA reflecting a flight to quality to dollar assets only. However, eventually when the global imbalances unwind, it could have disastrous consequences. As a result, countries with major currencies, for example, US dollar, Euro, Yen, and Pound Sterling would have to be more responsible for their economic policies in the future as their policies have far reaching negative externalities for other countries. However, the more important issue here is that global imbalances and international reserve currency are most likely more intertwined than generally perceived. Hence, similar imbalances, as we have just experienced, are also likely to arise in the future unless we take appropriate action.

On a different plane, China has already started engaging itself actively to promote its own currency, instead of the US dollar, for denomination of both its exports and imports and trade finance. This is reflected from the fact that the People's Bank of China (PBC) has signed bilateral currency swap arrangements with six other central banks totalling Yuan 650 billion between December 2008 and March 2009. Under a swap arrangement, a central bank can inject the swapped amount in a foreign currency (in the present instance, Yuan) into its domestic financial system, which would be borrowed by domestic commercial entities to pay for imports from the other country (that is, China). This would effectively avoid exchange rate risks, reduce the cost of fund transfer, and more importantly, while other central banks will not lose foreign exchange reserves as payments would be in Yuan that has been received under swap, China can also avoid accumulating US dollars as payments would be received in domestic currency. Arvind Subramanian (2011) in his latest book has highlighted that the rise of renminbi is conditionally imminent in the next 10 years or soon thereafter.

With respect to the proposal of replacing the US dollar by Special Drawing Rights (SDR) as the international reserve currency, it may be mentioned that SDR has only limited use as a reserve asset and its main function is to serve as the unit of accounting by the IMF and some other international organizations. The SDR is neither a currency, nor a claim on the IMF. Rather, it is a potential claim on the freely usable currencies of IMF members. Holders of SDRs can obtain these currencies in exchange for their SDRs in two ways: first, through the arrangement of voluntary exchanges between members and, second, from the IMF's designated members with strong external positions who would purchase SDRs from members with weak external positions.

The SDR could not become the reserve currency in the international monetary system for the following reasons: First, the fixed exchange rate system for which the SDR was developed changed to a floating rate regime shortly after the introduction of the SDR. This, combined with the internationalization of capital markets, reduced the need for a central reserve asset like the SDR and helps explain why so few SDRs have been allocated. Second, the SDR is not a market-based asset. It has always been administratively controlled by the IMF in almost every respect, from its valuation and yield to who may hold it and what it may be used for. These restrictions, along with the development of new financial instruments in the markets themselves, help explain why the use of the SDR has not developed in private markets.

On the whole, the global crisis resurrected deep-rooted concerns about the functioning of the international monetary system. The system has the inherent weaknesses of a setup with a dominant country-issued reserve currency, wherein the reserve issuer runs fiscal and external deficits to meet growing world demand for reserve assets and where there is no ready mechanism forcing surplus or reserve-issuing countries to adjust. The problem has amplified in recent years, in line with a sharp rise in the demand for reserves, reflecting in part the emerging markets' tendency to self-insure against costly capital account crises. It is suggested that on the demand side, alternative insurance arrangements that could mitigate the precautionary demand for reserves could be a part of the reform. On the supply side, a menu of alternative reserve assets that could offer sustained stability and efficiency must be given a consideration. These suggestions would require fundamental changes in the forms and degree of international cooperation.

INDIA'S EXCHANGE RATE REGIME

Since March 1993, the exchange rate in India is largely determined by demand and supply conditions in the market. The exchange rate policy in recent years has been guided by the broad principles of careful monitoring and management of exchange rates with flexibility, without a fixed target, or a preannounced target, or a band, while allowing the underlying demand and supply conditions to determine the exchange rate movements over a period, in an orderly way. Subject to this predominant objective, the exchange rate policy is guided by the need to reduce excess volatility, prevent the emergence of destabilizing speculative activities, help maintain adequate level of reserves, and develop an orderly foreign exchange market. It is pertinent to note that the classification of the exchange rate regimes done by IMF is based on the country's de facto regimes, which differ from their officially announced arrangements. The scheme ranks exchange rate arrangements on the basis of their degree of flexibility and the existence of formal or informal commitments to the exchange rate path. Under this classification, India's exchange rate regime is classified as managed float with no predetermined path for the exchange rate.

The reason why intervention by most central banks in forex markets has become necessary from time to time is primarily because of two reasons. A fundamental change that has taken place in recent years is the importance of capital flows in determining exchange rate movements as against trade deficits and economic growth, which were important in the earlier days. The latter do matter, but only over a period of time. Capital flows, on the other hand, have become the primary determinants of exchange rate movements on a day-to-day basis. Secondly, unlike trade flows, capital flows in gross terms which affect exchange rate can be several times higher than net flows on any day. The conduct of monetary policy and management in the context of large and volatile capital flows has proved to be difficult for many countries. As India liberalized its capital account in a carefully sequenced manner, since the 1990s, it too has been faced with similar problems. In general, the EMEs are facing the dilemma of grappling with the inherently increasing capital flows relative to domestic absorptive capacity. A freely floating exchange rate is argued to engender the independence of monetary policy.

In many developing countries, despite existence of significant inflation differentials, there is persistent pressure for exchange rate appreciation. This is due to the fact that positive forward prospects of the economic growth lead to higher capital inflows, which put upward pressure on the exchange rate and, in turn, create expectations for further exchange rate appreciation. Therefore, though, in the normal course, exchange rate movements should correct the capital flows, however, this has not been observed in the recent past. On similar lines, in India, the prevailing higher interest rate along with higher growth rate have created lower risk perception and given rise to arbitrage opportunities, which has attracted higher capital inflows. The absorption of capital flows is confined to the current account deficit, which at present is prevailing at a low level. Given this, large capital inflows are a stress on the real economy through pressures on exchange rate appreciation and sterilization. This not only adversely affects the exporters but also affects the profitability of the corporates through pressure on domestic prices, unless the productivity goes up commensurately. Since there are limits to sterilization, the capital account management becomes important.

* * *

The optimal exchange rate system is not an option but rather a decision determined by the failure of previous systems to deliver stability and sustained growth. Further, the optimal system may be imposed by exogenous developments such as the increased financial integration of the 1990s. Thus, the challenge confronting the policymakers is to pre-empt changes in the economic environment and to adjust the exchange rate and other policies consistently. Based on the experiences of various countries, consistency across policies is considered more important than the exchange rate system per se.

An NBER paper by Calvo and Mishkin (June 2003) titled 'A Mirage of Exchange Rate Regimes for Emerging Market Countries' argues that much of the debate on choosing an exchange rate regime misses the boat. The paper concludes that the choice of an exchange rate regime is likely to be of second order importance to the development of good fiscal, financial, and monetary institutions in producing macroeconomic success in emerging market countries. This suggests that less attention should be focused on the general question whether a floating or a fixed exchange rate is preferable, and more on these deeper institutional arrangements. A focus on institutional reforms rather than on the exchange rate regime may encourage emerging market countries to be healthier and less prone to crises than we have seen in recent years. It is because of the deeper institutional changes brought about by the EMEs in the wake of various EME currency crises of the 1990s, the present global economic crisis did not have a crippling impact on the most of the EMEs, including India, unlike many developed countries which faced significant stress on their economies. It is quite pertinent to note the views expressed by Jaffery A. Frankel that no single currency regime is best for all countries and that, even for a given country, it may be that no single currency regime is best for all time.

On the question of the appropriate exchange rate regime, a fixed exchange rate regime (even with a Currency Board) is clearly out of favour. The Brazilian and Argentinean crises, after the Asian crisis, came as a rude shock. Even strong Currency Board type arrangements of a fixed peg vis-à-vis the dollar were found to be unviable. Soon after the Asian crisis, the widely accepted theoretical position was that a country had the choice of either giving up monetary independence and setting up a Currency Board, or giving up the stable currency objective and letting the exchange rate float freely so that monetary policy could then be directed to the objectives of inflation control. There is a shift in this paradigm. The possibility of having a viable fixed rate mechanism has been generally discarded and the dominant view now is that for most countries floating or flexible rates are the only sustainable way of having a less crisis prone exchange rate regime.

Studies by the IMF and several experts show that by far, the most common exchange rate regime adopted by countries, including industrial countries, is not a free float. Most of the countries have adopted intermediate regimes of various types such as managed floats with no pre-announced path and independent floats with foreign exchange intervention moderating the rate of change and preventing undue fluctuations. By and large, barring a few, countries have managed floats and central banks intervene periodically. This has also been true of industrial countries. In the past, the US, the EU, and the UK have also intervened at one time or another. Thus, irrespective of the pure theoretical position in favour of a free float, the external value of the currency continues to be a matter of concern to most countries and most central banks.

2

Exchange Rate and Exchange Rate Policy

The external sector reform process in India has been carried forward by taking into account the width and depth of the market, the regulatory regime, capability of market participants to cope with changing regulations, and ease of administering thereof. India stands considerably integrated with the rest of the world today in terms of major openness indicators. Against this backdrop, the following section analyses, in retrospect, India's exchange rate story with particular focus on the policy responses during difficult times and the reforms undertaken to develop the rupee exchange market, during relatively stable times.

CHRONOLOGY OF REFORM MEASURES

History Prior to 1991

In the post-independence period, India's exchange rate policy has seen a shift from a par value system to a basket-peg and further to a managed float exchange rate system. During the period 1947 till 1971, India followed the par value system of exchange rate, whereby the Rupee's external par value was fixed at 4.15 grains of fine gold. The RBI maintained the par value of the rupee within the permitted margin of ±1% using the Pound Sterling as the intervention currency. Since the sterling–dollar exchange rate was kept stable by US Fed, the exchange rates of the rupee in terms of gold as well as the dollar and other currencies were indirectly kept stable. The devaluation of the rupee in September 1949 and June 1966, in terms of gold, resulted in the reduction of the par value of rupee in terms of gold to 2.88 and

1.83 grains of fine gold, respectively. Since 1966, the exchange rate of the Rupee remained constant till 1971 (Figure 2.1). The exchange control measures in this fixed exchange rate regime were guided by the Foreign Exchange Regulation Act that was initially enacted in 1947 and placed on a permanent basis in 1957. Based on the provisions of the Act, the Reserve Bank of India (RBI), and in certain cases the central government, controlled and regulated the dealing in foreign exchange payments outside India, export and import of currency notes and bullion, transfers of securities between residents and non-residents, acquisition of foreign securities, etc.[1]

With the breakdown of the Bretton Woods System in 1971 and the floatation of major currencies, the conduct of the exchange rate policy posed a great challenge to central banks as currency fluctuations opened up tremendous opportunities for market players to trade in currency volatilities in a borderless market. In December 1971, the rupee was linked with the Pound Sterling. Sterling being fixed in terms of US dollar under the Smithsonian Agreement of 1971, the rupee also remained stable against the dollar. In order to overcome the weaknesses associated with a single currency peg and to ensure stability of the exchange rate, the rupee, with effect from September 1975, was pegged to a basket of currencies. The currencies included in the basket as well as their relative weights were kept confidential by the RBI to discourage speculation.

Trading in the foreign exchange market began in 1978, when banks in India were allowed by the RBI to undertake intra-day trading in foreign exchange and were required to comply with the stipulation of maintaining 'square' or 'near square' positions only at close of business hours each day, unlike all times as previously. During this period, the exchange rate of rupee was officially determined by the RBI in terms of the weighted basket of currencies of India's major trading partners and the exchange rate regime was characterized by daily announcement, by the RBI, of its buying and selling rates to Authorized Dealers (ADs), for undertaking merchant transactions. The spread between the buying and selling rates was 0.5 per cent and the market began to trade actively within this range. As opportunities to make profits

---

[1] The Act was later replaced by a more comprehensive legislation, that is, the Foreign Exchange Regulation Act, 1973.

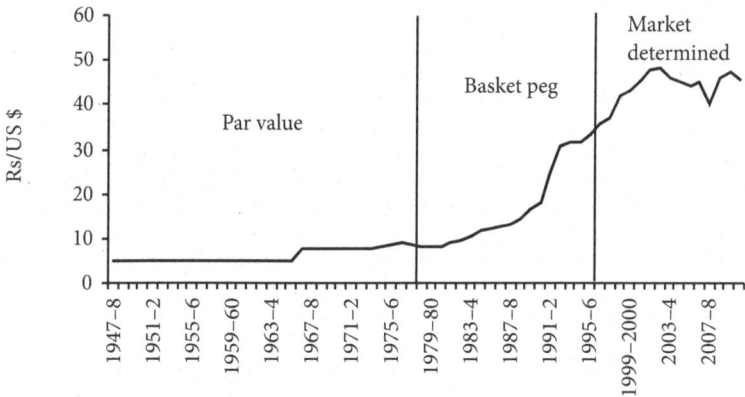

Figure 2.1   History of Rupee–Dollar Exchange Rate
Source: Reserve Bank of India.

began to emerge, trading volumes began to increase. For all practical purposes, however, the foreign exchange market in India till the early 1990s remained highly regulated with restrictions on external transactions, barriers to entry, low liquidity, and high transaction costs. The exchange rate during this period was managed mainly for facilitating India's imports. The strict control on foreign exchange reserves through the Foreign Exchange Regulations Act (FERA) had the dubious distinction of creating one of the largest and most efficient parallel markets for foreign exchange in the world, that is, the *hawala* (unofficial) market.

By the late 1980s and the early 1990s, it was recognized that both macroeconomic policy and structural factors had contributed to the balance of payment difficulties. Devaluations by India's competitors had aggravated the misalignment. The weaknesses in the external sector were accentuated by the Gulf crisis of 1990. The current account deficit widened to 3.2 per cent of GDP in 1990–1 and the foreign currency assets depleted to less than a billion dollars by July 1991. It was against this backdrop that India embarked on stabilization and structural reforms to generate impulses for growth.

Reform and Development Period: 1991–2 till Date

This phase was marked by wide ranging reform measures aimed at widening and deepening the foreign exchange markets and

Table 2.1   Chronology of the Indian Exchange Rate

Year	The Foreign Exchange Market and Exchange Rate
1947–71	Par Value system of exchange rate. Rupee's external par value was fixed in terms of gold with the Pound Sterling as the intervention currency.
1971	Breakdown of the Bretton Woods system and floatation of major currencies. Rupee was linked to the Pound Sterling in December 1971.
1975	To ensure stability of the Rupee, and avoid the weaknesses associated with a single currency peg, the Rupee was pegged to a basket of currencies. Currency selection and weight assignment was left to the discretion of the RBI and not publicly announced.
1978	RBI allowed the domestic banks to undertake intra-day trading in foreign exchange.
1978–92	Banks began to start quoting a two-way price against the Rupee as well as in other currencies. As trading volumes increased, the 'Guidelines for Internal Control over Foreign Exchange Business' were framed in 1981. The foreign exchange market was still highly regulated with several restrictions on external transactions, entry barriers, and transactions costs. Foreign exchange transactions were controlled through FERA. These restrictions resulted in an extremely efficient unofficial parallel (*hawala*) market for foreign exchange.
1990–1	Balance of Payments crisis.
July 1991	To stabilize the foreign exchange market, a two step downward exchange rate adjustment was done (9 per cent and 11 per cent). This was a decisive end to the pegged exchange rate regime.
March 1992	To ease the transition to a market determined exchange rate system, the Liberalized Exchange Rate Management System (LERMS) was put in place, which used a dual exchange rate system. This was mostly a transitional system.
March 1993	The dual rates converged, and the market determined exchange rate regime was introduced. All foreign exchange receipts could now be converted at market determined exchange rates.

Source: Reserve Bank of India.

liberalization of exchange control regimes. The immediate issue at hand was to address the Balance of Payments crisis of 1991. A conscious decision was taken to honour all debt without seeking rescheduling and several steps were taken to tide over the crisis:

(i)   a part of gold reserves was sent abroad to get some immediate liquidity

(ii)   non-essential imports were tightened by a variety of price based and quantitative measures

(iii)   the IMF, multilateral and bilateral donors were approached

(iv)   a macroeconomic stabilization programme was put in place

(v) India Development Bonds (IDBs) were floated in October 1991 to mobilize medium-term funds from non-resident Indians which yielded US$ 1.6 billion

(vi) credible commitments were made to bring about structural reforms.

The Report of the High Level Committee on Balance of Payments (Chairman Dr C. Rangarajan) laid the framework for a credible macroeconomic stabilization programme encompassing trade, industry, foreign investment, exchange rate, and foreign exchange reserves. With regard to the exchange rate policy, the committee recommended that consideration be given to:

(i) a realistic exchange rate

(ii) avoiding use of exchange mechanisms for subsidization

(iii) maintaining adequate reserve levels to take care of short-term fluctuations

(iv) continuing the process of liberalization on the current account

(v) reinforcing effective control over capital transactions.

The key to the maintenance of a realistic and a stable exchange rate is containing inflation through macroeconomic policies and ensuring net capital receipts of the scale assumed in Balance of Payments projections.

The initiation of economic reforms saw, among other measures, a two-step downward exchange rate adjustment by 9 per cent and 11 per cent, between 1 to 3 July 1991, to counter the massive drawdown in the foreign exchange reserves, to instil confidence in the investors and to improve domestic competitiveness. The two-step adjustment of July 1991 effectively brought to a close the period of the pegged exchange rate. Following the recommendations of the Rangarajan Committee to move towards the market determined exchange rate, LERMS was put in place in March 1992, involving a dual exchange rate system in the interim period. The LERMS was essentially a transitional mechanism and a downward adjustment in the official exchange rate took place in early December 1992 and ultimate convergence of the dual rates was made effective from 1 March 1993, leading to the introduction of a market determined exchange rate regime. Under the LERMS, all foreign exchange receipts on current account transactions (exports, remittances, etc.) were required to be surrendered to the ADs in full.

The rate of exchange for conversion of 60 per cent of the proceeds of these transactions was the market rate quoted by the ADs while the remaining 40 per cent of the proceeds were converted at the RBI's official rate. The ADs in turn were required to surrender to the RBI 40 per cent of their purchase of foreign currencies representing current receipts at the official rate of exchange announced by the RBI. They were free to retain the balance 60 per cent of foreign exchange for being sold in the free market for permissible transactions.

The dual exchange rate system was replaced by unified exchange rate system in March 1993. It was stipulated that all foreign exchange receipts could be converted at market determined exchange rates. The restrictions on a number of other current account transactions were relaxed. The unification of the exchange rate of the Indian rupee was an important step towards current account convertibility. The RBI, in conjunction with the Government, also gradually implemented wide ranging reform measures with an objective to remove market distortions and deepen the foreign exchange market. The experience with the market determined exchange rate system in India, since 1993, is generally described as 'satisfactory' as orderliness prevailed in the Indian market during most of the period. Episodes of volatility were effectively managed through timely monetary and administrative measures. A phase wise analysis of the post reform period is set out below.

EXCHANGE RATE—EPISODIC EVIDENCES

First Phase of Stability: March 1993 to July 1995

On unification of the exchange rates in 1993, the nominal exchange rate of the rupee against both the US dollar as also against a basket of currencies got adjusted to a lower level, which nullified the impact of all previous inflation differentials. The Real Effective Exchange Rate (REER) of the rupee in the months following the unification represented an equilibrium situation and this was also borne out by the fact that the current account was almost in balance in 1993–4. Exchange rate policy in the post-unification period was aimed at providing a stable environment by giving boost to exports and foreign investment in line with the envisaged premises of the structural and stabilization programme. This period is also marked by the setting up of the Sodhani Committee (1994) which, in its report submitted in May 1995, made several recommendations aimed at relaxing the regulations with a view to vitalizing the foreign exchange market. With the liberalization in the capital account, mainly in the area of foreign direct investment and portfolio investments, there was a surge in capital inflows during the financial years 1993–4 and 1994–5. The large inflows exerted appreciating pressure on the rupee. In order to obviate any nominal appreciation of the rupee which would erode export competitiveness, the RBI purchased a portion of such inflows and augmented the reserves; the foreign currency assets of the RBI rose from US$ 6.4 billion, in March 1993, to US$ 20.8 billion, in March 1995, representing over seven months of import cover. As a result, the exchange rate of the rupee reflected a prolonged period of stability and remained stable at Rs 31.37 per US dollar from March 1993 to July 1995. During this period, the sterilization operations were on a lower scale, resulting in somewhat larger growth in monetary aggregates. In other words, the focus of exchange rate policy in 1993–4 was on preserving the external competitiveness at a time when the economy was undergoing a structural transformation. The building up of the reserves was also a consideration as the crisis of 1991 was at the back of the mind of the policymakers.

First Phase of Volatility: August 1995 to March 1996

The prolonged stability in the exchange rate during 1993–5 witnessed some stress starting from the third quarter of calendar year 1995 in the wake of unfounded expectations about the external payments situation. Slowing down of capital inflows in the wake of the Mexican crisis, a moderate widening of the current account deficit on resurgence of activities in the real sector, and the rise of US dollar against other major currencies, after a bearish phase, were the main factors contributing to this phenomenon. The downward pressure on the rupee initially got intensified in October 1995 (exchange rate fell to Rs 35.65 per US dollar) and further in the first week of February 1996 (rupee touched record low of Rs 37.95 per US dollar). During this period, unidirectional expectations of a free fall of rupee reinforced normal leads and lags in external receipts and payments, vitiating orderly market activity. A panic demand for cover by importers and cancellations of forward contracts by exporters created persistent mismatches of demand and supply in both the spot and forward segments of the market. Forward premia rose sharply from 4 per cent in September 1995 to more than 10 per cent in October 1995, and further to around 20 per cent in February 1996. Furthermore, the bid-offer spread widened to about 20 paise with the spread being as wide as 85 paise on certain days, depicting tremendous buying pressure in the face of meagre supply. To eliminate the inconsistency of the RBI buying rate, it stopped publishing its quote on the Reuter screen with effect from 4 October 2005, offering only a buying quote to banks on specific request.

The RBI, in response, intervened in the market to signal that the fundamentals were in place, and to ensure that market correction of the overvalued exchange rate was orderly and calibrated. The tool was, however, sharpened to cover not only spot but also swap and forward market segments. Further, it was decided to keep a watch over the day-to-day merchant demands of the largest bank which alone handled about 50 per cent of the import payments. As the main buying requirement of this largest bank was in respect of a single public sector undertaking in the oil sector, a system was put in place to obtain information about the latter's daily requirement. Market intelligence and information gathering were strengthened and the RBI started obtaining direct price quotes from leading foreign exchange broking firms. Two basic approaches on intervention were adopted. On days when there was information about large all round demand, an aggressive stance was taken with intensive selling in larger lots till the rate was brought down decisively. On other occasions, continual sale of small/moderate amounts was to be effected to prevent unduly large intra-day variations. The first approach aimed at absorbing excess market demand, while the latter was aimed at curbing the 'ratchet effect'.[2] The size of the individual intervention deals was usually in the range of US$ 1–2 million, although larger size deals not exceeding US$ 5 million were resorted to, occasionally.

---

[2] The 'ratchet effect' means that in a bearish market situation, if the rate falls even due to situational factors it does not recover easily on reversal of those factors.

Direct intervention was supplemented by administrative measures announced in October 1995 and later in February 1996 (Annexure 1). All these measures enabled a strong recovery of the rupee in March–April 1996. Forward premia also declined in April 1996 as stability prevailed in the spot market and domestic interest rates began to ease. Although the RBI had intervened actively in the markets since October 1995, and the transactions did have an impact on the exchange rate and domestic liquidity situation, the net sales in the foreign exchange market between October 1995 and June 1996 broadly evened out and as such the intervention helped in smoothening the volatility rather than propping up the exchange rate. Further, while intervention initially impinged on domestic liquidity quite sharply, the overall impact remained broadly balanced with a small net injection of liquidity. Thus, the 1995–6 experience of volatility showed that while intervention signals the policy stance, the 'testing' of the commitment to the stated policy by the market could be best addressed by supportive measures as unveiled during October 1995 and February 1996.

This period also saw the implementation of some major policy initiatives aimed at further liberalizing the exchange control measures.

- The ceiling of Rs 15 crore on the aggregate overnight open position to be maintained by ADs was removed from January 1996 and ADs were given the freedom to fix their own foreign exchange overnight open position limits, subject to approval from the RBI.
- NRIs were permitted to invest funds on a non-repatriation basis in the Money Market Mutual Funds (MMMFs) floated with prior authorization from RBI/SEBI (February 1996).
- The RBI appointed a special committee to process all applications involving Indian direct investment abroad beyond US$ 4 million or those not qualifying for fast track clearance (September 1995).
- The RBI commenced functioning as a single window agency for receipt and disposal of proposals for overseas investments by Indian corporates, effective from December 1995. A reporting system for the same was also prescribed.
- The RBI set up a Market Intelligence Cell to study and closely monitor the developments in the Indian Foreign exchange market (October 1995).

Second Phase of Stability: April 1996 to mid-August 1997

The foreign exchange market witnessed remarkable stability during the period April 1996 to mid-August 1997. During this period, the spot exchange rate remained in the range of Rs 35.50–36.00 per US dollar. The stability in the spot rate was reflected in the forward premia (six month) as well, which remained range-bound within 6 to 9 per cent during the financial year 1996–7 and declined further during the first five months of the financial year 1997–8 within a range of 3 to 6 per cent following easy liquidity conditions. From the second quarter of calendar year 1996 onwards, capital flows were also restored and the loss of reserves was recouped within a short period of time.

In continuance of the reform process, this period marks the first formal move towards capital account liberalization whereby a committee on Capital Account Convertibility was appointed by the RBI on 28 February 1997, that submitted its report in May 1997. The Committee recommended a phased liberalization of controls on outflows and inflows over a three year period. The Committee also laid down three crucial preconditions in terms of fiscal consolidation, a mandated inflation target, and strengthening of the financial sector for moving towards capital account convertibility. Also, with a view to moving progressively towards capital account convertibility, the Union Budget for 1997–8 proposed introduction of a bill in 1997–8 to pass as an Act called the Foreign Exchange Management Act (FEMA) to replace FERA. Accordingly, the RBI drafted a new legislation FEMA that was consistent with full current account convertibility and the objective of progressive liberalization on the capital account.

Besides, this period also saw the implementation of some important foreign exchange market policy measures: setting up of Foreign exchange market Technical Advisory Committee (April 1996), Reconstitution of the Foreign Investment Promotion Board (FIPB), and proposal to set up Foreign Investment Promotion Council (FIPC) to promote FDI in India (July 1996), permission to ADs to offer a variety of hedging products, for example, interest rate swaps, currency swaps, forward rate agreements to their clients without prior approval of the RBI or the Government of India (August 1996), permission to FIIs to invest in GoI dated securities (March 1997), ADs permitted to offer forward contracts on the basis of past performance, and declaration of exposure (April 1997) and relaxation in External Commercial Borrowings (ECB) guidelines.

Second Phase of Instability—mid-August 1997 to August 1998

The year 1997–8 and the first quarter of 1998–9 posed severe challenges to exchange rate management due to the contagion effect of the South-East Asian currency crisis and other domestic factors. There were two periods of significant volatility in the Indian foreign exchange market: Phase I, from mid-August 1997 to January 1998, and Phase II, May 1998 till August 1998. Response to these episodes included intervention in both spot and forward segments of the foreign exchange market and adoption of stringent monetary and administrative measures, which were rolled back immediately on attainment of stability.

Phase I

Despite strong fundamentals, the rupee weakened in the last week of August, partly as a result of spillover effects of currency turbulence in South-East Asian markets. With inter-bank spot purchases (excluding sales by the RBI) exceeding inter-bank sales by a significant margin, the RBI sold foreign exchange worth US$ 978 million in September. In the forward market, excess demand conditions started emerging from August as importers rushed for cover to hedge large exposures which had remained uncovered in the earlier period[3] and exporters cancelled forward contracts. As the premia spurted (Table 2.2) reflecting both demand and supply mismatches and a hardening of the domestic interest rates, the RBI sold foreign exchange in the forward market as well and as a result its outstanding forward liabilities rose by US$ 904 million in September 1997.

In October 1997, the RBI allowed banks to invest and borrow abroad up to 15 per cent of their unimpaired Tier I capital, which led

---

[3] During late 1996 and early 1997, anticipation of stability, in general, and even appreciation of rupee in some quarters had led many market participants to keep their oversold or short positions unhedged and substitute some domestic debt by foreign currency borrowings to take advantage of interest arbitrage. In the wake of developments in South-East Asia and market perceptions of exchange rate policy, there was a rush to cover unhedged positions by the market participants.

Table 2.2 Forward Premia—Monthly Average (Per Cent Per Annum)

Month/Year	1-month	3-month	6-month
1997			
March	6.02	6.72	6.87
April	3.17	4.74	5.49
May	3.11	4.11	4.77
June	2.57	3.47	4.23
July	2.70	3.13	·3.63
August	5.07	5.19	5.50
September	6.90	6.82	6.63
October	4.23	5.08	5.52
November	6.51	6.90	6.89
December	9.42	9.22	8.60
1998			
January	21.05	15.82	12.79
February	12.70	15.85	14.57
March	8.81	9.10	9.58
April	3.67	5.31	6.91
May	6.49	7.37	8.20
June	9.59	10.23	10.10

Source: Reserve Bank of India.

to the resumption of capital flows and increase in volumes in the foreign exchange market, particularly in the outright forward and swap segments. This allowed the RBI to undertake both spot and outright forward purchases and liquidate its forward liabilities.

Thereafter, however, there was persistent excess demand and considerable volatility in the foreign exchange market. Market sentiment weakened sharply from November 1997 onwards in reaction to intensification of the crisis in South-East Asia, bearishness in domestic stock exchanges, and uncertainty. Between November 1997 and January 1998, the exchange rate of the Indian rupee depreciated by around 9 per cent. The RBI undertook wide ranging and steep monetary and administrative measures on 16 January 1998 in order to curb speculative tendencies among the market players and restore orderly conditions in the foreign exchange market (Annexure 1). As a result of the monetary measures of 16 January 1998, the stability in the foreign exchange market returned and, more importantly, the expectations of the market participants about further depreciation in the exchange rate of rupee were reversed. The monetary policy measures were successful because they had the impact of making forward premia prohibitively high and generating supply in the market, which further reinforced two-way expectations. The volatility in the market, as measured by month-wise coefficient of variation, reduced from 1.26 in January 1998 to 0.49 in February 1998 and further to 0.08 in March 1998. The exchange rate of the rupee vs the dollar which had depreciated to Rs 40.36/$ as on 16 January 1998 appreciated to Rs 39.50/$ on 31 March 1998. The six month forward premia which reached a peak of around 20 per cent in January 1998 came down to 7 per cent by the end of March 1998.

As normalcy returned in the foreign exchange market, the easing of monetary measures continued. The interest rate on fixed rate 'repos' (now 'reverse repo') was reduced to 7 per cent as on 2 April 1998 and further to 6 per cent on 29 April 1998. On 29 April 1998, the export refinance limit was also increased from 50 per cent to 100 per cent of the incremental export credit eligible for refinance. The Cash Reserve Ratio (CRR) and Bank Rate were also reduced to earlier levels. While it is generally accepted that India could escape the 1997 crisis unscathed, it needs to be recognized that this has been made possible due to the proactive policy responses taken by the RBI. The RBI acted swiftly to curb speculative activities and change market expectations. Direct intervention followed by administrative measures were undertaken initially but when the volatility continued and sentiment remained unchanged, monetary measures were undertaken to reverse unidirectional expectations.

Phase II

Management of the external sector continued to be a major challenge even in the post-Asian crisis period, particularly during May to June 1998 due to escalation of South- East Asian crisis, bearish domestic stock exchanges, uncertainties created by internal developments, and the strengthening of US dollar against major currencies, particularly the yen. Furthermore, during this phase, India was confronted with certain other developments like economic sanctions imposed by several industrial countries, suspension of fresh multilateral lending (except for certain specified sectors), downgrading of the country rating by international rating agencies, and reduction in investment by Foreign Institutional Investors (FIIs). As a result of these developments, the foreign exchange market again witnessed increased pressure during May–June 1998. The exchange rate of the rupee which was Rs 39.73 per US dollar at the end of April 1998, depreciated to Rs 42.92 per US dollar on 23 June 1998.

The RBI announced a package of policy measures on 11 June 1998 to contain the volatility in foreign exchange market (Figure 2.2).

These included:

(a)   announcement of the Reserve Bank's readiness to sell foreign exchange in the market to meet any mismatch between demand and supply

(b)   allowing FIIs to manage their exchange risk exposure by undertaking foreign exchange cover on their incremental equity investment with effect from June 12, 1998

(c)   advising importers as well as banks to monitor their credit utilization so as to meet genuine foreign exchange demand and discourage undue build-up of inventory

(d)   allowing domestic financial institutions, with the RBI's approval, to buy back their own debt paper or other Indian papers from international markets

(e)   allowing banks/ADs, acting on behalf of the FIIs, to approach RBI for direct purchase of foreign exchange, and

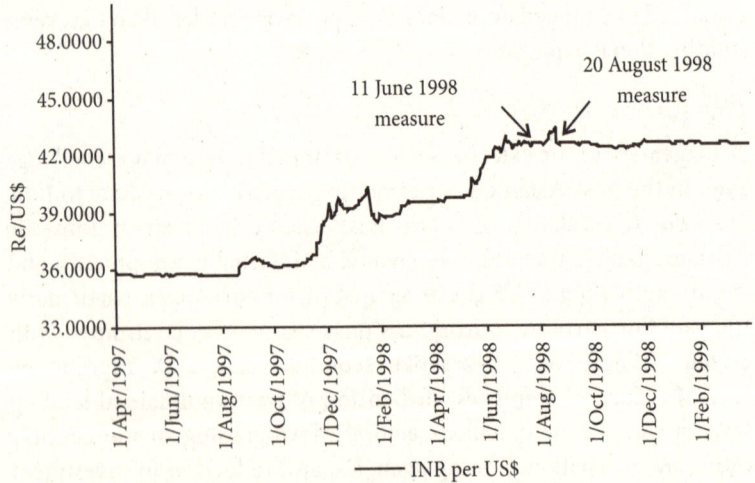

Figure 2.2   Movement in Exchange Rate
Source: Reserve Bank of India.

(f)   advising banks to charge a spread of not more than 1.5 per-
        centage points above LIBOR (London Inter Bank Offer Rate)
        on export credit in foreign currency as against the earlier
        norm of not exceeding 2–2.5 percentage points.

Responding to these policy measures, the foreign exchange market
returned to normalcy for some time but again came under stress in
August 1998.

With the deepening of the Russian financial turmoil and the fear
of the devaluation of Chinese Renminbi influencing the foreign
exchange market, there appeared excess demand pressures in August
1998 in the spot segment of the foreign exchange market. The Rupee
registered its lowest level of Rs 43.42 per US dollar on 19 August 1998.
Responding to these developments, the RBI announced a fresh package of measures on 20 August 1998 in order to prevent speculative
sentiments to build up pressure on the orderly functioning of the
market. These measures included:

(a)   a hike in the CRR from 10.0 per cent to 11.0 per cent
(b)   an increase in the repo rate from 5 per cent to 8 per cent
(c)   enhancement of forward cover facilities to FIIs
(d)   withdrawal of facility of rebooking the cancelled contracts
        for imports and splitting forward and spot legs for a commit-
        ment, and,
(e)   allowing flexibility in the use of Exchange Earners Foreign
        Currency (EEFC) accounts while restricting the extension of
        time limit for repatriation of export proceeds due to excep-
        tional circumstances.

A distinguishing aspect of the foreign exchange market interventions during the 1997–8 volatility episode was that instead of doing
the transactions directly with ADs, few select public sector banks were
chosen as intermediaries for this purpose. Under this arrangement,
public sector banks would undertake deals in the inter-bank market
at the direction of the RBI, for which it would provide cover at the
end of the business hours of each day. It was ensured that the public
sector banks' own inter-bank operations were kept separate from
the transactions undertaken on behalf of the RBI. Periodic on site
scrutiny of the records and arrangements of these banks by the RBI
was instituted to check any malpractice or deficiency in this regard.
The main reason for adopting an indirect intervention strategy in

preference to a direct one was that this arrangement would provide a cover for RBI's operations and reduce its visibility and, hence, would be more effective. However, the fact that RBI was intervening in the market through a few other public sector banks was not disclosed, though in due course of time it was known to the market. Besides, as a measure of abundant precaution and also to send a signal internationally regarding the intrinsic strength of the economy, India floated the Resurgent India Bonds (RIBs) in August 1998 and managed to raise US$ 4.2 billion through the scheme.

In retrospect, one could say that India was successful in containing the contagion effect of the Asian crisis due to swift policy responses to manage the crisis and a favourable macroeconomic situation. During the period of crisis, India had a low current account deficit, comfortable foreign exchange reserves amounting to an import cover of over seven months, a market-determined exchange rate, low level of short-term debt, and absence of asset price inflation or a credit boom. These positive features were the result of prudent policies pursued over the years, notably the cap on external commercial borrowings with restrictions on end-use, low exposure of banks to real estate and the stock market, insulation from large intermediation of overseas capital by the banking sector, close monitoring of off-balance sheet items, and tight legislative, regulatory, and prudential control over non-bank entities. Sound capital controls also helped in insulating the economy from contagion effect of the East Asian crisis. The ultimate result could be seen in terms of the volatility in the exchange rate of the Indian rupee which remained low during second half of the 1990s, when most of the Asian currencies witnessed high level of volatility (Table 2.3).

Phase of Relative Stability with Intermittent Event-related Volatility (September 1998–March 2003)

The measures announced by the RBI coupled with the success of the RIB issue changed the market sentiment and restored orderly conditions in the foreign exchange market. The rupee remained generally stable during September 1998 to May 1999 with the exchange rate varying in the range of Rs 42.20 to Rs 4290 per US dollar. This was also the period when the European Union countries adopted the Euro as

Table 2.3   Daily Exchange Rate Volatility for a Few Emerging Economies

(Annualized; in per cent)

Currency	1993–5	1996–2000	2001	2003	2004	2005	2006
Indian Rupee	7.5	4.3	1.6	2.1	4.7	3.5	4.0
South Korean Won	2.6	22.2	8.1	8.3	6.5	6.8	6.9
South African Rand	5.3	11.4	20.2	20.9	21.4	15.4	16.0
Turkish New Lira	29.3	5.4	63.1	16.2	12.2	10.4	16.6
Indonesian Rupiah	2.1	43.4	21.7	6.8	7.7	9.1	8.9
Thai Baht	1.7	18.3	4.9	4.4	4.3	4.7	6.2
New Taiwan Dollar	3.7	5.3	3.6	2.7	4.9	4.9	4.9
Singapore Dollar	3.7	7.4	4.5	4.5	4.6	4.4	3.9
Philippine Peso	6.8	12.9	17.6	4.1	3.1	4.1	4.6

Source: Reserve Bank of India.

their single currency. Consequently, the RBI also started monitoring movement of Rupee vis-à-vis Euro in addition to the dollar.

The rupee came under slight pressure during June–October 1999 due to the nervousness in the markets, induced by the heightened tension on the border, resulting in the RBI's intervention in the foreign exchange market. In order to reduce the temporary demand–supply mismatches, on 23 August 1999, the RBI indicated its readiness to meet fully/partly foreign exchange requirements on account of crude oil imports and debt service payments of the Government. In the period from November 1999 till March 2000, the rupee traded in a narrow band around Rs 43.50 per US dollar. Recovery in exports coupled with sustained portfolio inflows provided support to the exchange rate.

The period since April 2000 till March 2003 generally remained stable with intermittent periods of volatility associated with certain international developments. Sharp increase in international crude oil prices, cross-currency movements of the US dollar vis-à-vis other major international currencies, and reduced portfolio flows on account of successive interest rate increases in industrial countries during the first quarter of 2000–1 resulted in depreciation of the exchange rate to below Rs 44.00 per US dollar in May 2000 and further to below Rs 45.00 per US dollar during July 2000. In order to reduce uncertainty in the foreign exchange market, the RBI responded promptly with policy actions (Annexure 3). Besides, the introduction of the liquidity adjustment facility (LAF) effective from 5 June 2000 allowed the RBI an additional lever for influencing the short term liquidity conditions. Financing through India Millennium Deposits (IMDs) was resorted to as a pre-emptive step in the face of hardening of world petroleum prices and the consequent possible depletion of India's foreign exchange reserves.

Orderly conditions prevailed in the foreign exchange market for more than a year, from August 2000 till about early September 2001. The nervous sentiment of the foreign exchange market in the aftermath of 11 September 2001 terrorist attack in the US resulted in substantial rupee depreciation during 11–20 September 2001. Along with market sales, the RBI responded through a package of measures and liquidity operations during 15–25 September 2001. These measures included:

(a)   a reiteration by the RBI to keeping interest rates stable with adequate liquidity;

(b)   assurance to sell foreign exchange to meet any unusual supply–demand gap;

(c)   opening a purchase window for select Government securities on an auction basis;

(d)   relaxation in FII investment limits up to the sectoral cap/ statutory ceiling;

(e)   a special financial package for large value exports of six select products; and,

(f)   reduction in interest rates on export credit by one percentage point.

The exchange rate again came under some pressure following the attack on Indian Parliament on 13 December 2001. These twin pressures on the market resulted in the Rupee falling below Rs 48 per US dollar mark during this period. Tightness prevailed in the foreign exchange market for a short spell during April–May 2002 in view of tensions in Gujarat, rising crude oil prices, and border tension. The Rupee touched Rs 49 per US dollar in May 2002, the lowest exchange rate ever. During rest of the financial year 2002–3, the Rupee/Dollar exchange rate showed signs of firming up in view of the large foreign inflows into the economy.

This period was also marked by reform measures aimed at developing the institutional framework for effective functioning of the foreign exchange market in India. With a view to facilitating external payments in a liberalized regime, the new legislation FEMA was passed, which came into effect from 1 June 2000. The FEMA, which replaced the FERA, reflected a shift in policy emphasis: from conservation to management of foreign exchange consistent with the orderly evolution of trade and payments and the foreign exchange markets; from a 'citizenship' basis to a 'residency' basis in the conduct of foreign exchange transactions; and from criminal procedures of enforcement to civil procedures, all under a transparent framework promoting accountability. The RBI also set up the Clearing Corporation of India Limited (CCIL) in 2001. The CCIL, by providing for guaranteed settlement of transactions, is instrumental in lowering risks in Indian financial markets. CCIL commenced settlement of foreign exchange operations for inter-bank Rupee–Dollar spot and forward trades from 12 November 2002 onwards.

Period with Huge Capital Flows: 2003–4 to 2007–8

The Indian foreign exchange market had witnessed a massive surge in capital inflows since 2003–4. With excess supply conditions prevailing, the Rupee generally exhibited an appreciating trend against the US dollar during this period. The RBI had resorted to sterilization operations to tackle the large inflows. Faced with the finite stock of the Government of India securities with RBI, Market Stabilization Scheme (MSS) was introduced in April 2004, wherein Government of India Dated Securities/Treasury Bills were issued to absorb liquidity. Large scale purchases by the RBI to absorb excess supplies in the foreign exchange market resulted in large accumulation of foreign exchange reserves since end-March 2002. In addition, a number of other policy initiatives were periodically taken to offset the expansionary impact of external flows on the domestic money supply.

There were a few instances when the Rupee came under pressure associated mainly with FII outflows, global oil prices, and behaviour of the dollar in international markets. During the financial year 2004–5, the Rupee was under pressure from mid-May onwards when the excess supply situation changed because of the turbulence in equity markets on account of political uncertainty, leading to outflows by FIIs and rising global oil prices. On 17 May 2004, when the stock market exhibited a record fall, the RBI, in order to avoid any spillover to other market segments, for example, money, government and forex market, released two separate press releases indicating the constitution of an Internal Task Force to monitor the developments in financial markets and its willingness to provide liquidity. These announcements managed to restore orderly conditions in the market on that day. The rupee continued to remain under pressure almost till August 2004 during which period it depreciated by 4.3 per cent against the US dollar. The RBI made net market sales of US$ 2.7 billion during this period. The pressure on the rupee started easing from September 2004 onwards with the revival in FII flows, step-up in trade credits, and ECBs by importers. Remittances from exporters and heavy FII inflows continued to provide strength to the Rupee against the US dollar in the following months.

During 2005–6, orderly conditions generally prevailed in the foreign exchange market.[4] Pressure had built up on the Rupee from end-August 2005 under the impact of oil prices, sharp increase in the current account deficit, and strong US dollar. The exchange rate moved to Rs 46.33 per US dollar on 8 December 2005. With the revival of FII inflows and weakening of the US dollar in the international markets, the Rupee strengthened sharply beginning with the second half of December 2005, notwithstanding the IMD redemptions. Sales of US$ 6.5 billion during December 2005 on account of redemption of IMDs were recouped by purchases of US$ 10.8 billion during February–March 2006.

During 2006–7, the rupee initially depreciated against the US dollar reaching Rs 46.97 on 19 July 2006, reflecting higher crude oil prices and FII outflows. The rupee, however, strengthened thereafter on the back of moderation in crude oil prices, large capital inflows, and weakness of the US dollar in the international markets to reach Rs 43.14 per US dollar on 28 March 2007. The trend of rupee appreciation continued during 2007–8 in view of continuance of large capital inflows, fed rate cut, weakening of US dollar vis-à-vis other major currencies, and strong performance of the domestic economy. The RBI made net market purchases of foreign exchange of US$ 26.8 billion during

---

[4] The rupee witnessed some appreciation following the revaluation of the Chinese renminbi on 21 July 2005. The Rupee reached Rs 43.56 per US dollar on 18 August 2005.

2006–7 and US$ 78.2 billion during 2007–8. During January 2008, the RBI made net market purchases of US$ 13.62 billion, the highest purchase during any month in the current decade. Consequently, the foreign exchange reserves rose substantially to cross US$ 300 billion by end-March 2008. Since March 2008, however, there were some depreciation pressures on the rupee-dollar exchange rate in view of rising global oil prices and domestic inflationary pressures. The RBI, which had sold dollars last in December 2005, sold about US$ 1.5 billion during March 2008, after a gap of almost 27 months (though on a net basis, RBI made purchases). India's exchange rate is largely determined by domestic factors as reflected in the weak correlation between cross-country currency returns (Table 2.4). However, movement of the rupee vs the dollar is influenced to a limited extent by the movement in Euro and Pound Sterling.

Table 2.4   Cross Currency Correlations of Selected Economies (November 2006 to January 2008)

Currency	EURO	GBP	JPY	CHF	HKD	INR	SGD	MYR	PHP
EURO	1.00								
GBP	0.64	1.00							
JPY	−0.04	0.16	1.00						
CHF	−0.69	−0.30	0.37	1.00					
HKD	−0.07	0.00	0.12	0.14	1.00				
INR	−0.26	−0.26	−0.14	0.19	−0.03	1.00			
SGD	−0.65	−0.51	−0.07	0.44	0.10	0.24	1.00		
MYR	0.01	0.02	−0.05	−0.04	0.00	0.02	−0.03	1.00	
PHP	0.01	0.01	−0.06	−0.04	−0.01	0.03	−0.04	0.99	1.00

Source: Reserve Bank of India.

The period since 2003–4 saw a number of measures undertaken to deepen the foreign exchange market and impart flexibility to market participants, for example, residents and non-residents allowed to book forward contracts and participate in various hedging instruments for managing risks in foreign exchange market, new hedging instruments were made available, FIIs and NRIs permitted to trade in exchange traded derivative contracts subject to conditions, and so on. Besides, various liberalization measures were undertaken with a view to enhance transparency and greater dissemination of information to public. Simultaneously, procedural formalities were substantially minimized to avoid paper work and reduce compliance burden, while ensuring that Know-Your-Customer (KYC) guidelines are in place. Also, reflecting the RBI's objective of a regulatory shift from micro management of foreign exchange transactions to macro management of foreign exchange flows, the Exchange Control Department (ECD) of the RBI was renamed as the Foreign Exchange Department (FED) with effect from 31 January 2004.

The strength of India's external sector along with comfortable foreign exchange reserves provided the stage for further financial liberalization undertaken during this period: a comprehensive review of guidelines for ECBs (2004) led to significant liberalization of ECBs and capital account transactions were further liberalized guided by the Committee on Fuller Capital Account Convertibility, 2006. There was considerable debate on the exchange rate pass-through to prices during this period.

EXCHANGE RATE PASS-THROUGH TO INFLATION IN INDIA

Exchange Rate Pass-through to Inflation

An important aspect of the linkage between exchange rate changes with the domestic economy is the pass-through effect. Exchange rate pass-through can be defined as the degree of change in domestic prices due to change in exchange rates. Any movement of exchange rates is reflected as changes in import prices denominated in the domestic currency. Subsequently, the changes in the import prices find their way to producer and consumer prices. Pass-through elasticities are defined as the percentage change of domestic prices (import, producer, or consumer prices) resulting from a 1 per cent change of the exchange rate. If the response of import prices to exchange rate movements is one to one, the pass-through is said to be complete or full. If this condition is not met, then the pass-through is said to be incomplete, or partial.

Factors Affecting Exchange Rate Pass-through

Literature suggests that some of the important determinants of pass-through are:
- low global inflation and its lower volatility

- volatility of exchange rate
- share of imports in the domestic consumption
- trade to GDP ratio
- composition of imports
- Invoicing pattern of trade
- trade distortions from tariffs and quantitative restrictions.

Cross Country Experience

Literature suggests that many industrialized countries have experienced large exchange rate depreciations in more recent periods but despite that they were able to have a low inflation as exchange rate depreciations had much smaller effects on consumer prices than anticipated (Bailliu and Fujii 2004). A recent study by the European Central Bank (2007) covering 12 emerging markets in Asia, Latin America, and Central and Eastern Europe falsifies the conventional hypothesis that exchange rate pass-through to both import and consumer prices is always higher in emerging than in developed economies (Table 2.5).

Table 2.5   Accumulated Per Cent Response of Consumer Prices to 1 Per Cent Exchange Rate Shock

Country	4 Qtr Response	8 Qtr Response
China	0.08	0.77
Hong Kong	0.07	0.37
Korea	0.19	0.13
Singapore	−0.15	−0.06
Taiwan	0.01	0.01
Czech Rep.	0.61	0.77
Hungary	0.48	0.91
Poland	0.31	0.56
Turkey	0.09	0.12
Argentina	0.02	0.04
Chile	0.35	0.35
Mexico	0.76	1.39

Source: Zorzi et al. (2007).

A recent BIS study by Mihaljek and Klau (2008) provides estimates of the pass-through from exchange rate and foreign prices changes to inflation in fourteen emerging market countries for the period 1994 to mid-2006. For India, this study suggests that a 10 per cent change in its exchange rate could lead to a change in inflation up to 2 per cent.

Decline in Exchange Rate Pass-through in the Recent Period

The available literature and cross country experiences suggest that there is evidence that exchange rate pass-through to domestic inflation has tended to decline during the 1990s across a number of countries. There is also evidence that pass-through has also declined in developing countries during the 1990s and the extent of decline in these countries is estimated to be larger than that in advanced economies. There are several reasons attributed to this decline in pass-through of exchange rate. Some of the reasons are set out below:

- A key explanation for the decline in the pass-through is the increased commitment of monetary policy towards maintaining price stability. When a central bank is committed to price stability, the pass-through is lower because inflation expectations do not rise proportionally with the movement in the exchange rate. As the decade of the 1990s was one of low and stable inflation, the decline in pass-through may be correlated with this low inflation environment.
- Financial innovations such as availability of hedging products have also lowered pass-through by permitting importers to ignore temporary shocks.
- Another view suggests that the decline in the pass-through could be due to a change in the composition of imports towards sectors with low pass-through rather than a decline across all sectors.
- Available evidence for industrialized economies confirms that their import composition has shifted in favour of sectors with low pass-through such as the manufacturing sector.
- Another study suggests that the low observed pass-through might be due to disappearance of newly expensive goods from consumption and their replacement by inferior local substitutes.

- Another factor that has reduced the pass-through is related to globalization and 'Walmartisation'. The increased intensity of globalization and the commodification of many goods have, perhaps, reduced the pricing power of producers, particularly of low technology goods in developing countries, whereas the pricing power of large retailers like Wal-Mart has risen.

Exchange Rate Pass-through to Inflation in India

In RBI's *Report on Currency and Finance* of 2003–4, an analysis of exchange rate pass-through to domestic prices for the period 1976 to 2004 revealed the following results:
- A 10 per cent depreciation of the exchange rate increases whole-sale prices by 0.4 per cent. Almost 60 per cent of this pass-through takes place within one year while 80 per cent of pass-through is completed within two years of a shock to the exchange rate.   ·
- With regard to the sensitivity of inflation to exchange rate movements, it was estimated that an increase of 10 per cent in import price inflation raises domestic inflation by up to 1.1 percentage points. The effect is the minimum for consumer price index inflation (0.5 percentage points) followed by GDP deflator (0.8 percentage points) and wholesale inflation (1.1 percentage points).
- The study also estimated that exchange rate depreciation has the expected effect of raising domestic prices and the coefficient of exchange rate pass-through to domestic inflation ranges between 8–17 basis points, that is, a 10 per cent depreciation of the Indian rupee (vis-à-vis the US dollar) would, other things remaining unchanged, increase consumer inflation by less than one percentage point and the GDP deflator by 1.7 percentage points.
- The import prices in rupee terms can change on account of movements in the import prices in foreign currency or changes in exchange rate, or a combination of both. Segregating the influences of import prices in foreign currency on domestic inflation from that of the exchange rate movements could provide additional analytical insights in understanding the inflation process. The empirical results from the Report on Currency and Finance 2003–4 showed some differences between the pass-through

from import price to inflation and exchange rate movements to domestic inflation. While import prices impacted domestic inflation in the same year, the exchange rate movements seemed to affect WPI (wholesale price index) inflation with a lag of one year (two years in case of consumer price inflation).

- Another difference observed in the study was that the pass-through from exchange rates to inflation was somewhat larger than that of pass-through from import prices. In this context, it may be noted that most studies document that pass-through is high in a high-inflation environment.

- These estimates of the exchange rate pass-through are subject to a number of caveats. First, the study period has been characterized by a significant opening up of the economy. Second, the substantial decline in tariffs could have perhaps allowed domestic producers to absorb some part of the exchange rate depreciation without any effect on their profitability and non-tariff barriers could have reduced the exchange rate pass-through.

- The study notes that the estimates of pass-through would need to be evaluated on an ongoing basis, before a definitive conclusion is reached.

The above results were also confirmed with the findings of one study by Khundrakpam (2007) for the period August 1991 to March 2005. The study estimated the pass-through coefficients and found that a 10 per cent change in exchange rate leads to change in final prices by about 0.6 per cent in the short run and 0.9 per cent in the long run. The statistical tests on temporal behaviour of pass-through obtained from rolling regressions show that, unlike in the case of many countries, there was no evidence of decline in pass-through.

However, using the same methodology for the period April 1993 through June 2009, the estimated results show greater pass-through. For the extended data period, both the short-run and the long-run pass-through were found to be greater than that found in the earlier study by Khundrakpam (2007). The result shows a 10 per cent change in exchange rate increases domestic prices by 0.71 per cent in the short run and 0.99 per cent in the long run. To conclude, based on the result of several studies for India, the exchange rate pass-through to domestic prices for India is estimated to be small.

IMPACT OF GLOBAL FINANCIAL TURMOIL: 2008–9

Financial markets in India, which remained largely orderly from April 2008 to August 2008, witnessed heightened volatility from mid-September in view of concerns on deepening of the global financial crisis. Bankruptcy/sell-out/restructuring became more rampant, spreading from mortgage lending institutions to systemically important financial institutions and further to commercial banks and from the US to many European countries. Funding pressures developed in the inter-bank money market, equity markets weakened, and the rupee also came under pressure in the foreign exchange market. With a view to maintaining orderly conditions in the foreign exchange market, the RBI announced in mid-September 2008 that it would continue to sell foreign exchange (US dollars) through agent banks to augment supply in the domestic foreign exchange market or intervene directly to meet any demand–supply gaps. In the foreign exchange market, the Indian rupee generally depreciated against major currencies during 2008–9. The exchange rate of the rupee touched Rs 50.10 per dollar on 27 October 2008 as compared with Rs 39.99 per dollar at end-March 2008. The RBI scaled up its intervention operations during the month of October 2008. Despite a significant easing of crude oil prices and inflationary pressures in the second half of the year, declining exports, and continued capital outflows led by the global deleveraging process and the sustained strength of the US dollar against other major currencies, continued to exert downward pressure on the rupee. With the spot exchange rates moving in a wide range, the volatility of the exchange rates increased during this period. However, with the return of some stability in international financial markets and the relatively better growth performance of the Indian economy, there has been a revival in foreign investment flows, especially FII investments, since the beginning of 2009–10. Based on the exchange rate prevailing at the end of the financial year, the rupee appreciated by around 13 per cent in 2009–10 compared to a depreciation of 21.5 per cent in 2008–9. During the current year so far, up to 11 June 2010, the rupee depreciated by 3.6 per cent against the US dollar over end-March 2010. Though there has been some recovery in the forex turnover during 2009–10, it has not yet picked up to the pre-crisis levels.

Several measures were undertaken by the RBI to ease the forex liquidity situation. A rupee-dollar swap facility for Indian banks was introduced with effect from 7 November 2008 to give the Indian banks comfort in managing their short-term foreign funding requirements. For funding the swaps, banks were also allowed to borrow under the LAF for the corresponding tenor at the prevailing repo rate. The forex swap facility, which was originally available till 30 June 2009, was extended up to 31 March 2010; however, this was discontinued in October 2009. The RBI also continued with Special Market Operations (SMO) which were instituted in June 2008 to meet the forex requirements of public sector Oil Marketing Companies (OMCs), taking into account the then prevailing extraordinary situation in the money and foreign exchange markets. These operations were largely (Rupee) liquidity neutral. Finally, measures to ease forex liquidity also included those aimed at encouraging capital inflows, such as an upward adjustment of the interest rate ceiling on foreign currency deposits by non-resident Indians, substantially relaxing the ECB regime for corporates, and allowing non-banking financial companies and housing finance companies to access foreign borrowing.

- Interest rate ceilings on FCNR (B) and NR (E) RA deposits were increased by 175 basis points each from 16 September 2008 providing more flexibility to Indian banks to mobilize higher foreign exchange resources.
- The constraints on external commercial borrowings were eased through relaxing various conditions, viz., (i) enhancing all-in-cost ceilings for ECBs of average maturity periods of three to five years and over five years to 300 basis points above LIBOR and 500 basis points above LIBOR, respectively; subsequently, the requirement of all-in-cost ceilings under the approval route was dispensed with until December 2009; (ii) permitting ECBs up to US$ 500 million per borrower per financial year for rupee/foreign currency expenditure for permissible end-uses under the automatic route; (iii) the definition of infrastructure sector for availing ECB was expanded to include the mining, exploration and refinery sectors; (iv) payment for obtaining license/permit for 3G spectrum by telecom companies was classified as eligible end-use for the purpose of ECB; (v) dispensing with the requirement of minimum average maturity period of

seven years for ECB of more than US$ 100 million for rupee capital expenditure in the infrastructure sector; (vi) permitting borrowers to keep their ECB proceeds offshore or keep it with the overseas branches/subsidiaries of Indian banks abroad or to remit these funds to India for credit to their rupee accounts with AD category-I banks in India, pending utilisation for permissible end-uses; (vii) allowing non-banking financial companies (NBFCs) exclusively involved in financing of the infrastructure sector to avail of ECBs under the approval route from multilateral/regional financial institutions and government owned development financial institutions for on-lending to borrowers in the infrastructure sector, subject to compliance with certain conditions; and enabling housing finance companies registered with the National Housing Bank (NHB) to access ECBs subject to RBI approval and compliance to regulations laid down by NHB.

- Access to short-term trade credit was facilitated by increasing the all-in-cost ceiling to six-month LIBOR plus 200 basis points for less than three years' tenor. Furthermore, systemically important NBFCs not allowed hitherto, were permitted to raise short-term foreign borrowings.
- Interest rate ceiling on export credit in foreign currency was increased to LIBOR plus 350 basis points subject to banks not levying any other charges.
- AD category-I banks were allowed to borrow funds from their head office, overseas branches, and correspondents, and overdrafts in nostro accounts up to a limit of 50 per cent of their unimpaired Tier 1 capital as at the close of the previous quarter or US$ 10 million, whichever was higher, as against the earlier limit of 25 per cent.
- Indian companies were encouraged to prematurely buy back their Foreign Currency Convertible Bonds (FCCBs) under the approval or automatic route, at prevailing discounts rates, subject to compliance with certain stipulated conditions. Extension of FCCBs was also permitted at the current all-in-cost for the relative maturity.

The entire period since 1993, when we moved towards market determined exchange rates, reveals that as a whole the Indian rupee depreciated against the dollar. The rupee also depreciated against other major international currencies. Another important feature has been the reduction in the volatility of the Indian exchange rate during the last few years. Among all currencies worldwide, which are not on a nominal peg and certainly among all emerging market economies, the volatility of the rupee–dollar rate has remained lower.

Table 2.6 Movements of Indian Rupee 1993–4 to 2010–11

Year	Range (Rs per US$)	Average Exchange Rate (Rs per US$)	Daily Average Appreciation/ Depreciation	Coefficient of Variation (%)	Standard Deviation
1	2	3	4	5	6
1993–4	31.21–31.49	31.37	0.03	0.1	0.05
1994–5	31.37–31.97	31.40	−0.11	0.3	0.12
1995–6	31.37–37.95	33.46	−6.17	5.8	0.56
1996–7	34.14–35.96	35.52	−5.77	1.3	0.21
1997–8	35.70–40.36	37.18	−4.47	4.2	0.37
1998–9	39.48–43.42	42.13	−11.75	2.1	0.24
1999–2000	42.44–44.64	43.34	−2.79	0.7	0.10
2000–1	43.61–46.89	45.71	−5.19	2.3	0.15
2001–2	46.56–48.85	47.69	−4.15	1.4	0.13
2002–3	47.51–49.06	48.40	−1.48	0.9	0.07
2003–4	43.45–47.46	45.92	5.40	1.6	0.19
2004–5	43.36–46.46	44.95	2.17	2.3	0.31
2005–6	43.30–46.33	44.28	1.51	1.8	0.22
2006–7	43.14–46.97	45.28	−2.22	2.0	0.89
2007–8	39.26–43.15	40.24	12.53	2.1	0.83
2008–9	39.89–52.09	43.92	−12.36	7.8	3.58
2009–10	44.94–50.54	47.42	−3.16	2.8	1.34
2010–11	44.03–47.58	45.58	4.04	2.3	1.03

Source: Reserve Bank of India.

In recent years, the movement of the Indian rupee has been largely influenced by the capital flow movements rather than traditional determinants like trade flows. However, the rupee, in real terms, witnessed stability over the years despite volatility in capital flows and trade flows.

Thus, as can be observed, maintaining orderly market conditions have been the central theme of RBI's exchange rate policy. Despite several unexpected external and domestic developments, India's exchange rate performance is considered to be satisfactory. The RBI has generally reacted promptly and swiftly to exchange market pressures through a combination of monetary and regulatory measures along with direct and indirect interventions, and has preferred to withdraw from the market as soon as orderly conditions have been restored.

The various episodes of volatility of the exchange rate have been managed in a flexible and pragmatic manner. There are no set rules to handle such difficult situations. Rather, the policy responses have varied depending upon the need of the situation. The above analysis also underscores the need for central banks to keep instruments/policies in hand for use in difficult situations. An important aspect of policy response in India to the various episodes of volatility has been market intervention combined with monetary and administrative measures to meet the threats to financial stability, while complementary or parallel recourse has been taken to communications through speeches,

Table 2.7   Trend in External Value of the Indian Rupee

Year	Trade Based			
	REER	% Variation	NEER	% Variation
Base Year—1993–4				
1993–4	100.00	—	100.00	—
1994–5	104.32	4.3	98.91	–1.1
1995–6	98.19	–5.9	91.54	–7.5
1996–7	96.83	–1.4	89.27	–2.5
1997–8	100.77	4.1	92.04	3.1
1998–9	93.04	–7.7	89.05	–3.2
1999–2000	95.99	3.2	91.02	2.2
2000–1	100.09	4.3	92.12	1.2
2001–2	100.86	0.8	91.58	–0.6
2002–3	98.18	–2.7	89.12	–2.7
2003–4	99.56	1.4	87.14	–2.2
2004–5	100.09	0.5	87.31	0.2
Base Year—2004–5				
2005–6	103.1	–3.1	102.24	–2.2
2006–7	101.29	1.8	97.63	4.5
2007–8	108.52	–7.1	104.75	–7.3
2008–9	97.8	9.9	93.34	10.9
2009–10 (P)	94.74	3.1	90.94	2.6
2010–11 (P)	102.04	–7.7	93.56	–2.9

Source: Reserve Bank of India.
Notes: REER—Real Effective Exchange Rate; NEER—Nominal Effective Exchange Rate; P: Provisional

press releases (Reddy 2006). In line with the exchange rate policy, it has also been observed that the Indian rupee is moving along with the economic fundamentals in the post reform period.

Moving forward as India progresses towards a completely free capital regime and gets more and more integrated with the rest of the world, managing periods of volatility is bound to pose greater challenges in view of the impossible trinity of independent monetary policy, open capital account, and exchange rate regime. Preserving stability in the market would require more flexibility, adaptability, and innovations with regard to the strategy for liquidity management as well as exchange rate management. Also, with the likely turnover in the foreign exchange market rising in future, further development of the foreign exchange market will be crucial to manage the associated risks. Given the volatility of capital flows, it remains to be seen whether financial market development in a country like India can be such that this volatility does not result in unacceptable disruption in exchange rate determination with inevitable real and monetary sector consequences (Mohan 2007).

3

Foreign Exchange Market Structure and Turnover

Prior to the 1990s, the Indian foreign exchange market (with a pegged exchange rate regime) was highly regulated with restrictions on transactions, participants, and use of instruments. The period since the early 1990s has witnessed a wide range of regulatory and institutional reforms resulting in substantial development of the rupee exchange market. Market participants have become sophisticated and have acquired reasonable expertise in using various instruments and managing risks. The range of instruments available for trading has also increased. Against this background, this chapter discusses the structure of the foreign exchange market in India.

CURRENT RUPEE MARKET STRUCTURE

While analysing the exchange rate behaviour, it is also important to have a look at the market micro structure of the market where the Indian rupee is traded. Like any other market, trading in the rupee market involves some participants, a trading platform, and a range of instruments for trading. The current market setup is described below.

Market Segments and Players

The Indian foreign exchange market is a decentralized multiple dealership market comprising two segments, the spot and the derivatives market. In a spot transaction, currencies are traded at the prevailing rates and the settlement or value date is two business days ahead. The two-day period gives adequate time for the parties to send instructions to debit and credit the appropriate bank accounts at home and abroad. Derivatives market encompasses forwards, swaps, and options. The typical forward contract is for one month, three months, or six months, with three months being most common. Forward contracts for longer periods are not as common because they involve greater uncertainty. A swap transaction in the foreign exchange market is a combination of a spot and a forward transaction in the opposite direction. As in case of other EMEs, the spot market remains an important segment of the Indian foreign exchange market. With the Indian economy getting exposed to risks arising out of changes in exchange rates, the derivative segment of the foreign exchange market has also strengthened and the activity in this segment is gradually rising.

Players in the Indian market include:

(i)   Authorized Dealers (ADs), mostly banks who are authorized to deal in foreign exchange,[1]

(ii)   foreign exchange brokers who act as intermediaries between counterparties, matching buying and selling orders, and,

(iii)   customers, individuals and corporates, who need foreign exchange for trade and investment purposes.

Though customers are a major player in the foreign exchange market, but for all practical purposes they depend on ADs and brokers. In the spot foreign exchange market, earlier, foreign exchange transactions were dominated by brokers, but the situation has changed with evolving market conditions as now the transactions are dominated by ADs. Brokers continue to dominate the derivatives market. The RBI, like other central banks, is a market participant who uses foreign exchange to manage reserves and intervenes to ensure orderly market conditions.

---

[1] ADs have been divided into different categories: (i) All scheduled commercial banks, which include Public sector banks, private sector banks, and foreign banks operating in India belong to category I of ADs, (ii) All upgraded full fledged money changers (FFMCs), and select Regional rural banks and cooperative banks belong to category II of ADs and, (iii) Select financial institutions such as EXIM Bank belong to Category III of ADs.

The customer segment of the spot market in India essentially reflects the transactions reported in the balance of payments, both current and capital account. During the decade of the 1980s and 1990s, current account transactions such as exports, imports, invisible receipts, and payments were the major sources of supply and demand in the foreign exchange market. Over the last five years, however, the daily supply and demand in the foreign exchange market is being increasingly determined by transactions in the capital account such as foreign direct investment (FDI) to India and by India, inflows and outflows of portfolio investment, ECBs and their amortization, non-resident deposit inflows, and redemptions. It needs to be observed that in India, with the government having no foreign currency account, the external aid received by the Government comes directly to the reserves and the RBI releases the required rupee funds. Hence, this particular source of supply of foreign exchange, for example, external aid, does not go to the market and to that extent does not reflect itself in the true determination of the value of the rupee.

Related Institutional Bodies

The Foreign Exchange Dealers Association of India (FEDAI) plays a special role in the foreign exchange market as a developmental agency for smooth and speedy growth of the foreign exchange market in all its aspects. All ADs are required to become members of FEDAI and to execute an undertaking to the effect that they would abide by the terms and conditions stipulated by FEDAI for making foreign transactions. The FEDAI is also the accrediting authority for the foreign exchange brokers in the inter-bank foreign exchange market.

The Clearing Corporation of India Limited (CCIL) set up in 2001 is responsible for the settlement of trades in the Indian financial markets. It acts as a central counterparty to the trades done by its members, thereby absorbing their risk exposure from failed trades arising out of defaults by their counterparties. The CCIL has commenced settlement of foreign exchange operations for inter-bank USD/INR spot and forward trades since 8 November 2002 and for inter-bank USD/INR cash and tom trades from 5 February 2004. CCIL undertakes settlement of foreign exchange trades on a multilateral net basis through a process of innovation and all spot, cash, and tom transactions are

guaranteed for settlement from the trade date.[2] The CCIL's intermediation provides to its members benefits such as risk mitigation with
improved efficiency, lower operational cost, and easier reconciliation
of accounts with correspondents.

Hedging Instruments

The foreign exchange market in India today is equipped with several derivative instruments. Various informal forms of derivatives
contracts have existed since time immemorial though the formal
introduction of a variety of instruments in the foreign exchange
derivatives market started only in the post-reform period, especially
since the mid-1990s. These derivative instruments have been cautiously introduced as part of the reforms in a phased manner, both for
product diversity and, more importantly, as a risk management tool.
Recognizing the relatively nascent stage of the foreign exchange market then with the lack of capabilities to handle massive speculation,
the 'underlying exposure' criteria had been imposed as a prerequisite.
Exporters and importers were permitted to book forward contracts
on the basis of a declaration of exposure and past performance.

The foreign exchange derivatives products that are available today
in Indian financial markets can be grouped into three broad segments,
viz., forwards, options (foreign currency rupee options and cross currency options), and currency swaps (foreign currency rupee swaps
and cross currency swaps). Forwards and foreign exchange swaps
are relatively more popular derivatives instruments in the Indian
market. The cancellation and rebooking of forward contracts and
swaps, however, have been regulated in India with an intention that
excessive cancellation and rebooking should not add to the volatility
of the rupee. The Reserve Bank has been taking measures towards
eliminating such regulations. The use of options in India is gradually

---

[2] Every eligible foreign exchange contract, entered into between members, gets
novated or replaced by two new contracts—between CCIL and each of the two
parties, respectively. Following the multilateral netting procedure, the net amount
payable to, or receivable from, CCIL in each currency is arrived at, member-wise.
The Rupee leg is settled through the members' current accounts with the RBI
and the USD leg through CCIL's account with the Settlement Bank at New York.
CCIL sets limits for each member bank on the basis of certain parameters such as
Member's credit rating, Net Worth, Asset value, Management quality, etc.

picking up, though its volume is not much and bid-offer spreads are quite wide, indicating that the market is not very liquid yet.

In view of the experience gained by market participants in using various hedging instruments such as forward foreign exchange contracts, swaps and options, and improvements in liquidity and accounting systems relating to these instruments, a RBI-SEBI Standing Technical Committee on Exchange Traded Currency Futures was constituted to suggest a suitable framework to operationalize currency futures. Accordingly, guidelines were issued to allow resident individuals to trade currency futures in recognized stock/new exchanges. The directions permit scheduled commercial banks (AD Category–I) to become trading/clearing members of the currency derivatives segment set up by recognized stock exchanges, subject to their fulfilling certain prudential requirements. The exchange traded currency futures started trading first on the National Stock Exchange on 29 August 2008, followed by the Bombay Stock Exchange and the Multi Commodity Exchange, Stock Exchange (MCX-SX) on 1 October 2008 and 7 October 2008, respectively.

The Rupee Trading Platform

Spot trading in the Indian foreign exchange market takes place via the following platforms—FX CLEAR of the CCIL set up since August 2003, FX Direct, a foreign exchange trading platform launched by IBS Foreign exchange (P) Ltd. in 2002 in collaboration with Financial Technologies (India) Ltd., and two other platform by the Reuters, the D2 platform and the Reuters Market Data System (RMDS) trading platform. Both FX-CLEAR and FX Direct offer both real time order matching and negotiation modes for dealing. The Real Time Matching system enables real time matching of currency pairs for immediate and auto execution in both spot as well as forward instruments. It provides a real time two-way (both the participant as well as his counter party) risk management to mitigate participant counter party risk. In the Negotiated Dealing System, on the other hand, the participant is free to choose and negotiate with his counter party on all aspects of the transaction details, thereby, offering him flexibility to select the underlying currency as well as the terms of trade. These trading platforms cover the US dollar-Indian rupee (USD/INR) transactions and transactions in major cross currencies (EUR/USD, USD/JPY, GBP/USD, etc.), though USD/INR constitutes the majority of the foreign exchange transactions in terms of value. It is the FX CLEAR of the CCIL that remains the widely used trading platform in India.

In the forward market, trading takes place both in an over the counter (OTC) and in an exchange traded market with brokers playing an important role. The trading platforms include FX CLEAR of the CCIL, RMDS from Reuters, and FX Direct of the IBS.

FOREIGN EXCHANGE MARKET TURNOVER

Trading volumes in the Indian foreign exchange market have grown significantly over the last few years. The daily average turnover has seen an almost 10-fold rise during the 10-year period, from 1997–8 to 2007–8, from US$ 5 billion to US$ 48 billion. However, it displayed a declining trend during the crisis period 2008–9 and 2009–10 when the daily average turnover stood at US$ 47.6 billion and US$10.8 billion, respectively (Table 3.1).

Table 3.1   Turnover in the Foreign Exchange Market

Year	Turnover in US$ Billion			Share of Spot Turnover in Per Cent		
	Merchant	Inter-bank	Total	Merchant	Inter-bank	Total
1	2	3	4	5	6	7
1997–8	210	1,096	1,305	57.5	50.4	51.6
1998–9	246	1,057	1,303	51.1	48.6	49.1
1999–2000	244	898	1,142	60.6	49.2	51.6
2000–1	269	1,118	1,387	62.9	43.8	47.5
2001–2	257	1,165	1,422	61.8	38.1	42.4
2002–3	325	1,236	1,560	57.0	42.0	45.1
2003–4	491	1,628	2,118	52.5	48.2	49.2
2004–5	705	2,188	2,892	48.2	50.5	50.0
2005--6	1,220	3,192	4,413	45.0	52.6	50.5
2006–7	1,798	4,773	6,571	46.1	54.1	51.9
2007–8	3,545	8,704	12,249	45.9	51.2	49.7
2008–9	3,231	8,861	12,092	37.7	48.0	45.2
2009–10	2,710	7,645	10,355	38.9	53.9	50.0
2010–11	3,647	10,049	13,695	38.0	53.2	49.2

Source: Reserve Bank of India.

During 2009–10 (April–July), the daily average turnover picked up to reach US$ 49.8 billion. The pick-up in foreign exchange turnover has been particularly sharp from 2003–4 onwards, since when there has been a massive surge in capital inflows.

A look at segments in the Indian foreign exchange market reveals that the spot market remains the most important foreign exchange market segment, accounting for about 50 per cent of the total turnover. However, its share has seen a marginal decline in the recent past mainly due to a pick-up in turnover in the derivatives segment. The merchant segment of the spot market is generally dominated by the Government of India, select public sector units such as Indian Oil Corporation (IOC), and the FIIs. As the foreign exchange demand on account of public sector units and FIIs tends to be lumpy and uneven, the resultant demand–supply mismatches entail occasional pressures on the foreign exchange market, warranting market interventions by the Reserve Bank to even out demand and supply. However, as noted earlier, such intervention is not governed by a predetermined target or band around the exchange rate. Further, the inter-bank to merchant turnover ratio has halved from 5.2 during 1997–8 to 2.8 during 2009–10 reflecting the growing participation in the merchant segment of the foreign exchange market associated with growing trade activity, better corporate performance, and increased liberalization. Mumbai alone accounts for almost 80 per cent of the foreign exchange turnover.

It is noteworthy that the increase in foreign exchange market turnover in India between April 2004 and April 2007 was the highest amongst the 54 countries covered in the latest Triennial Central Bank Survey of Foreign Exchange and Derivatives Market Activity conducted by the Bank for International Settlements (BIS). According to the survey, daily average turnover in India jumped more than fivefold from US$ 7 billion in April 2004 to US$ 38 billion in April 2007. Global turnover over the same period rose by only 72 per cent from US$ 1.9 trillion to US$ 3.3 trillion. Reflecting on these trends, the share of India in global foreign exchange market turnover trebled from 0.3 per cent in April 2004 to 0.9 per cent in April 2007 (Table 3.2).

However, the daily average turnover in India declined to US$ 27 billion in April 2010 with a share of 0.5 per cent of the global turnover.

**Table 3.2   Global Foreign Exchange Market Turnover
(Daily Averages in April, in Billions of US dollars)**

	1998	2001	2004	2007	2010
Spot transactions	568	386	631	1,005	1,490
Outright forwards	128	130	209	362	475
Foreign exchange swaps	734	656	954	1,714	1,765
Currency Swaps	10	7	21	31	43
FX Options and Other products	87	60	119	212	207
Estimated gaps in reporting	61	28	107	129	
Total 'traditional' turnover	1,527	1,239	1,934	3,324	3,981
Memo					
Turnover at April 2010					
exchange rates	1,705	1,505	2,040	3,370	3,981
Total forex turnover of India	2	3.4	6.9	38.4	27.4
India's Share (%)	(0.1)	(0.2)	(0.3)	(0.9)	(0.5)

Source: Triennial Central Bank Survey on Foreign Exchange and Derivatives Market Activity in April 2010.

In April 2010, the average daily global market turnover rose by 20 per cent over April 2007 to US$ 4.0 trillion. It was seen that foreign exchange market activity became more global, with cross-border transactions representing 65 per cent of trading activity in April 2010 while local transactions accounted for 35 per cent. The percentage share of the US dollar has continued its slow decline witnessed since the April 2001 survey, while the Euro and the Japanese yen have gained relative to April 2007. Among the 10 most actively traded currencies, the Australian and Canadian dollars both increased in market share, while the Pound Sterling and the Swiss franc lost ground. The market share of emerging market currencies increased, with the biggest gains for the Turkish lira and the Korean won. The relative ranking of foreign exchange trading centres has changed slightly from the previous survey. Banks located in the United Kingdom accounted for 36.7 per cent, against 34.6 per cent in 2007, of all foreign exchange market turnover, followed by the United States (18 per cent), Japan (6 per cent), Singapore (5 per cent), Switzerland (5 per cent), Hong Kong SAR (5 per cent) and Australia (4 per cent).

Within the emerging market countries, traditional foreign exchange trading in Asian currencies generally recorded much faster growth than the global total between 2004 and 2007. Growth rates for Chinese renminbi, Hong Kong dollar, Indian rupee, Philippines peso, and Singaporean dollar exceeded 100 per cent between April 2004 and April 2007 (Table 3.3).

Table 3.3   Foreign Exchange Market Turnover in Select Economies Currencies, April 2010 (Daily Averages, in Billions of US dollars)

	1998	2001	2004	2007	2010
Chinese renminbi	0.2	0.0	0.6	9.6	19.8
Hong Kong dollar	79.9	68.4	106.0	181.0	237.6
Indian rupee	2.4	3.4	6.9	38.4	27.4
Indonesian rupiah	1.8	3.9	2.3	3.0	3.4
Korean won	3.6	9.8	20.5	35.2	43.8
Mexican Peso	8.7	8.6	15.3	15.3	17.0
Philippine peso	0.8	1.1	0.7	2.3	5.0
Russian Rouble	6.9	9.6	29.8	50.2	41.7
Singapore dollar	144.9	103.7	133.6	241.8	266.0
Turkish Lira	—	1.0	3.5	4.1	16.8
Thai baht	3.1	1.9	3.1	6.3	7.4

Source: Triennial Central Bank Survey on Foreign Exchange and Derivatives Market Activity in April 2010.

Looking at some of the comparable indicators, the turnover in the foreign exchange market has been about 7.2 times higher than the size of India's balance of payments (Table 3.4). With the deepening of the foreign exchange market and increased turnover, income of commercial banks through treasury operations has increased considerably.

Table 3.4   Foreign Exchange Market Turnover and BOP Size

Year	Foreign Exchange Market: Annual Turnover ($ Billions)	BOP Size ($ Billions)	Foreign Currency Assets ($ Billions)	Col 2 over Col 3 (Per Cent)	Col 2 over Col 4 (Per Cent)
1	2	3	4	5	6
2000–1	1,387	258	39.6	5.4	35.0
2001–2	1,422	237	51.0	6.0	28.0
2002–3	1,560	267	71.9	5.8	21.7
2003–4	2,118	361	107.4	5.9	19.7
2004–5	2,892	481	135.6	6.0	21.3
2005–6	4,413	663	145.1	6.7	30.4
2006–7	6,571	918	191.9	7.2	34.2
2007–8	12,249	1,416	299.2	8.7	40.9
2008–9	12,092	1,351	241.4	9.0	50.1
2009–10	10,355	1,369	254.7	7.6	40.7
2010–11	13,695	1,876	274.3	7.3	78.6

Source: Reserve Bank of India.

BEHAVIOUR OF FORWARD PREMIA

Apart from the spot segment, the foreign exchange market in India trades in derivatives such as forwards, swaps, and options. The typical forward contract is for one month, three months, or six months, with three months being the most common. Forward contracts for longer periods are not as common because of greater uncertainty. A swap transaction in the foreign exchange market is a combination of a spot and a forward in the opposite direction. Foreign exchange swaps account for the largest share of the total derivatives turnover in India followed by forwards and options. With greater opening up of the capital account, the forward premia is gradually getting aligned, with the interest rate differential reflecting growing market efficiency. However, in the Indian context, the forward price of the rupee is not essentially determined by the interest rate differentials, but it is also significantly influenced by:

(i)   supply and demand of forward US dollars

(ii) interest differentials and expectations of future interest rates, and,

(iii) expectations of future US dollar–rupee exchange rate (Figure 3.1).

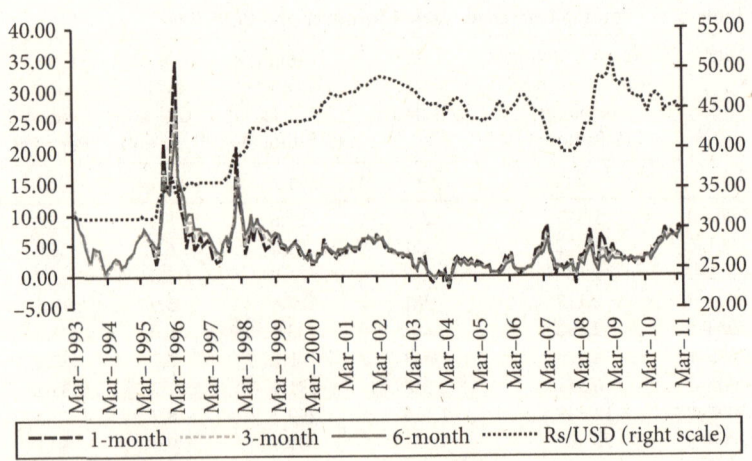

Figure 3.1   Movement of Forward Premia and USD
Source: Reserve Bank of India.

The deviation of the forward premia from the interest parity condition appears to increase during volatile conditions in the spot segment of the foreign exchange market. In recent times, however, reflecting the build-up of foreign exchange reserves, the strong capital flows, and the confidence in the Indian economy, forward premia have come down and are increasingly more reflective of the market sentiment.

Empirical studies in the Indian context reveal that foreign exchange premia of US dollar vis-à-vis the Indian rupee is driven to a large extent by the interest rate differential in the inter-bank market of the two economies combined with FII flows, current account balance, as well as changes in exchange rates of US$ vis-à-vis the Indian rupees (Sharma and Mitra 2006). Further empirical analysis for the period January 1995–December 2006 has shown that the ability of forward rates to correctly predict the future spot rates has improved over time and there is co-integration between the forward rate and the future spot rate as per RBI Report on Currency and Finance (RCF 2005–6).

With the opening up of the capital account, the forward premia is getting aligned with the interest rate differential reflecting market efficiency (Figure 3.2).

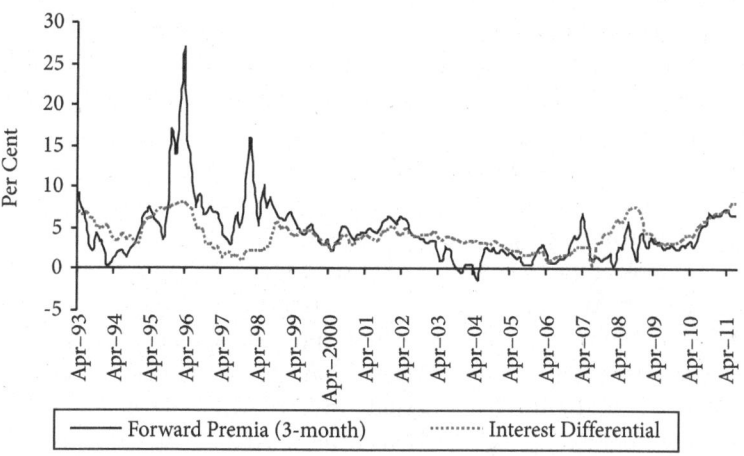

Figure 3.2 Movement of Forward Premia and Interest Rate Differential
Source: Reserve Bank of India.

While free movement in capital account is only a necessary condition for full development of forward and other foreign exchange derivatives market, the sufficient condition is provided by a deep and liquid money market with a well-defined yield curve in place.

Market Efficiency

With the exchange rate primarily getting determined in the market, the issue of foreign exchange market efficiency has assumed importance for India in recent years. There is evidence of enhanced efficiency in the foreign exchange market as is reflected in the low bid-ask spreads. The bid-ask spread of Rs/US$ market has almost converged with that of other major currencies in the international market. On some occasions, in fact, the bid-ask spread of Rs/US$ market was lower than that of some major currencies.

Besides maintaining orderly conditions, markets are perceived as efficient when market prices reflect all the available information so that it is not possible for any trader to earn excess profits in a systematic manner. The efficiency/liquidity of the foreign exchange market is often gauged in terms of bid-offer spreads. The bid-ask spread refers to the transaction costs and operating costs involved with the transaction of the currency. These costs include phone bills, cable charges, book-keeping expenses, trader salaries, etc., in the spot segment; it may also include the risks involved with holding foreign exchange. These costs/bid-ask spread may reduce with the increase in the volume of transaction of the currency.

In the Indian context the spread is almost flat and very low. In India, the normal spot market quote has a spread of 0.25 of a paisa to 1 paisa while swap quotes are available at 1 to 2 paise spread. A closer look at the bid-ask spread in the rupee–US dollar spot market reveals that during the initial phase of market development (that is, till the mid-1990s), the spread was high and volatile due to thin market participation with unidirectional behaviour of market participants (Figure 3.3). In the later period, with relatively deep and liquid markets, bid-ask spread has sharply declined and has remained low and stable, reflecting efficiency gains.

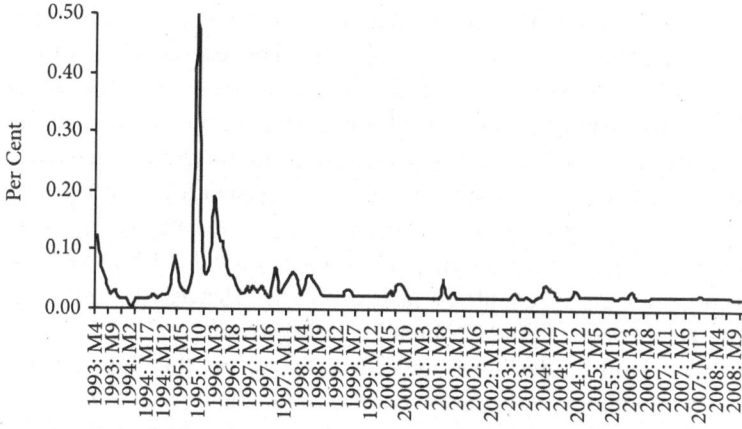

Figure 3.3   Bid-Ask Spread (Rs–US$) in the Spot Foreign Exchange Market
Source: Reserve Bank of India.

DEVELOPMENT OF THE NON-DELIVERABLE FORWARD MARKET

Along with the onshore spot and forward markets, the offshore non-deliverable forward (NDF) market is also assuming importance. The NDFs are synthetic foreign currency forward contracts on non-convertible or restricted currencies traded over the counter outside the direct jurisdiction of the respective authorities. These derivatives allow multinational corporations, portfolio investors, hedge funds, and proprietary foreign exchange accounts of commercial and investment banks to hedge or take speculative positions in local currencies. The settlement of the transaction is not by delivering the underlying pair of currencies, but by making a net payment in a convertible currency proportional to the difference between the agreed forward exchange rate and the subsequently realized spot fixing. These are generally settled in US dollar. The currencies that are traded in the Asian NDF markets are Chinese yuan, Korean won, Taiwanese dollar, Philippine peso, Indonesian rupiah, Malaysian ringgit, Thai baht, Pakistani rupee, and the Indian rupee.

While the Rs–US$ exchange rate NDF market has been around for over the last 10 years or so, the characteristics of this market seem to have evolved over this period reflecting onshore exchange controls and regulations. In the late 1990s, the NDF market was provided liquidity by foreign residents who had a genuine exposure to the Indian rupee but were unable to hedge their exposure in the domestic market due to existing controls. However, with the gradual relaxation of the exchange controls, reasonable hedging facilities are available to offshore non-residents who have exposures to the Rupee, especially when compared with the hedging facilities provided by some other competitor Asian countries such as China. Hence, the INR NDF market presently derives its liquidity largely from:

(i)   Non-residents wishing to speculate on the Indian rupee without any exposure to the currency, and

(ii)   arbitrageurs who try to exploit the differentials in the prices in the two markets without any outlay of capital on their part by two offsetting transactions.

Though an assessment of the volumes is difficult, it is estimated that the daily volumes for rupee NDF range around US$ 100 million in 2003–4 although NDF volumes have reportedly grown in the recent period. As compared with some other Asian currencies traded in the NDF market such as the Korean Won, Chinese Yuan, and the Taiwanese Dollar, turnover in INR NDF is small. While these volumes are not large enough to affect the domestic onshore market under regular market conditions, however, in volatile market conditions, these may impact on the domestic spot markets (RCF 2005–6).

In India, the spread is almost flat and very low in the spot segment of the foreign exchange market. The spread in the NDF segment remains higher than that of the spot and forward market reflecting lower liquidity in the NDF market. As compared with other Asian currencies, the spreads for Indian rupee NDFs remain lower than that of Indonesian rupiah and Philippine peso, but higher than that of Chinese renminbi and Korean won reflecting the higher liquidity available in the latter two currencies (Table 3.5).

The above discussion suggests that the foreign exchange market in India today is equipped with several derivative instruments, viz., forwards, options (foreign currency rupee options and cross currency options), and currency swaps (foreign currency rupee swaps and cross currency swaps). Various informal forms of derivatives contracts have existed since time immemorial though the formal introduction of a variety of instruments in the foreign exchange derivatives market started only in the post-reform period, especially since the mid-1990s. These derivative instruments have been cautiously introduced as part of the reforms in a phased manner, both for product diversity and, more importantly, as a risk management tool. Market infrastructure in terms of the trading platform has seen considerable improvement. All these have reflected in the market liquidity that has gone up significantly and market efficiency that has improved over the years.

Table 3.5   Bid-Ask Spreads in NDF Market for Select Asian Currencies (in Per Cent)

	1M NDF	3M NDF	6M NDF
Chinese Yuan			
Average	0.06	0.06	0.09
Min	0.01	0.01	0.01
Max	0.76	0.13	0.61
Korean Won			
Average	0.09	0.10	0.14
Min	0.01	0.02	0.02
Max	0.34	0.24	0.29
Indonesian Rupiah			
Average	0.51	0.73	1.09
Min	0.22	0.22	0.28
Max	1.92	2.73	3.13
Philippine Peso			
Average	0.22	0.23	0.39
Min	0.09	0.09	0.14
Max	0.51	0.51	0.75

Source: Reserve Bank of India.

4

Manifestations of the Global Financial Crisis

The recent global financial crisis was unprecedented in terms of its spread and intensity. It was the first of its kind in an increasingly integrated global economy, and challenged many of our fundamental beliefs. It could well be the watershed in the generally accepted framework of economic resilience and financial market stability. While crises have been part of the financial landscape for ages, it is now widely accepted that the nearest precedent to the recent crisis was the Great Depression of the 1930s in terms of its depth, geographical spread, intensity, and duration. No country was spared its wrath, although the impact has varied across nations. What started off as a sub-prime crisis in the US housing mortgage sector turned successively into a global banking crisis, global financial crisis, and a global economic crisis spreading from the littoral Atlantic regions across the world to Europe, Asia-Pacific, Latin America, and even to Africa.

The financial crisis became full blown in the second half of 2008, and has morphed through negative feedback to real activity, plunging the global economy into the deepest recession since World War II. The sharp deterioration in the global economic and financial situation continued despite wide ranging and often unorthodox policy responses, although they made some progress in stabilizing the financial markets.

As per IMF forecasts (September 2011), world GDP growth after declining by 0.7 per cent in 2009, grew at 5.1 per cent in 2010. However, the global growth is projected to decline to 4 per cent in 2011. The advanced economies after registering a growth of 3.1 per cent in 2010 (as against a decline of 3.7 per cent in 2009), are expected to slow down to 1.6 per cent in 2011, whereas the emerging and developing economies which slowed down to 2.8 per cent in 2009 (as against 6.0 per cent in 2008) grew at 7.3 per cent in 2010. They are expected to grow at 6.4 per cent in 2011.

GENESIS OF THE CRISIS

The recent global crisis was rooted in a combination of factors common to previous financial crises and some new factors. In an analysis post the crisis, a number of micro and macroeconomic factors have been listed in the literature as proximate causes of the crisis, the role of easy money, financial innovations, and global imbalances, on the one hand, to regulatory loopholes both at the national and global level, on the other. Easy credit combined with under pricing of risks, both by the households as well as financial intermediaries created bubbles in real estate, energy, and other sectors that had to face a disorderly unwinding. The analysis of the various causes of the crisis has sparked off a whole new debate on the relevance of various economic tenets and has challenged the economic doctrine that assumed the self correcting mechanism of the markets. There is also a view which holds the policy frameworks and growth strategies, pursued by economies in the various regions, responsible for the crisis.

Globalization and International Finance

A comparison of the recent crisis with the various episodes of crises in the past reveals that some semblance can be found amongst them with regard to the underlying causes. As in the past, the main causes of the recent crisis are linked to systemic fragilities and imbalances that contributed to the inadequate functioning of the global economy. Leading up to the crisis, these factors became more pronounced due to major weaknesses in financial regulation, supervision, and monitoring of the financial sector, along with inadequate surveillance and early warning. These, together with over reliance on market self-regulation and overall lack of transparency with distorted incentive structure led to excessive risk taking, unsustainable high asset prices, irresponsible leveraging, and high levels of consumption which were fuelled by easy credit and inflated asset prices. In terms of impact, the recent crisis seems to be more widespread than many other previous episodes and is considered to be closest to the Great Depression of the 1930s. The estimates of output and loss place this crisis above most of the episodes in the past, with a majority of the advanced and emerging market economies facing the downturn as a result of the rapid transmission of the crisis from the epicentre to the periphery. In fact, the same forces of globalization and international finance that had led to developments in poorer countries over the past decades also carried with them the seeds of contagion, which resulted in the international transmission of shocks.

The causes of the crisis were many and intertwined as such a pervasive crisis cannot be triggered by a single or isolated factor. In trying to understand the various causes of the crisis, different viewpoints have emerged. One view believes that the current disruption of financial markets is the long-run consequence of the easy global money and credit conditions that existed, particularly from the beginning of the decade. While the immediate cause of the financial crisis is attributed to the problems persisting in the sub-prime mortgage sector of the United States, the root cause lies in the persistence of global imbalances since the beginning of the current decade. The global imbalances interacted with the flaws in financial markets and instruments to generate the specific features of the crisis. Another view argues that if imbalances at the global level were the root cause, then why did the crisis originate in the United States (US) and not in other countries which were also partners of global imbalances? The excesses in the US financial system are, in fact, at the core of the current crisis and all other factors contributed to further aggravate the crisis. Finance has been the proximate factor behind most crises of the past and the recent crisis is no different.

Some are also of the opinion that one important cause of the crisis is the US Fed's maintenance of very low interest rates for a long time, leading to a housing and asset price bubble. An equally important cause has been the lack of recognition of asset prices in policy formulation. According to some, the Basel Accord is also a cause of the recent banking crisis and banks' efforts to circumvent the capital adequacy requirements of the Basel Accord caused the financial crisis. Leaders at the G-20 Summit in September 2009 blamed global imbalances, seeing them as more responsible for the crisis than the failure of global financial regulation. The roles of international financial institutions like the IMF with the responsibility of surveillance have also been questioned. It is lamented that the IMF failed in diagnosing and pointing out the vulnerabilities, both at the global level and at the level of systemically important advanced economies.

Global Current Account Imbalances

The large global current account imbalances also got reflected in the savings–investment behaviour in both emerging and advanced nations. This is why global imbalances are now universally ascribed to the 'savings glut' hypothesis, which states that the US current account deficit was driven by a savings glut in the rest of the world, especially in emerging market countries. The precautionary motive was the main reason behind the high savings in these economies. The absence of adequate safety nets and the consequent need for self-insurance, coupled with financial market underdevelopments in the emerging economies led private agents in these economies to oversave, particularly in countries such as China. The one child policy in China has also contributed to the rise in savings as children are substitutes for lifecycle savings. Besides, as per capita income increases at high rates, consumption usually does not keep pace with income and the savings rate tends to increase. Higher migration from the rural to urban areas added to the rise in savings as the consumption habits of the migrants remained unchanged, even though their incomes rose. Higher net savings by oil exporters are also believed to have contributed to the global savings glut. Consequent upon the sharp rise in oil prices, the current account surpluses of oil exporters, notably in the Middle East and also in countries such as Russia, Nigeria, and Venezuela, rose as oil revenues surged.

One view of the savings glut hypothesis is that there was an investment drought rather than a savings glut. The East Asian crisis has exerted permanent depressing effects on investment in these economies. While the savings rate in most East Asian EMEs, which has generally remained higher than in the industrialized countries, exhibited a modest decline, investment rates showed sharper declines, resulting in the widening of the savings–investment gap in the EMEs.

A corroborative view is that the consumption glut in the advanced countries has exacerbated the current account disequilibrium across the world. Excess consumption combined with higher leveraging in a loosely regulated and unsupervised financial system fuelled the housing bubble.

The global imbalances were accentuated by the excessively loose monetary policy in advanced economies, especially the US. To some extent, the lack of adequate exchange rate flexibility in some EMEs, which gave rise to excess liquidity and low interest rates, exacerbated the problem. The real interest rate in the US was consistently below 1 per cent from mid-2001 up to the end of 2005; indeed, for much of this period it was negative. It was generally accepted that the Fed had followed an excessively loose monetary policy in 2002–6. The low interest rate regime had a variety of effects. Low interest rates combined with ample liquidity, provided the impetus for strong credit growth in a number of economies and led to a build-up of domestic imbalances. The credit boom created grounds for rapid financial innovations and increased risk taking behaviour.

Underpricing of Risks

Even as financial imbalances were building up, however, macroeconomic stability was maintained, a reflection of Great Moderation, which encouraged underpricing of risks. Monetary policy failed to respond to this asset price inflation, guided by the now notorious Greenspan orthodoxy, according to which, first, asset price bubbles are hard to identify on a real time basis and the fundamental factors that drive asset prices are not directly observable. Second, monetary policy is too blunt an instrument to counteract asset price booms. And third, a central bank cannot presume to know more than the market because financial markets are all-efficient, rational, and self-correcting. Thus, it was considered more cost effective for monetary policy to wait for the bubble to burst and clean up afterwards, rather than prick the bubble in advance. Thus, global imbalances accompanied by a 'savings glut' in the emerging economies and loose monetary policy in the US and other advanced economies, led to an era of low real interest rates and rapid search for yield that resulted in many of the financial excesses. Both these factors were clear precursors of unsustainable bubbles, which were ignored in general because of the pre-crisis phase of high global growth with low inflation. Theoretically, the period after 2000 can be characterized as a period when both the IS and the LM curves shifted to the left, thus, maintaining output at low interest rates.

Concerns had been expressed that the continued widening of global imbalances could have a disorderly unwinding with a sudden stop of capital flows from emerging markets to the US that would trigger a crisis in the US leading to substantial dollar depreciation. However, the trigger for the crisis did not come from the global imbalances but from the housing bubble in the US economy. Even as financial imbalances were building up, macroeconomic stability was maintained, which, in turn, encouraged underpricing of risks.

Regulatory Weaknesses

Financial innovations, regulatory arbitrage, lending malpractices, excessive use of the originate-and-distribute model, together with securitization of sub-prime loans and their bundling into AAA tranches, without risk being adequately assessed, culminated into excessive leverage of financial market entities in the US. The sub-prime crisis is also viewed as the best example of several weaknesses in the regulatory structure of financial institutions in terms of lax supervisory oversight and relaxation of normal standards of prudent lending. Several issues have been highlighted in this regard—lack of counter-cyclical regulation, inability to recognise systemic risks, the need for prudential regulation, non-recognition of off-balance-sheet items of banks, operation of non-banks beyond the regulatory purview, the complex and non-transparent nature of new financial instruments, and regulatory oversight of systemically important financial institutions. Regulators in the financial sector did not have adequate skills to cope with rapid growth in the variety and complexity of innovations in financial products in the markets. Despite the prevalence of a well established regulatory structure in terms of capital requirements and risk assessments, financial institutions found it relatively easy to move to activities outside the regulatory perimeter. While the regulatory capital requirements did limit the build-up of leverage on bank balance sheets, bank managers engaged in various off-balance sheet activities to increase risk and return without increasing the capital they were required to hold.

IMPACT AND MANIFESTATIONS OF THE CRISIS

Due to the rapid global integration and deep and complex interconnections between financial institutions, the crisis which emerged in the US sub-prime housing market manifested itself across assets, markets, and economies. During the initial stages of the crisis, the impact was manifested in terms of the mounting losses on the exposure of banks and financial institutions to the sub-prime mortgages and structured finance products. These losses were exacerbated by lack of liquidity in the markets for those instruments, which led to substantial reductions in their mark-to-market valuations.

With the collapse of Lehman Brothers, the crisis entered a turbulent new phase in September 2008, after which it rapidly developed into a crisis of confidence and engulfed the whole financial system in the US. Subsequently, it spread to other developed economies resulting in a number of European bank failures, declines in various stock indices with consequent large reductions in the market value of equities and commodities, failure of key businesses, fall in consumer wealth, and a significant drop in economic activity. Moreover, the deleveraging of financial institutions, as assets were sold to pay back obligations that could not be refinanced in frozen credit markets, further accelerated the liquidity crisis. In this phase, bank losses and write-downs became more closely linked and the impact was felt in terms of a surge in borrower defaults on the back of worsening macroeconomic performance.

In view of the soaring demand for liquid funds in the wake of the contraction in the money market mutual fund sector, global inter-bank markets came under pressure squeezing banks' access to short-term funding. Money markets, which were already strained, failed to recuperate despite massive central bank liquidity injections. As a result, inter-bank rates spiked to historic highs. The movements in other major markets such as those for Euro and Sterling funds also showed similar signs, albeit moderately. Thus, the turmoil transcended from credit and money markets to the global financial system more broadly. The contagion also spilled over to the emerging markets, which saw broad based asset price declines amidst depressed levels of risk appetite. While policy intervention on an unprecedented scale helped to stabilize the money market conditions, credit growth, however, continued to remain sluggish, particularly in the advanced economies even in the recent months.

The stock market is another segment of the financial sector that has borne much of the heat of the global financial crisis. During the recent financial crisis, equity markets all over the world witnessed high volatility and sharp declines in prices. However, in contrast to other markets, the impact of the crisis was more pronounced on the EME stock markets compared to their mature counterparts.

There had been rapid transmission of shocks from the US and Europe to the rest of the world. The impact of the crisis was felt in almost all the economies of the world in varying degrees. The crisis spread to EMEs through all four channels: trade, finance, commodity, and confidence channels. In the EMEs, the slump in export demand and tighter trade credit caused deceleration in aggregate demand, reversal of capital flows led to equity market losses and currency depreciations, global liquidity tightening resulted in lower external credit flows, and market rigidities and erosion of confidence led to widening of credit spreads. In the financial sector, the estimates for global write-downs of loans and securities held by banks over 2007–10 amounted to US$ 2.3 trillion (World Economic Outlook, April 2010).

Global trade linkages and financial integration had given the financial market crisis a global form as the increasingly integrated global trading and financial system magnified and accelerated the transmission process. The impact of the global financial crisis spilling over to the real sector reflected in falling income, shrinking demand, and deceleration in trade in major advanced economies such as the US, Euro area, the UK, and Japan, and led these into recession by the fourth quarter of 2008. Emerging market economies looked relatively resilient during the initial months of the crisis, benefiting from large capital inflows and benign macroeconomic conditions. However, with the slowdown in economic activities in advanced economies becoming more entrenched, shrinking global trade and intensifying turbulence in global financial markets, the contagion spread to the EMEs. As a result, the crisis quickly spread around the world, pushing the global economy into a severe and synchronized recession. In the real economy, the final impact of the crisis was reflected in deteriorating global growth outlook as can be observed from the successive revisions in the growth projections for 2009 from 3.8 per cent in April 2008 to (–) 1.1 per cent in October 2009, which was revised further to (–) 0.6 per cent in April 2010.

Volatility in the financial markets along with the slowdown in economic activities in the advanced economies was transmitted to the EMEs through both trade and financial channels on account of the increased global integration witnessed in recent years. Over the past quarter century, the growth in world trade at about 6 per cent was almost double the rate of growth of world output. Apart from trade liberalization, this can also be attributed to rapid developments and integration in financial markets. But the same developments also widened the scope for economic turmoil when global conditions deteriorated. For instance, trade finance which is now being increasingly used for financing trade was severely affected during the crisis as financial markets tumbled.

During the recent financial crisis, the slowdown of international trade has mirrored that of economic activity. International trade flows, which had grown robustly in recent decades mainly on account of waves of liberalization, suddenly abated by the end of 2008 and then strongly contracted in some areas, further propagating the effects of the crisis across countries. According to the IMF's estimates, world trade (goods and services) contracted by 10.7 per cent in 2009 after recording a subdued growth of 2.8 per cent in 2008. World trade volumes fell on three other occasions after 1965 (0.2 per cent in 2001, 2.0 per cent in 1982, and 7.0 per cent in 1975), but none of these episodes approached the magnitude of decline observed in 2009. The decline in world trade volume was much higher than the earlier plunge, showing the large impact of the recent financial crisis through the increased integration of global trade across countries.

At the same time, the officially recorded remittance flows to developing countries reached US$ 317 billion in 2009, down 6 per cent from US$ 338 billion in 2008. For the first time since the 1980s, remittances to developing countries declined, albeit modestly, in 2009. Apart from trade, the sub-prime crisis spread through the financial channel, especially through capital flows. Total capital flows to developing countries declined from around US$ 1.2 trillion during 2007 to

US $ 780 billion during 2008, mainly on account of sharp declines in portfolio equity and debt flows. On the other hand, FDI flows continued to grow, although at a decelerated pace. In Europe and Central Asia, the trend of rapid increase in debt flows during recent years reversed significantly during 2008, making it one of most vulnerable regions during the current crisis. In contrast to FDI flows, portfolio flows to the emerging market and developing economies witnessed a massive reversal during the second half of 2008, reflecting the process of global deleveraging and risk aversion on the part of global investors. Disruptions in emerging market portfolio flows became more widespread following the collapse of Lehman Brothers in mid-September 2008. The reversal in portfolio equity inflows, notably in Asia, led to weakening of emerging market currencies, widening of spreads on international sovereign bonds, and a sharp rise in domestic bond yields in many EMEs.

To sum up, the transmission of the global financial crisis to the real economy was routed mainly through the decline in world trade, especially in the second half of 2008 and early 2009. The decline in trade flows was further accentuated by the sharp reduction in commodity prices in line with the decline in demand. The trade channel of the transmission of global crisis played a particularly important role in economies that had greater integration in global trade, such as the East Asian economies. Along with shrinking trade flows, net private capital flows to emerging and developing economies witnessed a sharp reversal during 2008 with many of the EMEs facing much tighter limits on external financing as global deleveraging and increasing risk aversion curtailed investor interest in these markets. Countries with larger current account and fiscal deficits, and sectors with significant foreign exchange exposures on their balance sheets, were more affected by the tightening of external financing conditions and withdrawals of capital. Despite a modest decline in remittance inflows in 2009, these flows have remained more resilient compared to private debt and equity flows, though the adverse developments turned out to be more serious for some small, poor countries where it makes up a relatively large share of GDP. Finally, in the course of 2009, global imbalances contracted to some extent with reduction in current account deficits/surpluses of several countries, notably the US and China.

POLICY RESPONSE TO THE CRISIS

In the recent crisis, reacting to funding problems and incipient runs, the first round of responses to the current financial crisis came mostly from central banks and regulatory authorities. Since the intensification of the financial crisis in September 2008, central banks and governments, globally, acted in a decisive and concerted manner to contain the adverse effect of the financial crisis on the real economy and promote its recovery. More broadly, authorities followed multifaceted strategies involving continued provision of liquidity and extended guarantees of bank liabilities to alleviate funding pressures, making available public funds for bank recapitalization, and announcing programmes to deal with distressed assets. At the same time, with inflation concerns dwindling and risks to the economic outlook deepening, central banks used a range of conventional and unconventional policy tools to support the economy and ease credit market conditions. As concerns about the extent of the downturn and the limits to monetary policy mounted, governments turned to fiscal policy to support demand.

To address the twin problems of financial crisis and fall in aggregate demand, both feeding on to each other, it was increasingly viewed that the policy packages should have two components. One component aimed at bringing the financial system back to health and the other at reviving aggregate demand, keeping in view the obvious interactions and synergies between the two. In a highly integrated global economy, coordinated monetary and fiscal policy in responding to the crisis had to be at an unprecedented level to be effective. Governments and central banks have been remarkably flexible in recognizing that a hasty response in some countries had the risk of increasing moral hazard in others, while, on the other hand, a delay by some countries in joining the others bore dangers of diluting the impact of the response. Monetary policy responses, which began in terms of policy rate cuts by individual central banks, became more coordinated afterwards. This was reflected in the provision of cross-border liquidity through swap arrangements by major central banks as well as several rounds of policy rate cuts. Dealing with the solvency risks being faced by systemically important institutions together with funding liquidity pressures in interbank markets became important for policymakers.

Monetary Measures

Central banks initially focused on their own markets. But given the effects on cross-border confidence as well as the need for foreign currency liquidity in many markets, they rapidly developed a number of channels of cooperation. These included coordinated policy announcements and foreign currency swap lines. Monetary policy in response to the drying up of global liquidity was extremely responsive and cooperative. On 8 October 2008, six major central banks undertook the first ever round of coordinated action in policy rate cuts. Similar swift action followed from other central banks as well. By the end of May 2009, the Federal Reserve, the Bank of Japan, the Bank of England, the Bank of Canada, and the Swiss National Bank had brought policy rates close to zero.

Notwithstanding the swift and sizeable easing in policy rates, the limitations of interest rate as a policy instrument came to surface in many countries. With persisting strains in the financial markets and the rise in credit and liquidity risk premia, the transmission mechanism was greatly hampered. Though banks generally passed reductions in their funding costs on to their customers, they tightened credit standards substantially offsetting the impact of rate cuts on overall financial conditions. As policy rates reached historically low levels in many advanced economies, the zero lower bound became a binding constraint, making it impossible to follow policy rules that called for negative nominal interest rates in view of widening output gaps and falling inflation rates.

Amidst this complex and challenging environment, central banks were forced to look beyond the interest rate channel and explore all possible ways to restore the functioning of the credit markets and ease financial conditions. Though these liquidity easing measures were mostly in line with the standard central bank lender of last resort function, their range and magnitude were well above traditional levels. Major central banks provided enhanced term funding to a wider range of institutions and against a wider collateral than in the past. In some cases, they stepped in to provide direct lending to distressed institutions and took other exceptional measures to improve funding conditions in credit markets. As the crisis deepened and the interest rate channel became ineffective, the central banks in these countries were forced to go for quantitative easing. This response was focused directly on alleviating tighter credit conditions in the non-bank sector and easing broader financial conditions.

There have been two approaches to this quantitative easing. In the first approach, funds were provided to non-banking institutions to improve liquidity and reduce risk spreads in specific markets such as commercial paper, asset-backed securities, and corporate bonds. In the second approach, central banks purchased government or government guaranteed securities from banks or other institutions in order to ease liquidity conditions. The relative emphasis given to private versus public sector securities and bank versus non-bank markets differed across countries. The quantitative easing involving government securities tended to be more important in bank-centred systems (Japan and the UK). Credit easing with private securities generally played a larger role in market-centred systems (the US).

Prior to September 2008, EMEs were grappling with capital inflows and inflationary pressures and were tightening liquidity conditions by actually raising policy rates. As the financial crisis engulfed the EMEs, central banks in these countries embarked on both conventional and unconventional measures in response to the sudden tightening of global liquidity conditions. EMEs undertook several liquidity easing and foreign exchange measures, although their use of credit easing and quantitative easing has been more limited. As exchange rates in these economies came under pressure with the intensification of stress in the global dollar markets and net capital inflows began to reverse, they initiated foreign exchange liquidity easing measures. It was only at the beginning of November 2008 that policy interest rates were reduced in many EMEs, indicating that conventional domestic monetary policy easing lagged behind unconventional measures.

Central banks in many EMEs resorted to liquidity injections and frequent cuts in policy rates from a much higher level. Central banks in several EMEs resorted to cuts in reserve requirement ratios, the introduction of reserve averaging, and hike in exemption thresholds with a view to ease domestic liquidity shortages. Most of them also eased the terms of existing standing and market-based liquidity providing facilities, viz. extension of maturities, easing collateral requirements, and increasing the frequency of auctions. Several central banks provided domestic liquidity to targeted institutions for on-lending to market entities. Central banks in EMEs eased the terms of existing foreign exchange facilities, that is, extending maturities and broadening the collateral. They also put in place new foreign exchange facilities such as dollar repo and swap facilities. The list of counterparties was widened to include non-banking financial institutions and key non-financial institutions (for example, exporters or energy importers). Foreign exchange liquidity limits were also relaxed including removal of ceilings on bank purchases of offshore foreign exchange and easing of capital inflow limits. In addition, some central banks lowered the required reserve ratio for bank foreign currency liabilities and shifted the currency structure of required reserves away from foreign exchange. In order to ease foreign exchange liquidity conditions, central banks in countries like Brazil, Korea, Mexico, and Singapore had dollar swap arrangements with the Federal Reserve.

As a consequence of unprecedented support extended to bring about normalcy in the financial systems, central bank balance sheets in the advanced economies swelled much more than in the EMEs. This could pose several policy challenges and risks in the future. Yet, central bank actions across countries managed to address the immediate funding needs of the banks and restore some normalcy. However, the monetary policy measures could not stop solvency concerns of some systemically important financial institutions. This led to severe market dislocation with adverse implications on the real sector. Thus, governments were compelled to take several actions to prevent collapse by extending large-scale fiscal support to financial institutions.

Fiscal Measures

The present global crisis, as in the past, has been characterized by the twin problems of financial instability and fall in aggregate demand, feeding into each other. Thus, the fiscal policy response has consisted of two components with obvious synergies between them. The first component has been the crisis management strategy directed at bringing the financial system back to health. The strategy has involved providing direct financial support and/or deposit insurance/guarantee to troubled financial institutions in order to make them solvent and stabilize the financial system. The second step has been to activate discretionary fiscal measures to support aggregate demand in order to contain economic slowdown.

Fiscal support to the financial sector included a combination of upfront government support by way of capital injection and purchase of assets, lending by the treasury, and providing guarantees for bank deposits, inter-bank loans and bonds. Capital injections were made to directly address the solvency problem. Asset purchases were aimed at repairing impaired assets. Treasury lending to financial institutions was to ensure that these institutions were not starved of funds. Guarantees on deposit and debt were provided with the intention of providing assurance to depositors and lenders. The intended upfront government support to financial institutions in the advanced countries had been much larger than in the EMEs. As on June 2009, it ranged from 0.7 per cent of GDP in Italy to a high of 20.0 per cent in the UK, with the majority of them providing far more than 5.0 per cent of GDP. For the EMEs, the upfront government support ranged from nil, in a number of them, to 3.5 per cent of GDP in Hungary. The average support for the advanced G-20 countries is estimated at about 5.5 per cent of GDP. For emerging G-20 countries, the average is placed at 0.4 per cent of GDP.

The recent crisis has led to a resurrection of fiscal policy as a counter-cyclical instrument of macroeconomic stabilization. The average size of the fiscal stimulus packages on account of direct response to the crisis for those OECD countries carrying out a stimulus package over the period 2008–10 is estimated to be 3.5 per cent of area-wide GDP in 2008. However, there has been wide variation in the size of the fiscal stimulus measures across countries, partly reflecting divergence in the severity of the crisis, the initial fiscal position, and the size of automatic stabilizers. Five countries (Australia, Canada, Korea, New Zealand, and the US) have announced packages larger than 4.0 per cent of GDP. During 2009, all the G-20 countries announced fiscal stimulus measures ranging from 0.2 per cent of GDP (Italy) to 4.1 per cent of GDP (Russia), and in about half of them the size was close to 2.0 per cent of GDP or more.

While the impact of fiscal stimulus on growth may be uncertain, the level of deficit and debt would increase substantially. On the assumption of a stronger resumption in economic growth, the overall fiscal deficit for the advanced G-20 countries in 2012 has been projected to be higher by 1.8 percentage points over the level of 2008. For the emerging G-20 countries, the same will be higher by 2.0 percentage points. During the same period, the debt ratios are expected to rise by 27 percentage points in the advanced economies. For emerging market economies, it is expected to decline slightly after some initial increase. Should the downside risks materialize, the situation, however, would become even worse. It is even maintained that given the prolonged downturn, fiscal stimulus should go beyond the measures already announced, provided that there is enough fiscal space. This has raised fiscal sustainability concerns and other related implications in the medium to long-term. The problem would be more serious in countries that are already facing the looming challenges of population ageing. The prospective cost in terms of pensions and healthcare together could be more than ten times the costs of the crisis. Therefore, a credible exit strategy, with necessary institutional arrangements, would be required.

Financial Policies

The international community showed exemplary cooperation in fighting the worst impact of the crisis. Recognizing the severe resource constraints faced by low income countries, a number of initiatives have been taken by the G-20 and Bretton Woods institutions. These initiatives were:

(i)   increased funding for multilateral financial institutions,

(ii)   widening the access for developing and emerging economies to multilateral funding, and,

(iii) improvements in the terms and conditions of multilateral lending.

In the London Summit of the G-20 in April 2009, an additional international support of US$ 1.1 trillion was secured to increase the funding from multilateral financial institutions to strengthen the global financial safety net. This included:

(i)   trebling the resources available to the IMF to US$ 750 billion,

(ii)   mobilization of an additional US$ 100 billion for Multilateral Development Banks (MDBs), and,

(iii)   US$ 250 billion of trade financing from various public and private institutions, including credit agencies.

The present crisis has demonstrated the urgent need for effective financial regulation and supervision. The imminent requirement to restore confidence and rebuild trust in the financial system gave way to a broad based initiative towards financial reforms. A reassessment of crisis management arrangements has been undertaken, apart from potential medium-term changes in the conduct of financial sector policy. The medium-term changes are mainly in the area of minimal capital requirements, liquidity requirements, other prudential constraints on permissible liabilities and assets, reporting requirements, and governance requirements. Certain other areas of the regulatory framework, such as the treatment of certain aspects of liquidity risk and the securitization framework, have also been revisited. In developing financial sector initiatives, there is a broad underlying consensus among authorities regarding the goal to create a financial system that is less leveraged, better capitalized, and more transparent, and features stronger incentives for all participants in the system. The focus of the financial sector reforms has been on building a stronger and globally more consistent supervisory and regulatory framework for the financial sector in future, which will support sustainable global growth. It has been emphasized that regulation and supervision of financial institutions should take into account the increasing inter-linkages in the financial sector, as also the, greater need to contain systemic risks. The focus is on better and effective regulation rather than on tighter regulation.

THE INDIAN CONTEXT

Impact on India

During the initial phase of the crisis, the impact on the Indian financial markets was rather muted; however, since mid-September 2008, the impact on the Indian financial markets amplified. In fact, the banks' negligible engagement in off-balance sheet activities and illiquid securitized assets, which remained at the heart of the recent global financial crisis in advanced economies, protected India from early turmoil in international financial markets. Nonetheless, India could not remain unscathed and the global developments affected its financial and real activities in the second half of 2008-9.

India's financial markets—equity markets, money markets, forex markets, and credit markets—had all come under pressure from a number of directions. First, the substitution of overseas financing by domestic financing brought both the money market and credit market under pressure. Second, the forex market came under pressure because of reversal of capital flows as part of the global deleveraging process and, simultaneously, corporates were converting the funds raised locally into foreign currency to meet their external obligations. Third, the Reserve Bank's intervention in the forex market to manage the volatility in the rupee further added to liquidity tightening. Fourth, Indian banks as well as corporates were finding it difficult to raise funds from external sources as a consequence of the global liquidity squeeze and, as a result, pressure escalated sharply on banks for the credit requirements of corporates. Also, in their frantic search for substitute financing, corporates withdrew their investments from the domestic money market mutual funds, putting redemption pressure on the mutual funds, and, down the line, on NBFCs where the mutual funds had invested a significant portion of their funds. Finally, India also witnessed large capital outflows, exchange rate depreciation, protracted contraction in merchandise exports, and a steep fall in equity prices in the second half of 2008-9. All these factors resulted in a sharp deceleration in the growth of the Indian economy in the second half of 2008-9.

Channels of Global Integration

The globalization process in India was strengthened and reinforced in the 1990s and 2000s due to several important developments. First, trade openness (goods and services trade) increased substantially with the trade-GDP ratio doubling since 1999–2000. Second, services, which were largely considered non-tradable, turned increasingly tradable, mainly due to off-shoring led by rapid innovations in information technology, labelled as Information Technology-Enabled Services (ITES) and Business Process Outsourcing (BPO). Third, the trade channel of global integration has been, concomitantly, supported by the migration channel with the competitive edge of human resources in knowledge based services. The rising importance of the human channel, which operates directly through remittances and indirectly through trade in goods and services, in strengthening India's global integration is reflected in the widening gap between exports and imports of goods and services and current account receipts and payments as a percentage of GDP, which increased from about 2 per cent in 1990–1 to around 7 per cent during 2008–9. Fourth, the economy became more open to external capital flows as the gross capital account-GDP ratio witnessed a more than threefold increase during the same period. Fifth, higher capital account openness also strengthened the integration of domestic markets with global markets, which was reflected in the stronger correlations of domestic interest rates, equity, and commodity prices with their global counterparts. These developments also facilitated the role of expectations in transmitting global shocks to the domestic economy. Sixth, even in commodity producing sectors, global integration came through prices and not necessarily through physical trade in commodities as global price movements have an important expectation impact on domestic prices. Finally, greater synchronization of the domestic business cycles with the global cycles implied that the external shocks could have a greater and more rapid impact on the domestic economy.

Until the global crisis, the Indian economy exhibited remarkable resilience to various adverse external developments despite the increasing openness of the economy since the 1990s. There were several reasons for this resilience. First, domestic demand played a dominant role in the growth process. Second, domestic demand was led by private consumption during the first four decades after independence. Third, a large part of investment demand was supported by domestic savings. Fourth, the services sector, led by domestic demand, contributed to the stability of overall economic growth. Fifth, in the financial sector, the banking sector, accounting for a major share of the financial intermediation process, did not have significant exposure to international financial markets.

Unlike the episode of the late 1990s, the recent global crisis led to a change in the perspective on the Indian economy. Global developments became important for the economy due to the significant increase in trade and finance openness. The share of exports and imports in the aggregate demand in India has risen sharply during the current decade as compared to the 1980s and 1990s. On the other hand, the share of private consumption has fallen during the same period. As a result of the compositional shift in aggregate demand, the Indian economy has become more vulnerable to external shocks compared to the earlier period. This is clearly visible in the decline in the growth rate of the Indian economy as the recent global crisis gathered momentum with widespread impact across sectors. The growth rate of the Indian economy moderated sharply to 6.8 per cent in 2008–9, declining by 2.8 percentage points from the peak in 2006–7. At the same time, there was also significant moderation in the growth rates of private consumption and investment activities.

Channels of Transmission

Although the growth of the Indian economy started slowing down from the last quarter of 2007–8 and the trend continued in subsequent quarters taking a cue from world growth, slowdown accentuated in the third and fourth quarter of 2008–9 before improving somewhat during the first quarter of 2009–10. In fact, the Indian economy was already on the moderate growth trajectory of the business cycle from the fourth quarter of 2006, but the current global crisis made the slowdown more pronounced from the third quarter of 2008–9.

There was a sudden change in the external environment following the failure of Lehman Brothers in mid-September 2008. The global financial crisis and deleveraging led to reversal and/or modulation of capital flows, particularly foreign institutional investor (FII) flows, ECBs and trade credit. Large withdrawals of funds from the equity markets by the FIIs reflecting the credit squeeze and global deleveraging resulted in large capital outflows during September–October 2008, with concomitant pressures in the foreign exchange market across the globe, including India. The cascading effect of the global financial crisis on the domestic foreign exchange market was felt through the dollar liquidity shocks emanating from the lower level of net capital flow and contracting exports. After Lehman's bankruptcy, the rupee depreciated sharply, breaching the level of Rs 50 per US dollar on 27 October 2008.

The money market was orderly during the first half of 2008–9, with call rates remaining generally within the informal corridor of reverse repo and repo rates. The call money rates edged up in tandem with the hikes in liquidity adjustment facility (LAF) repo rates in stages till August 2008, reflecting monetary policy tightening on inflation concerns and hovered around the upper bound of the corridor during the second quarter (up to mid- September 2008). In mid-September 2008, the failure of Lehman Brothers and a few other global financial institutions led to the freezing of money market activities in major financial centres; and Indian markets were also indirectly affected. In response to the crisis, the Reserve Bank provided substantial dollar liquidity to curb excessive volatility in the foreign exchange market, which had a tightening impact on rupee liquidity. Such operations by the Reserve Bank in the foreign exchange market along with transient local factors such as build-up in government balances, following quarterly advance tax payments, adversely impacted domestic liquidity conditions and the call money rate moved above the repo rate till the end of October 2008.

Indian stock markets started decelerating from their peak on 8 January 2008 (the BSE Sensex was at 20,873), despite relatively robust macroeconomic fundamentals. In fact, of late, the movements in Indian stock markets have been highly synchronized with advanced and EMEs. The inter-temporal cyclical synchronization of Indian stock markets with select advanced and EMEs has gone up significantly during recent periods. This increasing cyclical synchronization of Indian stock markets reflects the increasing financial globalization of the Indian economy over the past few years, which has been propelled by large FII inflows. The BSE Sensex dipped by about 38 per cent to 12,860 at end-September 2008 from a peak of 20,873 on 8 January 2008, reflecting the initial impact of the crisis. Subsequently, it declined further by about 37 per cent to touch a new low of 8,160 on 3 March 2009 from the end-September 2008 level. The decline in the BSE Sensex from the peak to the new low was to the extent of 61 per cent. The volatility in Indian stock markets has also increased in synchronization with global stock markets since the beginning of 2008. The volatility, measured in terms of the standard deviation of daily stock market indices (BSE Sensex and Nifty), shot up sharply in January 2008, October

2008, and May 2009, reflecting global events and domestic developments (RBI 2009).

In the backdrop of a sharp global economic slowdown arising from the world economic crisis, India's merchandize trade could not maintain the growth momentum attained during the period 2002–3 to 2007–8. India's merchandize exports during 2008–9 amounted to US$ 166.7 billion, posting a sharp reduction in growth to 2.4 per cent from 28.9 per cent during 2007–8. Exports which were buoyant till August 2008 (33.7 per cent growth during April–August 2008) witnessed a moderation in growth to 13.5 per cent in September 2008 and subsequently showed decline in all the remaining months of 2008–9, thereby exhibiting deceleration in overall export growth in 2008–9. Imports during 2008–9 at US$ 283.8 billion also witnessed a sharp deceleration in growth to 12.9 per cent from 35.4 per cent a year ago. Imports which showed a high growth during the first half of 2008–9 (44.8 per cent during April–September 2008) decelerated to 7.6 per cent in October 2008 and 10.2 per cent in November 2008 and subsequently exhibited continuous decline since December 2008, reflecting slowdown in domestic economic activity. Trade deficit during 2008–9 stood at US$ 117.1 billion and showed a substantial rise of US$ 28.5 billion (32.3 per cent) over US$ 88.5 billion in 2007–8. Though both exports and imports growth decelerated in 2008–9, the moderation in export growth was sharper than that in import growth, thereby giving rise to a steep increase in the trade deficit.

Volatile capital flows have been a central issue during the crisis and continue to be so now as the crisis ebbed. The EMEs saw a sudden stop and reversal of capital flows during the crisis as a consequence of global deleveraging. India has experienced both 'floods' and 'sudden stops' of capital flows. Net capital flows to India increased from as low as US$ 7 billion in 1990–1 to US$ 45 billion in 2006–7, and further to US$ 107 billion during 2007–8, the year just before the crisis. They dropped to as low as US$ 7 billion in 2008–9 at the height of the crisis. Capital flows are estimated to have recovered to around US$ 50 billion in 2009–10. Accordingly, the rupee exhibited greater two-way movements with Rupee/US dollar exchange rate appreciating by 12.9 per cent from Rs 50.95 per dollar at end-March 2009 to Rs 45.14 per dollar as at end-March 2010.

During this crisis, the impact of the financial channel was more distinct with sharp decline in portfolio inflows, external commercial borrowings, trade credit, and overseas borrowings of banks. Foreign direct investment and non-resident deposits, however, displayed resilience. A sharp contraction in Indian corporates' overseas borrowings significantly impacted domestic investment activity. Access to trade finance was severely affected for many EMEs due to tightness in overseas liquidity. Some improvement is discernible with the return of a degree of stability in the international financial markets and a recovery in the industrial sector in many advanced countries. India's balance of payments made a turnaround, gaining strength mainly from elevated private remittances coupled with a sharp bounce back in portfolio investment and buoyant NRI deposit inflows during 2009–10.

The banking sector in India, as in most of the EMEs, displayed buoyancy during the current global financial meltdown. The strength and resilience in the balance sheets of Indian banks was derived from them being well capitalized and having greater exposure to domestic conventional assets, unlike advanced countries where the banking sector had extensive exposure to sub-prime mortgage markets (particularly, in the US) and other exotic structured products. Furthermore, the banking sector in India, unlike advanced countries, is dominated by commercial banking and not investment banking. The direct effects of the global financial crisis on the Indian banking and financial system were almost negligible due to the limited exposure to riskier assets and derivatives, and the relatively low presence of foreign banks. Prima facie, Indian banks faced the stress because foreign investors pulled out of the economy and created a liquidity crunch. There was suddenly less money available to borrow or lend. The tightened global liquidity situation in the period immediately following the failure of Lehman Brothers in mid-September 2008, coming as it did on top of a turn in the credit cycle, increased the risk aversion of the financial system and made banks cautious about lending. At the same time, corporates and retail investors exerted redemption pressures on mutual funds, some of which got transmitted to NBFCs due to their dependence for funds on mutual funds. Thus, despite not being hit on the balance sheets, banks and other financial institutions were impacted by the indirect spillovers of the crisis during 2008–9.

POLICY RESPONSE IN INDIA

Before the intensification of the global financial meltdown from September 2008, both monetary and fiscal policy measures in India were guided by an overriding intention to contain spiralling inflationary expectations that were largely driven by international commodity prices. Monetary policy was striving to dampen the demand side pressures through monetary tightening. At the same time, fiscal policy was attempting to ease supply side constraints with a slew of measures, such as slashing excise and customs duties and encouraging imports of necessary goods, among others. India's policy response to the crisis was aimed at containing the contagion from the outside, to keep the domestic money and credit markets functioning normally and see that the liquidity stress did not trigger solvency cascades. In particular, three objectives were pursued with respect to the financial sector: first, to maintain a comfortable rupee liquidity position; second, to augment foreign exchange liquidity; and third, to maintain a policy framework that would keep credit delivery on track so as to arrest the moderation in growth. Besides the challenges thrown by the global financial meltdown, policy responses also involved the challenge of balancing short-term mitigation and medium-term sustainability.

The unprecedented global developments in the second half of 2008–9 forced the government to adopt an expansionary fiscal stance to cushion the economy from the effects of the global crisis. This shift in the fiscal policy stance was in line with the international trend to minimize the adverse effects of the global crisis and also consistent with mainstream views that in situations of deep and prolonged economic downturn, as in the present context, fiscal policy could play a leading role in stabilization. Although financial markets in India experienced heightened volatility in sync with international developments generating collateral damages, the banking system remained strong and well capitalized. The stress tests conducted on Indian banks suggest that they can withstand significant shocks arising from large potential changes in credit quality, interest rate, and liquidity conditions. Therefore, the fiscal policy in India did not have to extend support to the banking sector in the form of capitalization/

financial bailout, which was rampant in most advanced economies. Thus, the fiscal response has been highly weighted towards containing the economic slowdown by raising aggregate demand through discretionary fiscal policy. The depth and extraordinary impact of this crisis, however, clearly indicated the need for counter-cyclical public spending and, accordingly, the central government invoked the emergency provisions of the FRBM Act to seek relaxation from fiscal targets and launched fiscal stimulus packages in December 2008 and January 2009.

The fiscal policy measures undertaken in the form of three fiscal stimulus packages during the second half of 2008–9 constituted tax cuts, encouraging investment on infrastructure, and increased expenditure on both investment and consumption, with the latter accounting for the major share. The expansionary fiscal stance continued in the Union Budget for 2009–10. On the whole, the fiscal stimulus measures appear to have given more emphasis to support consumption demand rather than investment demand. The fiscal deficit increased to 6.0 per cent of GDP in 2008–9 from 2.7 per cent of GDP in 2007–8.

The monetary policy response was in terms of easing liquidity into the system through conventional measures such as cutting policy rates cash reserve ratio (CRR), reverse repo, and statutory liquidity ratio (SLR), and open market operations (OMO), and unconventional measures, viz., opening refinance facilities to SIDBI and EXIM Banks and clawing back prudential norms in regard to provisioning and risk weights. The total amount of actual/potential liquidity injected was Rs 5,85,000 crore. There are, however, some key differences between the actions taken by the RBI and the central banks in many advanced countries. First, in the process of liquidity injection, the counterparties involved were banks; even liquidity measures for mutual funds, NBFCs, and housing finance companies were largely channelled through the banks. Second, there was no dilution of collateral standards which were largely government securities, unlike the mortgage securities and commercial papers in the advanced economies. Third, despite a large liquidity injection, the RBI's balance sheet did not show an unusual increase, unlike global trends, because of release of the earlier sterilized liquidity. Fourth, the availability and deployment of multiple instruments facilitated better sequencing of monetary and liquidity measures. Finally, the experience in the use of pro-cyclical provisioning norms and counter-cyclical regulations ahead of the global crisis helped enhance financial stability.

Taken together, the measures put in place by RBI and the Government of India, since mid-September 2008, ensured that the Indian financial sector continued to function in an orderly manner. The cumulative amount of primary liquidity potentially available to the financial system through these measures was over US$ 122 billion or about 11 per cent of GDP. This sizeable easing has ensured a comfortable liquidity position starting mid-November 2008 as evidenced by a number of indicators. The monetary policy in India, like most other countries, had instituted both conventional measures and unconventional measures to be accommodative for containing the spillovers emanating from the recent global financial crisis. In the backdrop of firming up recovery and risk of rising food prices impinging on inflationary expectations, the monetary policy started its first phase of exiting its accommodative stance with reversing some of the unconventional measures during October 2009.

Table 4.1   Liquidity Injection/Availability during September 2008–9

Measure/Facility	Amount (Rs crore)	% of GDP (2008–9)
1. CRR Reduction	1,60,000	2.9
2. Unwinding/Buyback/De-sequestering of MSS Securities	1,59,044	2.9
3. Open Market Operations (purchases)*	1,04,128	1.9
4. Term Repo Facility	60,000	1.1
5. Increase in Export Credit Refinance	22,328	0.4
6. Special Refinance Facility for SCBs (Non-RRBs)	38,500	0.7
7. Refinance Facility for SIDBI/NHB/EXIM Bank	16,000	0.3
8. Liquidity Facility for NBFCs through SPV**	25,000	0.4
9. Total (1 to 8)	5,85,000	10.5
Memo item:		
SLR Reduction	40,000	0.7

Notes: * Includes Rs 57,487 crore of OMO purchases against the proposed OMO purchases of Rs 80,000 crore during the first half of 2009–10.
** Includes an option of Rs 5,000 crore.

From the perspective of EMEs, including India, a prominent lesson of this crisis is that with increasing globalization of trade, finance, and labour they are more strongly integrated with advanced economies than ever before. Consequently, any crisis that affects a major country or group of countries in the global economy or financial system will have implications for EMEs as well, sooner or later, depending on the nature and magnitude of the crisis. Thus, policymakers need to enhance their capacity to pre-empt the potential of such global shocks while formulating their policies.

CRISIS RESOLUTION IN EURO AREA

The peripheral Eurozone slid into a deep, structural, and multifaceted crisis characterized by large fiscal deficit, enormous public debt, and consistently eroding competitive position manifested in a gradually deteriorating current account balance. The problem first came to the surface in 2009 when Greece slipped into recession with GDP contracting by 2 per cent and unemployment rate rising to 9.5 per cent. Assessing the situation, on 22 April 2010, Moody downgraded Greece's sovereign rating to A3 followed by Standard & Poor which downgraded Greece's and Portugal's long-term debt to BB+ (junk) and A−, respectively, sparking off a marked dip in confidence in global equity markets. Several Greek banks were also downgraded subsequently which delimited their access to international financial markets.

At the core of the Greek problem lay the large magnitude of the twin deficits. First, the country's heavy dependence on foreign borrowing amidst slowing growth and reduced global risk appetite had heightened concerns over long standing fiscal and external imbalances. Second, the country's incapacity to correct the situation through changes in the exchange rate coupled with no fiscal latitude raised questions about Greece's ability to honour its outstanding debt obligations undermining global confidence in Greek economy. Third, elevated concerns of the situation spilling over to adjoining economies with equally fragile fiscal and financial sectors namely Portugal, Ireland, Italy, and Spain (PIIGS) raised serious concerns since early 2010. Fourth, systemic concerns emanated from the large holdings of sovereign debt paper with European banks.

The problems of the region are mostly structural and they existed even prior to the crisis. The global crisis only amplified the chronic weaknesses in the system and accelerated the downturn in the

economies. A large part of the fragile fiscal position in these economies is attributable to a low domestic saving rate. Expenditure on
retirement benefits due to an ageing population, tax evasion coupled
with steady depletion of growth promoting expenditure in education,
research, and infrastructure has resulted in a bloated public sector
structure in the countries over the years. Due to low domestic saving
rate, public debt has to be financed from foreign sources, resulting
in wide current account deficit and a growing external debt. Thus,
the fiscal problem got intertwined with the external deficit and debt
problem and the twin deficits fed each other in a self-fulfilling cycle.
This is directly traceable to a large trade deficit, reflection of their
continuously depleting price, and product competitiveness in international markets.

In May 2010, the European Union (EU) had announced concrete
stabilization measures for the euro area which comprised of a (i) €110
billion joint EU–IMF package for Greece; (ii) creation of the European
Stabilization Mechanism (ESM) and; (iii) stringent fiscal consolidation measures by a number of member states. In parallel with the
announcement of the ESM, the European Central Bank (ECB) took
action to stabilize euro area sovereign debt markets through sterilized
purchases of sovereign debt of certain countries. The G7 countries also
announced the reactivation of bilateral dollar swap lines between the
US Federal Reserve and ECB, Bank of England, and Swiss National
Bank. On 4 August 2010, the European Financial Stability Facility
(EFSF) became fully operational, increasing investor confidence by
providing an additional source of support. However, despite sincere
efforts, there was an underlying concern about member countries'
ability to endure the concomitant adjustment costs that accompany
the fiscal austerity measures.

Approximately one year later, the worst expectations about Euro
area have actually come true. First, Greece missed its deficit targets
and IMF forecast Greek debt levels to snowball to unsustainable levels in the near term. Second, there are emerging concerns about the
repayment capacities of Ireland and Portugal. With large fiscal deficits
and continued low growth, Portugal became the third euro area sovereign to seek financial assistance in April 2011 amidst political turmoil
in the country over a fiscal austerity package. Third, relatively stronger
economies like Italy have reported uncomfortable public debt levels

with a public debt burden of 120 per cent of national income and with €900 billion of debt maturing over the next five years. Fourth, all three countries namely, Greece, Ireland, and Portugal have been downgraded by major credit rating agencies during the period undermining investor confidence in the region. Fifth, there have been concerns about the sufficiency of EFSF funding.

In this background, to work out an international bail-out for Greece and a more comprehensive solution to the sovereign debt crisis now engulfing other parts of the bloc, the Eurozone leaders held an emergency summit on 21 July 2011. The salient points emerging from the meeting are set out below.

(i)   The EU agreed to extend a new programme for Greece worth €109 billion. The EU called on the IMF to continue to contribute to Greek financing. A new dimension to the new programme is that EU is also hoping to enlist some voluntary support from the private sector to fully cover the financing gap. The net contribution from the private sector is estimated at €37 billion.

(ii) The maturity of future loans to Greece from the EFSF was extended from the current 7.5 years to a minimum of 15 years and up to 30 years with a grace period of 10 years.

(iii) The rate of interest charged on EFSF loans will be equivalent to that of Balance of Payments facility (currently 3.5 per cent) with a lower bound of EFSF funding cost.

(iv) The implementation of the programme in Greece will be under strict surveillance of the European Commission in liaison with the ECB and IMF.

(v)   The leaders approved the European Commission's proposal to set up a task force to work with Greek authorities to target the structural funds on enhancing competitiveness, job creation, and training.

(vi) The leaders reiterated their determination to continue to provide support to other countries in the Eurozone such as Ireland and Portugal under programmes, provided they successfully implement those programmes. The concessional lending rates and flexible maturities agreed to for Greece shall apply equally to these two countries.

(vii)   The leaders resolved that all member states will adhere strictly to agreed fiscal targets, improve competitiveness, and address macroeconomic imbalances. Under this, public deficits in all countries will be brought below 3.0 per cent by 2013 at the latest.

(viii)   As a follow-up to the bank stress tests, member states will also provide backstops to banks as appropriate.

(ix)   To improve the effectiveness of EFSF and ESM, they are allowed to act on the basis of a precautionary programme, finance recapitalization of financial institutions through loans to governments, and intervene in the secondary markets during exceptional financial market circumstances.

US RATINGS DOWNGRADES: GLOBAL IMPLICATIONS

The US had been enjoying 'triple A status' since 1967 and had faced the warning of a downgrade only once in 1995 when the country had US$4.9 trillion in debt which is nearly US$ 10 trillion less than now. The protracted stand-off between US politicians over raising the US debt ceiling culminated in the worst outcome for the global economy on the 7 August 2011 when global credit rating agency, Standard & Poor's (S&P) downgraded the US long-term rating from AAA to AA+. Standard and Poor's has been of the view that the downgrade reflects that the fiscal consolidation plan that the Congress and the Administration recently agreed to, falls short of what would be necessary to stabilize the government's medium-term debt dynamics. More broadly, the downgrade reflects that the effectiveness, stability, and predictability of American policymaking and political institutions have weakened at a time of ongoing fiscal and economic challenges to a greater degree than when S&P assigned a negative outlook to the rating on 18 April 2011.

According to the US Congressional Budget Office, currently the US deficit stands at around 9.3 per cent of GDP in 2011 and the ratio of the public debt (the debt held by the public) to GDP equals 69.0 per cent of GDP. The massive debt was a result of unsustainable tax cuts between 2001–3, two expensive international wars costing over US$15 trillion between 2002–9, discretionary spending worth over US$600 billion, fiscal costs of backstopping and bailing out banks during the global crisis of 2007 amounting to US$220 billion and fiscal stimulus worth US$700 billion under the Troubled Asset Relief Programme (TARP). About 2.5 per cent of the deficit is cyclical and would fall in tune with the business cycle when the economy returns to potential growth. However, the structural part of the deficit is about 6.8 per cent of GDP which would require some discretionary policy action from the US government. The Republicans and Democrats had earlier agreed to a cut in US government spending of US$2.1–2.4 trillion spread over the next 10 years, which is way short of the US$4 trillion target, proposed previously.

The predominance of the US dollar as the global reserve currency has perennially been argued to be the 'Achilles heel' of the global imbalance debate. Theoretically, the US downgrade should encourage central banks and fund managers across the world who have been parking money in US treasuries to look for other safe havens which, in turn, may gradually but partly resolve the long drawn global imbalance debate that central banks accumulating large reserves in US dollars have been investing in US treasuries reducing yields and fuelling risky investments in the US. Likewise, the debate on multiple reserve currencies may also acquire momentum in due course. However, past experience shows that, although emerging economies might be willing to shift their portfolios away from US dollar to other currencies, they have not been able to find viable alternatives which may lead them to continue with the current portfolios, as of now.

RECOVERY AND THE WAY FORWARD

The response of the global community through quick and prudent policies followed by continuous monitoring at the national and international level, with a remarkable degree of international cooperation, brought the sharp contraction of the global economy during late 2008 and early 2009 to an end. By the end of 2009, most economies started to grow again and international trade began to revive, although, uneven across regions, the pace of recovery has been faster than previously anticipated. However, in May 2010, the global financial system once again experienced instability as market concerns intensified against high sovereign debt and fiscal deficits of some European countries. In view of the fresh concerns over 'fiscal sustainability', in general, growth in the second quarter of this year was lower than in the first quarter. Looking forward to the second-half of this year, many uncertainties cloud the global economic outlook. The task of economic recovery and repair, thus, seems to be far from complete and this highlights the importance of carrying forward the reform process initiated in the light of the recent global crisis.

The financial crisis has brought a number of weaknesses in macro-economic policy, financial regulation, and global financial architectures into the open. The reform agenda is enormous, much remains to be done, and new questions have come up for the design of more stable national and global financial systems. While there are many lessons for financial reforms going forward, there remains much to be done in areas such as competition policy for a stable financial system, approaches to consumer protection in financial services, and the political economy of financial regulation, financial openness, and financial crises.

The G-20 leaders have the task of steering the collective action in policies that would ensure a lasting recovery and a brighter economic future. Apart from progressing with the strict guidelines for financial regulatory reforms and reform of the International Financial Institutions, launching of the 'Framework for Strong, Sustainable, and Balanced Growth' as a multilateral process, where G-20 countries together set out objectives and the policies needed to get there, has been a milestone in a collective effort to restore the economies. And, most importantly, they undertake a 'mutual assessment' of their progress toward meeting those shared objectives. With this, the G-20 Mutual Assessment Process or the 'MAP' involves a new approach to policy collaboration, entirely conceived and owned by G-20 members. The aim is to ensure that the collective policy action will benefit all. Like any new initiative, the MAP will be fully fleshed out over time, in a large part through learning by doing.

The EMEs are recovering strongly and inflation pressures there are rising. In view of the beginning of the recovery, some EMEs, including India, have already begun to exit from their expansionary monetary policy stance. Going forward, the exit policies are expected to progress at varying rates across countries, depending upon the country-specific circumstances. The EMEs need to carry out their own due diligence to ensure that systemic risks are monitored within their countries.

Large capital inflows are considered to be a key contributing factor in many financial crises in EMEs in the past. Given low policy rates in the major financial centres, many EMEs are concerned that their stronger growth prospects could attract destabilizing capital inflows, leading to currency appreciation. The recent experience of EMEs with capital flows seems to point towards the potential role for prudential measures to reduce systemic risk associated with large capital inflows. Some continue to keep policy rates low and resist exchange rate appreciation by conducting large-scale intervention in foreign exchange markets. Such policies tend to be associated with a sizeable expansion in bank balance sheets, rapid credit growth, and asset price overshooting. The risks of domestic overheating, thus, increase. To promote more balanced domestic and global growth, some EMEs could rely more on exchange rate flexibility and on monetary policy tightening. In addition, prudential tools have an important role to play in enhancing the resilience of the financial system to domestic and external financial shocks. In contrast, while capital controls may have a limited and temporary role, they are unlikely to be effective over the medium term. Recent experience suggests a cautious approach to the pace and scope of capital account liberalization as there is a strong linkage among capital account liberalization, domestic financial sector reform, and the design of monetary and exchange rate policy.

So far as the Indian economy is concerned, it looks poised to recover smartly after facing the most severe global recession in recent decades extraordinarily well. One of the major reasons cited for the Indian economy being less vulnerable to the global crisis is its lower exposure to trade and global finance, despite the increased exposure to the global economy. It may, however, also be noted that the economic reform measures of the 1990s, especially the financial sector reforms which led to significant strengthening of the banking sector, have helped India to become more resilient to shocks of various kinds. Nevertheless, India was also fortunate in escaping a potentially more severe impact from the global crisis. A powerful series of counter measures by the major economies arrested the financial panic and allowed for the global financial markets and the global demand to stabilize. India might not have recovered at such a pace had the global conditions worsened. The quick response from the Indian authorities also benefited India to tread on the growth path once again.

Nonetheless, given the fragility of global economic recovery and the still high risk of financial and other shocks in the global environment, India needs to address its policy towards further strengthening economic resilience. Currently, the dominant concern from the monetary policy point of view is high inflation. With growth taking a firm hold, the balance of the policy stance has to shift decisively to containing inflation and anchoring inflationary expectations. The risk of capital flows runs both ways. It is quite possible that EMEs, including India, receive more flows than they need, because of accommodative monetary policies of advanced country central banks for an extended period, posing challenges for monetary and exchange rate management, while on the other hand, an uncertain global situation could significantly reduce the flow of capital into EMEs constraining domestic investment which is critical to achieving and sustaining high growth rates. The ability to meet the fiscal consolidation targets would also hold the key to the performance of the Indian economy in the post crisis new world order.

5

Approach to Capital Account Liberalization

One of the most significant developments in the world economy in the 1990s has been the spectacular surge in international capital flows. There was increasing recognition that gains from international portfolio diversification, albeit less than that accrued from international trade, could still be significant. Capital flows to EMEs have increased significantly in the period preceding the recent crisis, reflecting both the push and pull factors. The pull factors included strong growth, reduction in inflation, macroeconomic stability, opening up of capital accounts, and buoyant growth prospects in EMEs. The stance of monetary policy in the advanced economies has been the major push factor with the loose monetary policy and search for yield in the advanced economies, encouraging large capital inflows to the EMEs. Innovations in information technology have also contributed to the two-way movement in capital flows to the EMEs.

It is recognized in the literature that large and persistent inflows of capital could become a potential threat to financial stability, in case the prolonged benign interest rate environment in advanced economies encourages investment in risky assets in the EMEs, in the quest for higher returns. Similarly, large and sudden reversals of capital flows can create disorderly conditions in the foreign exchange market causing depreciation of the exchange rate. If unaccompanied by automatic stabilizers and countercyclical prudential parameters in the financial system, the situation may cascade into a crisis in no time as the current experience has shown.

Further, the problem lies not only with respect to the absolute size of the flows but also with the accompanying volatility. Volatile capital flows tend to exacerbate the uncertainty surrounding financial markets, particularly during a downturn in the markets, leading to herd behaviour, and market crashes. It is also observed that whether the crisis originates in emerging or advanced economies, capital flows generally reverse from EMEs. In fact, global capital inflows are characterized by 'sudden stops' with painful adjustments in output and consumption. Reversals of capital flows from the EMEs, as again shown by the current financial crisis, are quick, necessitating a painful adjustment in bank credit and collapse of stock prices. Such reversals also result in the contraction of the central bank's balance sheet. This is accentuated by the difficulties in domestic assets accretions, compensating for the depletion of reserves which tend to take place at a faster rate. These developments can then lead to banking and currency crises, large employment and output losses, and huge fiscal costs. Thus, the boom and bust pattern of capital inflows can, unless managed proactively, result in macroeconomic and financial instability.

With more and more countries adopting capital account liberalization and the exponential rise in scale and variety of cross border financial transactions since the 1990s, there has been an alarming rise in the rampant episodes of exchange rate volatility manifesting itself in frequent currency crises. Further, the positive effect of capital flows on investment is achieved only at the expense of higher asset price volatility. The impact of shocks to portfolio capital flows in raising asset price volatility has been empirically established.

CAPITAL ACCOUNT CONVERTIBILITY

Currency convertibility refers to the freedom to convert the domestic currency into other internationally accepted currencies and vice versa. Convertibility, in that sense, is the obverse of controls or restrictions on currency transactions. While current account convertibility refers to freedom in respect of 'payments and transfers for current international transactions', capital account convertibility (CAC) would mean freedom of currency conversion in relation to capital transactions in

terms of inflows and outflows. Article VIII of the IMF puts an obligation on a member to avoid imposing restrictions on the making of
payments and transfers for current international transactions. Article
VI (3), however, allows members to exercise such controls as are
necessary to regulate international capital movements, but not so as
to restrict payments for current transactions or which would unduly
delay transfers of funds in settlement of commitments.

The committee on Fuller Capital Account Convertibility (FCAC)
(2006) put forth the following working definition of CAC:

> CAC refers to the freedom to convert local financial assets into foreign
> financial assets and vice versa. It is associated with changes of owner-
> ship in foreign/domestic financial assets and liabilities and embodies
> the creation and liquidation of claims on, or by, the rest of the world.
> CAC can be, and is, coexistent with restrictions other than on external
> payments.

Recognizing the incompatibility of full capital mobility, monetary
policy autonomy, and exchange rate stability, central banks across the
world have worked towards resolving this 'impossible trinity', though
the importance given to each objective has changed during the past
century. Tracing out the history, one observes that the period since the
1870s till the outbreak of the World War I was the period of the gold
standard when there were no capital controls and monetary independence had been given away to take care of the policy trilemma. Free
movement of capital was sacrificed during the period from 1945 till
the end of Bretton Woods system that was marked by imposition of
capital controls by most economies, even the developed ones, including the US.

Capital Account Liberalization (CAL) was undertaken over a
period of years in advanced countries including the Euro area, particularly after the breakdown of the Bretton Woods system of fixed
exchange rates in the mid-1970s. During the 1980s and 1990s, many of
the EMEs also undertook capital account liberalization. This was followed by episodes of huge capital inflows into some of these countries,
the magnitude of which became unmanageable and destabilizing for
many EMEs. Based on the cross-country experience in capital account
liberalization, especially since the East Asian crisis of 1997, the mainstream thinking both at the academic and policy levels has changed in

the recent years. The risks of full CAL arise mainly from inadequate preparedness before liberalization in terms of domestic and external sector policy consolidation, strengthening of prudential regulation, and development of financial markets, including infrastructure, for orderly functioning of these markets. Most currency crises arise out of prolonged overvalued exchange rates, leading to unsustainable current account deficits. A transparent fiscal consolidation is necessary and desirable to reduce the risk of currency crisis. Short-term debt flows react quickly and adversely during currency crises. Domestic financial institutions, in particular banks, need to be strong and resilient. The quality and proactive nature of market regulation is also critical to the success of efficient functioning of financial markets during times of currency crises.

Theoretical Base

The case for CAL is often made on the premise that it promotes growth among resource constrained developing countries which need external capital to sustain an excess of investment over domestic saving. CAL also promotes macroeconomic stability by smoothing consumption and investment over alternating phases of the business cycle. Financial openness fosters efficiency by enabling residents to base investment and consumption decisions on world interest rates and prices. CAL also offers the opportunity of using the world market to diversify portfolios of savers and investors.

A number of studies have confirmed that financial globalization can contribute significantly to promoting growth in developing countries by augmenting domestic savings, reducing cost of capital, transferring technology, developing the domestic financial sector, and fostering human capital formation (Prasad et al. 2003). At the same time, however, it has been recognized that sudden and large surges in capital flows cause several concerns. Large capital flows could push up monetary aggregates, engender inflationary pressures, destabilize exchange rates, exacerbate the current account position, adversely affect the domestic financial sector, and disrupt domestic growth trajectories, if and when such flows get reversed or drastically reduced (Hoggarth and Stern 1999). Volatility of capital flows, particularly portfolio flows, and their consequent impact on the emerging market economies has been well documented. It is widely recognized now that although global capital flows have a potential for improving efficiency, they also can trigger instability. Developing countries as a group have tended to be more vulnerable to instability arising out the volatility of short-term capital flows, the risk of large capital outflows, export of domestic saving from capital scarce developing countries, and weakening the ability of domestic authorities to tax financial activities, income, and wealth. There is also the potential risk of the 'Dutch disease' due to large capital inflows as real exchange rate appreciation can divert resources from tradable to non-tradables in the face of rising external liabilities. Inefficient financial markets with asymmetric information carry the risk of financial bubbles. Global interdependence is marked by common shocks and a confidence channel transmits these shocks to various parts of the world. Thus, while financial globalization can, in theory, help to promote growth, there is, however, no robust empirical evidence as yet that it can help developing countries to improve growth rates and reduce macroeconomic volatility (Prasad et al. 2003).

Benefits of Capital Account Liberalization

The origins of the theoretical controversy over the benefits of capital account liberalization can be traced to the basic question—are financial markets predominantly efficient or do information asymmetries and real sector rigidities render them inefficient? Proponents of the efficient markets hypothesis argue that an open capital account could bring with it greater financial efficiency, specialization, and innovation by exposing the financial sector to global competition.

Gruben and McLeod (2001) found that greater financial openness across a large number of countries and the significant decline in global inflation could contribute to higher growth. Capital account liberalization could, in combination with other policies, play a significant role in the take-off of less developed countries, and to the extent that it does, it would have large benefits (Gourinchas and Jeanne 2002). Developing countries need external capital to sustain an excess of investment over domestic savings and an open capital account could attract foreign capital. Residents get the opportunity to base their investment and consumption decisions on world interest rates and world prices for tradables which could enhance their welfare. By setting prices right, an open capital account enables aggregate savings and investments to be optimized, leading to both allocative efficiency and competitive discipline. Capital flows permit nations to trade consumption today for consumption in the future, that is, to engage in inter-temporal trade (Eichengreen et al. 1999). Again, by offering the opportunity of using the world market to diversify portfolios, an open capital account permits both savers and investors to protect the real value of their assets through risk reduction. On the other hand, capital controls could encourage hidden capital flight and/or diversion of savings into real assets and gold, leading to sub-optimal use of internal resources.

In the neoclassical framework, capital flows contribute to growth primarily by supplementing domestic savings. In the endogenous growth framework, the contributions to growth attributed to capital flows comprise the spillovers associated with foreign capital in the form of technology, skills, and introduction of new products as well as positive externalities in terms of higher efficiency of domestic financial markets, resulting in improved resource allocation and efficient financial intermediation by domestic financial institutions. Since the spillovers and externalities associated with different forms of foreign capital could vary, a pecking order approach to the composition of capital flows is often pursued by prioritizing the capital flows based on the growth enhancing role of each form of capital.

Costs of Capital Account Liberalization

Several arguments, on the other hand, are put forward against the liberalization of the capital account, viz., potential macroeconomic instability arising from the volatility of short-term capital movements; the risk of large capital outflows, and associated negative externalities; export of domestic savings from capital scarce developing countries; and weakening the ability of authorities to tax domestic financial activities, income, and wealth. There is also the potential risk of the 'Dutch disease effect' due to large capital inflows and appreciating real exchange rate, diverting resources from tradable to non-tradable sectors in the face of rising external liabilities. Inefficient financial markets with asymmetric information could also lead to risk of financial bubbles. Besides, premature liberalization could lead to currency substitution and capital flight, balance of payments crises, currency depreciation, and domestic inflation. It is argued that monetary contraction not only slows economic activity through the normal interest channels, but can also threaten the health of the economy through the banking system (Kaminsky and Reinhart 1999).

The growing global macroeconomic imbalance, as evidenced by the large and sustained current account deficit of the US, suggests that markets may at times allocate global savings differently from what is perceived by the policymakers as appropriate and sustainable in the long-run. Like the effect on resource allocation, the beneficial effects of capital account liberalization on growth are ambiguous. There is no evidence that countries without capital controls have grown faster, invested more, or experienced lower inflation (Rodrik 1998).

Unlike the ambiguity surrounding the resource allocation argument, there is greater unanimity on the point that open capital account exerts pressures to discipline domestic macroeconomic and financial environment. Disciplinary effects of an open capital account on the fiscal deficit suggest that complete freedom for outward capital mobility could be associated with a reduction in the budget deficit (Kim 1999). Gourinchas and Jeanne (2002) emphasized that many EMEs may benefit from the discipline effect rather than the conventional resource allocation effect. If the benefits of capital market liberalization are smaller for the poorest countries than for the middle income countries, the same is probably also true of the costs (Gilbert 2000).

Furthermore, controls on outflows are viewed by markets as an additional risk factor and their prolonged use has often been associated with capital flight. Fischer (1998) insisted that currency controls, no matter how well executed, impose distortions on the economy and the longer they are in place, the more serious they tend to get. Another fact that weighs against capital controls relates to their efficacy. Capital controls are not very effective, particularly when the current account is convertible, as current account transactions create channels for disguised capital flows. Capital controls intend to insulate domestic financial conditions from external financial developments. The influence of external financial conditions, however, has been increasing over the years, even in countries with extensive capital controls. As the costs of evading the controls have declined and the attractiveness of holding assets in offshore markets has increased, capital controls are becoming increasingly ineffective. As per the squeezing on a balloon argument, capital being fungible, restrictions on one form of capital and not on others would quickly lead to displacement of flows to the uncontrolled segment (Quirk and Evans 1995).

A review of the empirical studies on the effectiveness of both variants of control suggests that in almost 70 per cent of the cases where the controls on outflows were used as a preventive measure, a large increase in capital flight was observed after their imposition (Yoshitomi and Shirai 2000). The support for using curative control came from Krugman (1998) who suggested temporary use of controls amidst a crisis to avoid the adverse effects of a high interest rate defence of the exchange rate. Krugman justified temporary capital controls on the ground that the costs of any resulting distortions were likely to be lower than the alternative costs to the economy on account of higher interest rates and economic slump. The qualifications to this argument were fourfold:

(i)   controls should disrupt ordinary business as little as possible,
(ii)   controls must be used as a temporary measure as distortions associated with controls tend to grow over time,
(iii) controls may cause the greatest damage when the intention is to defend an overvalued exchange rate, and
(iv)   controls must aid reforms and they should not be viewed as an alternative to reform.

Bhagwati (1998) asserted that full capital mobility was not a necessary condition for free trade. He advocated capital controls as a stopgap measure as part of the solution for Asia on grounds that it allowed these countries to adopt more expansionary monetary and fiscal policies and, hence, promoted a faster recovery of the real economy. Such a recovery could be expected to reduce the problems of insolvency and closure in the corporate sector, and non-performing loans in the banking system. Stiglitz (1998) contended that the cost of disruption due to swings in expectations is invariably high for developing countries. Thus, there exists a case for more direct intervention in less sophisticated economies. Given the nature of international financial transactions, developing countries ought to give themselves as much freedom as they can to place prudential controls on the more volatile forms of capital movements, in particular, portfolio capital and short-term flows (Agosin 1998). Gilbert and Vines (2000) felt that '...within a cost-benefit framework, the benefits are seen as more modest than had previously been supposed, while the Asian crisis has increased our estimates of the potential costs of liberalisation.'

While no conclusive end to the debate appears to be in sight, there is a general consensus that the case for capital account convertibility would rest on the circumstances and economic conditions specific to a country, as also the extent of development of its markets and institutions. In the absence of an all-or-nothing case for or against capital account convertibility, several countries have experimented with various types of capital controls in different situations. The experiences of these countries provide useful lessons for theorists and policymakers alike.

History and Trends in Capital Account Liberalization: 1914–2009

Capital account liberalization, which is at the root of the surge in capital flows, has a long precedent. The history of capital flows dates back to the pre world war period when raw materials was exported from the colonies of Asia and Africa to the more prosperous and advanced economies like Britain, France, and Germany, and in search of higher yields, capital flowed back into the colonies in the form of 'investments'. After World War II, the process of capital account liberalization was formalized and marked by establishment of proper institutions, legal codes, as well as emphasis on achieving political consensus. By 1958, full current account convertibility had been achieved in most advanced countries. Starting from the 1960s, many advanced countries had just begun dismantling capital controls when their attempts were hindered by the problems in the Bretton Woods system. The fixed exchange rate system of the Bretton Woods, the loss of confidence in the role of US dollar, along with higher interest rates in Europe, led to capital outflows away from the US towards European countries. The US, that had generally adopted liberal policies with regard to capital account in the post war period, introduced capital controls on account of these speculative outflows. Controls in the form of Interest Equalisation Tax (1963),

Voluntary Guidelines limiting foreign lending and investment (1965), and Voluntary Guidelines limiting foreign direct investment (1968) were introduced. Most of these controls were eliminated after the end of Bretton Woods system. Since then (1974 onwards) the US has followed a liberal capital regime with limited control mainly pertaining to security concerns.

Unlike the US, the move towards capital account liberalization amongst European countries has not been very smooth. It has been marked by alternate phases of controls and relaxations and has ranged over one-and-a-half decade (UK liberalized in 1979, while Greece in 1994, Table 5.1).

Table 5.1   Abolition of Capital Controls—Developed Countries

Country	Year of Abolition of Capital Controls
United States	1974
European countries	
United Kingdom	1979
Germany	1981
Netherlands	1986
Denmark	1988
France	1989
Sweden	1989
Italy	1990
Belgium	1990
Austria	1991
Finland	1991
Spain	1992
Portugal	1992
Ireland	1993
Greece	1994
Japan	1991
Australia	1985
New Zealand	1985

Source: Bakker and Chapple (2002) and IMF, *Annual Report on Exchange Arrangements and Exchange Restrictions*, various issues.

Liberalization of capital transactions in European countries, for example, was formally laid down in the Treaty of Rome in 1957. Analogous to the process in Asia, capital account liberalization in Europe was a gradual institutionalized process. The year 1958 marked the beginning of a move towards capital account liberalization with the setting up of the European Economic Commission (EEC) that provided for the eventual freedom of capital movements in Europe. The commitment to the opening up of the capital account remained weak throughout the 1960s, marked by 'one step forward and two step backwards approach', despite a formal treaty in place. The UK became the first European country to implement liberalization of capital movements in 1979, 24 years after the signing of the Treaty of Rome. The process gradually culminated in the Single European Act of 1987 with a directive in 1988 'which contained concessions in the form of longer transition periods for member states which were not ready to give up capital controls in the near future.'

The move towards complete capital account liberalization and the period post capital account liberalization in developed countries has not been without problems/risks. For example, in UK, that followed a fast move towards account liberalization, while inflows increased marginally, the immediate post liberalization period saw a substantial hike in capital outflows in UK. Economic growth in UK improved during the 1980s and inflation fell. Towards the end of 1980s, UK witnessed a period of industrial unrest and an asset price bubble developed. Exchange rate remained volatile at times, though there was no backtracking towards capital control measures ever. The UK at present has no restrictions on capital transactions in money, capital, and derivatives market and with respect to personal capital transactions and institutional investors. The authorities have, however, retained the power to impose restrictions on inward direct investment if it hinders national interest.

The generalized move towards capital account liberalization, in the 1980s in advanced countries, coincided with a general shift towards more market oriented economic policies aimed at achieving non-inflationary growth. While the OECD code on capital account liberalization provided a helpful instrument for exerting pressure on member countries to lift controls, the political willingness of the European countries to move towards EU encouraged the lifting of all controls. As mentioned earlier, the move towards complete capital account liberalization and the period of post liberalization in developed countries has not been without problems.

Outside Europe, Japan, Australia, and New Zealand have also imposed controls on short-term capital flows for extended periods.

Japan's approach towards capital account liberalization remained inconsistent till 1979, with controls imposed and subsequently eased in 1967, 1973, and 1979. As a result, investment inflows generally remained low. Subsequently, Japan followed a very gradual approach towards liberalization, ranging over a decade from 1979 to 1991. Australia and New Zealand, on the other hand, are examples of rapid move to capital account liberalization. On the back of the foreign exchange crisis of 1984, New Zealand liberalized all restrictions within a year (mid-1984 to mid-1985). Prior to the move, New Zealand followed a regime of pervasive capital controls, exchange rate peg, and import controls on a wide range of products.

Developing Countries Experience

The decade of 1980s and 1990s witnessed growing pressures on the developing countries to open up to foreign capital flows (through World Bank and IMF conditionality, WTO rules, membership of regional trade agreements, etc.). Many emerging economies maintained unrestricted capital accounts in the 1980s and 1990s. This was followed by episodes of huge capital inflows into these countries, the magnitude of which became unmanageable and destabilizing for the EMEs. Sterilization operations were usually the first policy response to such inflows. However, such operations typically entailed costs to the central bank and attracted further inflows as they tended to keep interest rates high. Recognizing the ineffectiveness of sterilization operations beyond a point and succumbing to the appreciation pressures due to huge inflows, many of these emerging economies backtracked from the liberal capital account measures and imposed restrictions—both price and non-price based measures.

The country experience with respect to tackling post liberalization inflows and outflows has been varied. Some of the countries have backtracked to limit short-term capital inflows, viz., Brazil (1993–7), Chile (1991–8), Malaysia (1994), and Thailand (1995–7). Malaysia (1998), Thailand (1997–8), and Indonesia have backtracked by reimposing controls on capital outflows to prevent flight of capital (Ariyoshi et al. 2000). Some developing countries, however, have not resorted to backtracking to tackle post capital account liberalization inflows/outflows, but have resorted to other means. It was these capital account crises in some of the East Asian and Latin American countries that contributed to a more nuanced approach towards capital account liberalization, that is, capital account liberalization should proceed more cautiously and with appropriate sequencing.

In the case of most of the developing economies that went in for re-imposition of controls subsequent to capital account liberalization, while controls temporarily relieved the pressures on the balance of payments, they did not provide lasting protection when the fundamental causes of the imbalances remained unaddressed.

During the 1980s and 1990s, IMF and Multilateral Development Banks became the mouthpiece of the 'Washington Consensus' educating economies about the virtues of free capital mobility. As Stanley Fischer of the Fund puts it 'IMF was so convinced with the benefits accruing from the free capital flows that at its Interim Committee meeting in April 1997, IMF agreed to broaden its mandate to include liberalization of international capital movements as a central purpose of the Fund.' The subsequent crisis in East Asia in 1997, however, halted such moves of the IMF. It motivated introspection into the fundamental policy of open capital account in political and academic circles. The East Asian crisis fuelled an international discourse on the costs and benefits of capital account liberalization.

Although current account liberalization is among the IMF's official purposes outlined in its Articles of Agreement, the IMF has no explicit mandate to promote capital account liberalization. According to the Report of the Independent Evaluation Office of the IMF on its approach to capital account liberalization:

> ... the IMF has given greater attention to capital account issues in recent decades, in light of the increasing importance of international capital flows for member countries' macroeconomic management. The IMF encouraged countries that wanted to move ahead with capital account liberalization, especially before the East Asian crisis. However, there is no evidence to suggest that it exerted significant leverage to push countries to move faster than they were willing to go. ... The IMF pointed out the risks inherent in an open capital account as well as the need for a sound financial system, even from the beginning. These risks, however, were insufficiently highlighted, and the recognition of the risks and preconditions did not translate into operational advice on pace and sequencing until later in the 1990s.

The varied experience of the developing countries that went in for capital account liberalization in the 1980s and 1990s could be summarized as follows:

(i)   The liberalization of the capital account was gradual in most of the advanced economies in the run up to full convertibility, combined with strengthening financial systems and prudential regulations. Even after 'fully' liberalizing the capital account, these countries continued to maintain certain capital controls.

(ii) Experience of some of the Asian and Latin American economies, which went in for liberalization of their capital account in the 1980s and later backtracked by imposing controls, shows that even after full capital account convertibility, there is a need for safety valves in the form of regulatory safeguards to meet potential capital account crises.

(iii) Gradual process of capital account liberalization does not eliminate the risks of crisis or pressures in the foreign exchange market. These risks, however, get minimized when an integrated approach to reform is taken involving macroeconomic stabilisation and institutional strengthening.

(iv) Capital controls could temporarily relieve the pressures on the balance of payments but they cannot provide lasting protection when the fundamental causes of the imbalances remain unaddressed. Moreover, partial system of capital control that seeks to discriminate between types of flows or destinations provides incentives for circumvention and is vulnerable to diversion of capital flows to unregulated financial markets.

(v)   Though fiscal consolidation may not by itself be a sufficient condition to prevent a crises, it has been a necessary component of liberalization and its absence can lead to instability. Limiting fiscal imbalances and preventing excessive build-up of domestic debt is essential to avoid chances of backtracking subsequently from capital account liberalization.

(vi) Emerging market economies have managed heavy inflows subsequent to liberalization through sterilization, though later most of them have re-imposed capital controls faced with the limitations of sterilization.

DEFINING CAPITAL CONTROLS

Capital controls can be defined as restrictions on the free movement of capital. Countries use these controls to restrict volatile movements of capital entering (inflows) and exiting (outflows) their country. Capital controls are recognized to take the form of taxes, price or quantity controls, or outright prohibitions on international trade in assets. Thus, broad forms of capital controls are direct or administrative controls and indirect or market-based controls.

Direct controls which are also known as quantity controls restrict capital transactions and associated payments, and transfer of funds through outright prohibitions, explicit quantitative limits, or an approval procedure. Direct/administrative controls seek to directly affect the volume of cross border capital transactions. Direct controls are generally associated with administrative obligation on the banking system to control flows.

Quantity restrictions on capital flows may include rules mandating ceilings or requiring special authorization for new or existing borrowing from foreign residents. Administrative controls may also take the form of a government agency approving transactions for certain types of assets. Access to certain types of investment may be outrightly restricted.

Indirect or market-based controls discourage capital flows by varying the cost of capital. Such controls may assume various forms such as dual or multiple exchange rate system, explicit or implicit taxation of cross border financial flows (for example, Tobin tax), and various other price-based measures. Depending on the specific type, market-based controls may either affect only the price or both the price and the volume of a given transaction.

Tobin Tax

Named after the economist James Tobin, the Tobin tax was proposed in the 1970s and was intended to put a penalty on short-term speculation on currencies. This is a tax on all trade in currency across borders. The original tax rate Tobin proposed was 1 per cent, which was subsequently lowered to between 0.1 per cent and 0.25 per cent. Several countries like Brazil, Chile, and Colombia have used variants of Tobin tax to discourage heavy short-term capital inflows. It has been argued that it helps reducing exchange rate volatility and consequently curtails the intensity of 'boom-bust' cycles due to international capital flows. Tobin tax is criticized on several counts. First, the tax does not distinguish between the different types of flows or transactions, whether permanent or temporary, debt or non-debt, long-term or short-term, or between export receipts, or import payments. Second, the tax can be evaded easily through the modern financial instruments like derivatives and it also reduces liquidity in the markets. It is also noteworthy that the burden of a Tobin tax is inversely proportional to the length of the transaction, that is, the shorter the holding period, the heavier the burden of tax.

Unremunerated Reserve Requirement

The quantity-based control which attracted the attention worldwide is Unremunerated Reserve Requirement (URR). Such a measure requires the parties to deposit some percentage of their inflows with the central bank with no interest earning for a specified period of time. In other words, the URR is a requirement to hold an unremunerated fixed-term (mostly one year) reserve at the Central Bank, equivalent to a fraction of capital inflows in select categories. Hence, the URR is equivalent to a tax per unit of time that declines with the permanence or maturity of the affected capital inflows.

The Central Bank of Chile imposed URR on select inflows during June 1991–September 1998. Various features of the URR were altered during this period. In May and July 1992, the URR was raised to 30 per cent and the holding period was fixed at one full year, regardless of the term structure of the credit. In 1998, with declining capital inflows, the Central Bank reduced the URR to 10 per cent in late June, and later the URR was set at zero in September. In 2001, the authorities removed all remaining restrictions on the capital account. The imposition of URR in Chile changes the composition of capital flows and reduced the short-term capital flows successfully.

Colombia too resorted to URR to discourage short-term capital inflows in September 1993. In an effort to target short-term inflows, the URR was limited to loans with maturities up to 18 months. The URR was subsequently modified several times to better target short-term inflows (with higher rates applied to shorter maturities). On 6 May 2007, the authorities introduced capital controls as part of a new strategy to slow the appreciation of the peso. The primary measure included a URR of 40 per cent on external borrowing. The capital controls were extended in late May 2007 to portfolio inflows. Investors were given the option of early withdrawal of funds from the URR, but with substantial penalties ranging from 9.4 per cent of the reserve requirement (for immediate withdrawals) to 1.6 per cent (if held for five months). Controls were subsequently relaxed in September 2008 as the minimum stay requirement on FDI was revoked and finally eliminated in October 2008. As in Chile, following the Asian crisis, the URR was substantially reduced to contain exchange rate pressures. The capital controls in Chile/Colombia were effective in reducing the short-term capital inflows and in changing the composition of the flows.

Why Capital Controls?

As a result of large swings in capital flows witnessed in the recent period, the old debate on capital controls has revived. The literature points out several reasons why countries at different points in time have imposed capital controls. Some of them are as follows:

(i)   To discourage capital outflows during the time of crisis so as to reduce the pressure of sharp depreciation of domestic currency.

(ii) To prevent overvaluation of the currency. Further, restrictions are also put to limit short-term inflows in response to concerns about macroeconomic implications of increasing size and volatility of capital inflows.[1] Volatility of capital inflows could hurt the monetary stability of an economy and could make the financial system more vulnerable.

(iii) Reducing reliance on sterilization which involves quasi fiscal costs. Continuous sterilization may increase interest rate gap between EMEs and advanced economies and, thereby, encourage further inflows. Moreover, as inflows increase, there would be an appreciating pressure on the domestic

[1] See Annexure 1.

currency. The appreciation of the domestic currency would lead to loss of export competitiveness and worsening the balance of payment position.

(iv) To modify the composition of inflows, in particular to discourage short-term banking inflows, especially those denominated in foreign currency.

(v) Limiting debt creating flows, which are considered more risky than equity flows.

(vi) To decouple domestic interest rates from foreign interest rates with the aim of restoring some monetary independence under the fixed or highly pegged exchange rate regime.

(vii) To reduce foreign demand for domestic assets without resorting to expansionary monetary policy or revaluation. This allows a lower rate of inflation than would otherwise be possible (for example, German Bardepot scheme, 1972–4).

(viii) Reducing domestic demand for foreign assets without taking recourse to contractionary monetary policy or devaluation. This allows a higher rate of inflation than otherwise would be possible (for example, US interest equalization tax, 1963–74).

(ix) To support domestic investment by restricting capital outflows, particularly by countries that lack resources.

RECENT DEBATE ON CAPITAL CONTROLS

Large swings in capital inflows over a very short period of time beyond the absorptive capacity of the economy pose the risk of excess liquidity fuelling asset prices, raising inflation and inflationary expectations, and adversely affecting the competitiveness of industry through sharp currency appreciation. Abrupt reversals in such capital flows cause even greater problems. All these impose significant adjustment costs and complicates monetary and exchange rate management in the EMEs. It may be noted that the large capital inflows in the current year so far has already resulted in currency appreciation in many EMEs, notably in Brazil, Taiwan, Russia, Indonesia, Thailand, etc. Against this backdrop, the issue of capital control, especially the imposition of financial transaction tax (Tobin Tax), to mitigate the adverse impact of large swings in capital inflows to EMEs, as witnessed in the recent period, is being widely debated among policymakers, multilateral forums like G-20, G-77, IMF, and also in academic circles.

On the issue of management of capital flows, the Bretton Woods institutions also seem to have drifted somewhat from their earlier approach which relied more on capital account openness. The IMF Managing Director, Dominique Strauss-Kahn (2009), remarked that

[a] related challenge to exit strategies is managing capital flows to emerging markets... Countries have a number of policy options in their toolkits. In many countries, appreciation should be the key policy response. Other tools include lower interest rates, reserves accumulation, tighter fiscal policy, and financial sector prudential measures. Capital controls can be part of a package of measures. We are completely open-minded. But we should recognise that all tools have their limitations. Again, we should be pragmatic.

According to the World Bank (2009), 'Capital restrictions might be unavoidable as a last resort to prevent or mitigate the crisis effects... Capital controls might need to be imposed as a last resort to help mitigate a financial crisis and stabilise macroeconomic developments.' Nijathaworn (2009) recommended that, given the risk of formation of asset price bubbles associated with large capital flows, risk management of banks must continue to be strengthened and regulators must be prepared to use macro-prudential measures proactively as and when necessary to reduce such risk. This means credit standards and bank capital rules must remain vigilant regardless of the abundance of liquidity. Subramanian and Williamson (2009) prescribe that institutions like the IMF must recognize that capital inflows can pose serious macroeconomic challenges that may require a different cyclical response.

Additionally, there has been a growing intellectual support for the use of Tobin tax from influential quarters. Lord Adair Turner, head of the Financial Services Authority (FSA), suggested the introduction of a tax on financial transactions. The then UK's Prime Minister, Mr Brown, in his speech, inter alia, talked about global financial levies. Since the Turner-Brown proposal for use of financial transactions tax, the world has seen growing support from many important quarters, including Paul Krugman, Paul Volcker, the former US Federal Chief, and also India's former Governor of the RBI, Dr Y.V. Reddy.

Dr Reddy suggested that this idea could be examined for the forex market and the securities transaction tax system could be suitably modified and extended to transactions in participatory notes, though they are traded abroad. While Tobin's original proposal aimed at discouraging speculative capital flows by taxing international capital, the Turner-Brown suggestion aims at a tax on all financial transactions, both domestic and international and, hence, the emphasis is more on containing excesses in the financial system rather than managing the challenges for domestic liquidity and exchange rate associated with large (speculative) capital flows.

Subramanian has also proposed a similar tax that could be more appropriate and effective. First, it should have counter-cyclical macro-prudential focus, that is, the tax should be used only when surges in capital flows amplify risk of asset bubbles and exchange rate appreciation. Second, it should be applied in a coordinated manner in G-20 to avoid the risk of countries using the tax shifting the burden of excessive inflows to countries which refrain from using such taxes.

RECENT EXPERIENCE ON CAPITAL CONTROL

In the recent period, many countries have imposed restrictions on capital flows to contain the impact of such speculative flows, particularly on the movement of exchange rates. Brazil has imposed some variants of Tobin tax in the recent period. Similarly, Taiwan, Indonesia, and South Korea have also imposed some form of capital controls to restrict speculative flows.

Brazil

In response to heavy portfolio inflows and substantial exchange rate appreciation during the preceding seven months, Brazil imposed a 2 per cent entry tax (IOF) on foreign inflows to domestic bond and equity markets on 19 October 2009. Other types of capital flows, including direct investment and dollar borrowing by Brazilian banks and firms, were not directly affected. This is not the first time that Brazil resorted to capital controls on portfolio inflows—it had levied a 1.5 per cent tax on bonds (but not equity) inflows until October 2008, which were withdrawn in response to the financial crisis. As per the Brazilian finance ministry, the measure was intended to combat speculation in capital markets and to counteract the appreciation of the Brazilian real which was damaging export industries and employment.

The experience with the exchange rate and reserve accumulation since October 2009 has been mixed. During the period, factors other than the IOF have been impacting the exchange rate and the pace of reserve accumulation such as weakening on the current account, the dollar's appreciation against the Euro, and deterioration in global market sentiment. Nominal currency appreciation against the dollar more or less halted after the imposition of the tax, but the Brazilian real continued to appreciate against the Euro. The exchange rate of Brazilian real depreciated somewhat, from 1.74 per US$ in October 2009 to 1.80 at end-June 2010, showing some appreciation during July to 1.75 on 29 July 2010. Daily volatility was essentially the same before and after 19 October 2009. Foreign reserves continued to accumulate but at a reduced pace of about US$ 100 million a day, compared with a little more than US$ 200 million per day in the seven months before the tax was imposed. Equity flows, which had reached a record pace in July–October 2009, diminished after October, while the debt inflows after diminishing up to March 2010 have started to pick up.

There is some evidence of diversion of foreign investment flows from investments for which the IOF would have a significant impact, to those where it would not. One route for circumvention could be through the domestic derivatives market, where the effective incidence of the tax would be much lower than in the bond market. The existence of liquid forward currency markets, both onshore and offshore, provides an unusual opportunity for analysing the effect of capital controls on cross border arbitrage.

South Korea

On 13 June 2010, South Korea announced New Macro-Prudential Measures to mitigate volatility of capital flows which are to be implemented by mid-July 2010. These measures are much wider in scope than foreign exchange liquidity controls announced earlier in 2009. The controls are specifically aimed at regulating capital flows and stabilizing its currency. Another objective of these policy measures is to curb the country's rapidly growing short-term foreign debt. The June 2010 announcements have two major components.

Implementing Macro-Prudential Measures

The new macro-prudential measures have three parts:

1. *Introducing New Ceilings on Foreign Exchange Derivatives Positions*: These entail new restrictions on currency derivatives trades, including foreign exchange (FX) forward, FX swap, cross currency interest rate swap (CCIRS), non-deliverable forward (NDF), etc. New ceilings have been imposed on domestic banks and branches of foreign banks dealing with forex forwards and derivatives. For Korean banks, there will be a limit on currency forwards and derivatives positions at 50 per cent of their equity capital. For foreign banks, the ceilings will be set at 250 per cent of their equity capital against the current level of around 300 per cent.

Under the existing trading rules in Korea, banks can buy forex derivatives contracts without any limits. Many banks also rely heavily on borrowings from overseas to cover potential losses arising from forward trading. As a result of this, the forex derivatives trading substantially contributed in the rise in short-term overseas borrowings and external debt during 2006 to 2007. The new restrictions will be implemented in a flexible manner.

   (a) The ceilings will be adjusted on a quarterly basis depending on the future economic conditions, market situation, and the impact on the business activities, etc.

   (b) The measures will come into effect with a three-month grace period considering the burden of banks to decrease FX derivatives positions at once.

   (c) Furthermore, the principle of 'grandfathering' will be considered: For example, in case the existing FX derivatives position is more than the positions of the New Ceilings, the banks can maintain their existing positions of FX derivatives for maximum two years.

2. *Reinforcing the Regulations on the Use of Foreign Currency Bank Loans*: The authorities have further restricted the use of

bank loans in foreign currency. This has been done primarily to make sure that foreign currency bank loans are for overseas use only. As an exception, only the small- and medium-sized enterprises have been allowed to use foreign currency financing for domestic use to the extent that total foreign currency loans remain within the current levels. This policy measure is highly significant since excessive foreign currency bank loans are considered to be major sources of systemic risks in many emerging markets.

3. *Improving FX Soundness of Financial Institutions*: The Korean authorities have further tightened the existing regulations on foreign currency liquidity ratio of domestic banks. The domestic banks will monitor the soundness of foreign currency liquidity on a daily basis and report it to authorities every month.

The authorities have also recommended foreign banks operating in Korea to establish liquidity risk management mechanisms as they are a major source of foreign currency liquidity. According to the Bank for International Settlements, foreign banks account for the bulk (60 per cent) of short-term external liabilities of all banks operating in Korea.

Improving Crisis Response Capabilities

This would entail enhancing the ability to absorb volatility of capital flows in a long-term view through:

(i) Monitoring capital flows through establishment of a head-quarter inside the Korea Centre for International Finance (KCIF) as part of developing an early warning system; and

(ii) Establishing global financial safety nets through international cooperation. The agenda of global financial safety nets will be pursued as part of the 'Korea Initiative' at the Seoul G20 summit to be held in November 2010.

At the same time, the funding system and the monitoring ability of the Chiang Mai Initiative Multilateralization (CMIM) will be advanced to improve crisis response capabilities of the Asian region. Meanwhile, the Korean authorities have explicitly ruled out imposition of any financial transactions taxes (such as in Brazil) or unremunerated reserve requirements (such as in Chile).

Indonesia

Just three days after the announcements by the Bank of Korea, Bank Indonesia announced a policy package on on 16 June 2010 Strengthening Monetary Management and Financial Market Development. These new measures are aimed at strengthening the effectiveness of monetary operations, maintaining financial market stability as well as to deepen the financial markets, but also reflect the growing concerns in Indonesia over short-term capital inflows. However, Bank Indonesia has specified that this policy package is not in any way related to capital control measures and is consistent with the free foreign exchange system adopted by Indonesia thus far. The following policy measures were announced:

(i)   Widening of the overnight inter-bank money market rate corridor effective 17 June 2010.

(ii)   Revisions of regulations on banks' FX net open positions (NOP), effective 1 July 2010.

(iii)   Imposing a minimum one month holding period for Bank Indonesia certificates both in primary and secondary markets, effective 7 July 2010.

(iv)   Introduction of term deposits as non-securities monetary instrument, effective 7 July 2010.

(v)   Issuance of the nine and twelve month SBI (Bank Indonesia Certificates), effective second week of August 2010 and Second week of September 2010, respectively, and

(vi)   Implementation of the triparty repurchase (repo) of Government debt securities in 2011.

New regulations on banks' NOP is intended to increase the number of transactions and the depth of the domestic foreign exchange market to support the rupiah exchange rate stability while keeping in consideration prudential aspects of banking. The On Balance Sheet NOP limit of maximum 20 per cent of capital is abolished; however, the overall NOP is still maintained at 20 per cent of capital. The existing real time compliance on NOP limit is further relaxed into 30 minutes window time. This policy became effective from 1 July 2010. Analysts believe that these policy measures may deter hot money inflows into the country. Yet, they expect tougher measures in the future if volatility in capital flows persists. Some analysts also expect that the new curbs may shift capital flows to other financial assets such as government and corporate bonds.

INDIA'S APPROACH TOWARDS CAPITAL ACCOUNT LIBERALIZATION

India's approach towards liberalizing the capital account has been one of gradualism by treating the liberalization as a continuous process rather than a single event. The lessons from the East Asian and other financial crises of 1990s have brought about a marked shift in the approach towards CAL, particularly among developing countries. The opening up of the capital account in India was an integral part of the well sequenced economic reforms programme initiated in 1991. Unlike Latin American countries, India adopted a gradualist approach towards CAC, the incentive framework/blueprint for which was provided by two reports—Report of the High Level Committee on Balance of Payments (C. Rangarajan 1993) and the Two Reports on Capital Account Convertibility (S.S. Tarapore, 1997 and 2006). The Reports recommended a compositional shift in private capital inflows from short-term to long-term debt, non debt creating flows, strict regulation of short term external commercial borrowings, and gradual liberalization of outflows. The reports recognized that it is imperative that the movement to full capital account convertibility be preceded by structural and institutional reforms to strengthen the fiscal and the financial sector. Hence, capital account liberalization was regarded as a process rather than an event.

Recognizing the macroeconomic implications of volatility and possibility of reversals associated with capital inflows as experienced by many EMEs, India has adopted a policy of managing the capital account with a preference for non-debt flows, de-emphasis on short-term debt flows, and adequate foreign exchange reserves, which has ensured the sustainability of capital flows and minimized contagion that could have arisen from financial crises elsewhere. In the recent period, restrictions on capital outflows have subsequently been relaxed. This approach of gradual capital account liberalization by India has remained consistent with the hierarchical criteria with regard to the nature of inflows (with preference for direct investment over portfolio inflows, inflows, in general, being less restricted compared to outflows and outflows associated with inflows being relatively free) as well as treatment of outflows in the order of corporates, financial intermediaries, and individuals.

The strategy has been to encourage non-debt creating and long-term capital inflows and discourage short-term and volatile flows. A hierarchy was worked out in the sources and types of capital flows. The priority has been to liberalize inflows relative to outflows, but all outflows associated with inflows have been totally freed. Capital account liberalization has moved in tandem with other reforms. The extent and timing of capital account liberalization is properly sequenced with other concomitant developments such as strengthening of the banking sector, fiscal consolidation, market development and integration, trade liberalization, and the changing domestic and external economic environment. Even during the crisis, there has not been any deviation from the calibrated approach to CAL. In retrospect, this calibrated approach has paid India rich dividends. India plans to continue its gradualist approach as it enables harmonization and synchronization with reforms in other sectors of the economy.

In recent years, there has been a distinct shift from debt to non-debt creating flows like FDI and foreign portfolio investment. In this hierarchy of preferences, emphasis is also given to maintaining a diversified capital account (such as FDI, portfolio flows, ECBs, and NRI deposits), so that synchronized outflows under each segment could be avoided.

Foreign direct investment is freely allowed in all sectors subject to specified sectoral ceilings. These ceilings have been revised upwards from time to time, depending on the technological needs. Since 2000, all industries, except for a small list in the strategic sector, have been brought under the automatic route where prior approval is not required. Some sensitive sectors however continue to be under the approval route for FDI and some sectors are subject to sectoral FDI caps. Further, FDI in India is subject to certain pricing guidelines as well as reporting guidelines which are specified by the RBI under FEMA, 1999, from time to time. FDI has mostly penetrated the engineering goods, chemicals, services, and IT. Indian companies are allowed to raise resources through the issue of ADR/GDR provided the eligibility of the issuer company is aligned with the requirements under the FDI policy. The issue of Sponsored American Depository Receipt (ADR)/Global Depository Receipt (GDR) requires prior approval of the Ministry of Finance.

In terms of policy liberalization, foreign portfolio investments have acquired prominence over FDI. The FIIs, under the extant FEMA regulations SEBI registered FIIs (which can include foreign banks, FIs, hedge funds, PE funds etc.) can invest in India in listed shares (including fully and mandatorily convertible preference shares) and convertible debentures (fully and mandatorily convertible debentures) under the Portfolio Investment Scheme (subject to individual FII cap of 10 per cent and an overall FII cap of 24 per cent—which can be increased to the FDI sectoral cap by passing of a board resolution followed by a general body resolution to that effect. SEBI registered FIIs can also invest in listed non-convertible debentures (NCDs) and commercial paper issued by Indian companies under the overall corporate debt limit of US$ 15 billion, as well as Government securities up to a limit of US$ 5 billion. Equity flows, once liberalized, have generally been left to be conditioned by domestic and global developments (notwithstanding the sectoral caps), and accordingly portfolio flows have been volatile, and influenced significantly both the capital market and the foreign exchange market. There has, however, never been any reversal of policies relating to equity flows; unlike in several other EMEs which liberalized faster to reverse later in order to deal with volatility induced by capital flows. Certainty about the policy environment, thus, has been an important feature of Indian approach to liberalization. FII participation in the government and corporate debt markets has been subject to ceilings which are revised from time to time.

Unlike equity flows, however, debt flows such as NRI deposits and ECB, have been modulated depending on the overall cycle of net capital flows, through the use of price based measures (such as linking the interest rate to LIBOR) and some administrative measures (such as end use norms for ECB). While during surges in capital inflows some outflows relating to residents are liberalized, during moderation in overall inflows the NRI deposits and ECB windows have been made more attractive.

To enable Indian corporates to take advantage of the propitious terms of contract in international financial markets, ECBs have been allowed within prudent limits subject to end-use restrictions which prohibit investment in stock market and real estate sector to eschew the possibility of building up of speculative bubbles in these sectors. The ECB policy clearly favours long-term borrowings and restricts short-term borrowings. The permissible area for ECB has been gradually expanded from the exclusive thrust on infrastructure sector to services sector like hospitals, hotels, and software companies. Further, ECB limits and norms for pre-payment have been used as flexible instruments to modulate ECB flows in tandem with domestic liquidity needs and global financial market developments.

Hurdles with respect to capital outflows have also been mitigated over a period of time. For example, avenues for direct overseas investment through joint ventures and wholly owned subsidiaries have been opened up; mutual funds have been allowed to invest overseas; and exporters and exchange earners have also been given permission to maintain foreign currency accounts and use them for permitted purposes. Further, outward FDI flows have also witnessed a sharp growth in recent years. Indian companies have been investing in joint ventures and wholly owned subsidiaries in countries like Singapore, Mauritius, Cyprus, and Netherlands. Policy reforms in overseas direct equity investment has facilitated global expansion of Indian companies in sectors like manufacturing, non-financial services, trading, and financial services. However, residents, and more particularly the resident individuals continue to face stringent restrictions on investing abroad. Lately, they have been allowed some elbow room for asset diversification through the Indian Depository Receipts (IDR) route. Under the IDR route, foreign companies have been allowed to list their depository receipts on Indian stock exchanges and mobilize capital from India.

Broadly, under the current regime, foreign corporates and institutions have been allowed a reasonable amount of convertibility, while NRIs have been allowed to invest in India, subject to severe procedural and regulatory impediments. Admission of capital inflows is subject to a hierarchy of preferences with direct investment preferred over portfolio flows, rupee denominated debt preferred over foreign currency debt, and medium and long-term debt preferred over short-term debt. In a nutshell, the CAL process in India has been linked to macroeconomic conditions, financial sector developments, risk management capabilities of financial institutions, and depth of domestic financial markets.

FUTURE OF CAPITAL ACCOUNT LIBERALIZATION IN INDIA

With the global economic recovery setting in, there has been a pronounced recovery in net private capital inflows to EMEs. From a situation of large outflows during 2008, the momentum has quickly shifted in the other direction. In the large part, this is because the outlook for emerging markets, in aggregate, is perceived to be very bright relative to that for mature economies. Higher growth, wider interest rate spreads, and fiscal excesses of advanced economies rather than EMEs, in the context of containment of the impact of global financial crisis, are some of the factors attracting capital flows to the EMEs in a big way in the recent period. These macro conditions have the potential to lead to another extended boom in financing flows to emerging economies. It is important that public policy makes a conscious choice in terms of a hierarchy of capital flows by pitching for more stable components of capital flows. While direct investments need to be encouraged, the composition of portfolio investment, which could be volatile, requires a closer look.

It is evident that while the controls on capital inflows have proved somewhat effective in containing pressures on foreign exchange markets, the experiments with controls on outflows by the EMEs, particularly in the crisis situation, did not help in alleviating the exchange market pressures. While controls to limit short-term inflows could be helpful in specific circumstances, the use of such measures for limiting long-term inflows could hurt domestic investment and growth. Temporary uses of capital controls are effective and can improve the financial environment. However, persistent use of such capital control measures entails costs to the economy. It is important to recognize that neither is the use of capital controls uniform nor are the results identical. Additionally, their impact can be subdued by global conditions. In case of pressures arising out of capital outflows, the controls in the form of numerous restrictions on the banks' external transactions were not fully effective as they were circumvented in many instances. Offshore markets for the domestic currency (for example, non-deliverable forward (NDF) markets) proved to be an important source of speculation and, in some instances, hindered the efficacy of capital control measures.

The country experiences in regard to the use of capital control measures highlight that there is no unanimity on the exact form of controls and past experiences also do not strongly support the effectiveness of such controls imposed by different countries. The issue of imposition of financial transaction tax, to mitigate the adverse impact of sharp swings in capital flows to EMEs, is a complex one and needs to be viewed with utmost caution as such a move has the potential to disrupt market discipline, could have moral hazard connotations, and could impair capital flows to developing countries. Even if such a levy were to be imposed, the necessary precondition is to have in place internationally accepted and credible measures to curb/control short-term volatile capital flows as opposed to unilateral measures by various countries, which may often be at cross purposes.

It is noteworthy that in the Indian context, the opening up of capital account has been a process and has been sequenced in line with other structural and financial reforms undertaken since the early 1990s. There is a preference for hierarchy in capital flows, long-term to short-term and equity to debt flows. With the current account balance of India in deficit, unlike in many other Asian EMEs, capital flows are needed to finance such deficits. However, capital flows in excess of such financing needs pose risks for the markets and the economy and, hence, calls for their effective management through use of multiple instruments available at the disposal of the RBI and the Government.

Indian banks have weathered the global crisis and are regarded as healthy and sound institutions. Macro prudential regulation, which are recommended worldwide today as an ideal regulatory specification, has been the hallmark of India's banking regulation for years. Although we may sound victorious and prescient, we cannot rest on our laurels. The global environment changes fast and particularly speedily for the financial sector. We realize that we have to continuously strive to improve the competitive efficiency of our commercial banking system, which accounts for three-fourths of the business of the financial sector.

The global crisis has demonstrated that the fiscal policy plays a dominant role in alleviating the problems of an economy resulting from the crisis. The Government should not only be in a position to wield its financial power to gather resources but also should have credible mechanism to recover spent resources. A major building block of such fiscal strength is an unwavering faith in the fiscal institution. In pursuance of this, India instituted the Fiscal Responsibility and Budget Management Act, 2003. Fiscal expansion undertaken during 2008–9 and 2009–10, in response to the crisis, is currently being consolidated within the realms of this Act. The fiscal deficit is budgeted to decrease during the next two years.

Professor Eswar Prasad of the Cornell University has expressed that although India's strategy of cautious and calibrated CAL has reduced its vulnerability to crises, it has limited indirect benefits that accrue from financial integration. Excessive caution in further opening up of capital account may, thus, be holding back financial sector reforms and reducing the independence and effectiveness of monetary policy. There is no gain in saying that India could achieve the conflicting triad of exchange rate stability, independent monetary policy, and capital mobility only because of the conservative approach towards opening up the capital account. However, our semi-insulation should not be construed as abhorrence for experimentation. The increasing liberalization of capital account enabled faster integration of the Indian economy with the global economy as manifested in the rising share of capital flows in the GDP. The sum of gross inflows and outflows, both under the current and capital account of India's balance of payments, had surpassed the total GDP in 2006–7 and stood at around 112 per cent of GDP in 2008–9. In fact, India's financial integration with the world has been as deep as India's trade globalization, if not deeper (Subbarao 2009a). India's Eleventh Plan unequivocally recognizes that India's target for 9.0 per cent inclusive growth would materialize in an environment characterized by greater global engagement. In other words, India is committed to achieve the threesome—inclusive growth, price stability, and financial stability—within an open economy framework. However, with deficit in both trade and current account, and capital flows driving the exchange rate under a flexible framework, the strategy towards CAL needs to be chosen carefully.

India's recent experience with CAL suggests that the country has received capital inflows far greater than warranted by the current account deficit. Experience tells us that unless managed properly, excess inflows can spillover into uncharted risky territories that can threaten the macroeconomic and financial stability, and hinder the growth process. This calls for expansion of the absorptive capacity of the economy where the financial system will have a seminal role to play. An immediate requirement of India's growth process today is a 'big push' to the infrastructure sector. It is well recognized that long-term financing of infrastructure cannot be left only to banks and, hence, the financial system needs to device novel financial instruments and develop new markets that are well equipped to bear the risks associated with long-term lending. There is an urgent need to further deepen and broaden the financial markets which can be realized effectively through greater involvement with the rest of the world. In short, a continued CAL process is desirable both from the growth and stability point of view.

Further, with greater openness, the probability of large capital out-flows or sudden stops is also expected to rise. It has to be recognized that foreign exchange reserves can only be a partial antidote to capital flow volatilities. While the issue of adequacy of reserves still remains incalculable and polemical, the sources of reserve accretion need greater attention. Reserves accumulated through capital inflows are prone to easy evaporation in the event of loss of market confidence. In this context, we appreciate the changing approach of multilateral institutions towards opening up of the capital account. EMEs would like to preserve their autonomy to impose selective capital controls. We would welcome Fund's efforts to examine the implications and negative externalities of large and volatile capital flows and any work that the Fund does to reduce the volatility of capital flows.

6

Capital Flows and Central Bank Intervention in the Foreign Exchange Market

Until the 1970s, capital flows were confined to the industrial economies. Post 1970, the nature, composition, purpose, and direction of capital flows underwent overwhelming changes, with the dimensions of the flows being a function of the global developments in each period. After the decade of the 1970s, the developing economies witnessed four distinct waves of capital flows. During the first wave, between the 1970s to early 1980s, capital flows were dominated by debt flows in the form of syndicated bank lending, mostly to Latin American economies which had begun to open up their capital accounts abruptly during this period. The flows were interrupted by the Chilean Crisis of 1982.

The second wave of surge in capital flows began in the mid-1980s and continued till the Asian crisis of 1997. The flows during this period were dominated by FDIs, which was complemented by portfolio flows during the early 1990s. The capital flows during this period were inspired by two major developments. One, several countries including India undertook capital market reforms and liberalized entry and participation norms for FIIs. Further, privatization and mergers and acquisition activity was undertaken in full measure during this period in many Latin American economies. Two, the intellectual underpinnings of capital account liberalization were sown during this period. As a result, many EMEs maintained unrestricted capital accounts in the 1980s and 1990s, resulting in large capital inflows, the magnitude of which became unmanageable and destabilizing for them. This also led to re-imposition of capital controls in many cases.

The third wave of global surge in capital flows began after the Asian financial crisis. A distinct feature of capital flows in the current decade (before the unravelling of the recent crisis) is that capital flows have generally been significant in case of countries with current account surpluses. In this phase, India has also received significant capital inflows, especially during 2003–4 to 2007–8, even with current account deficits. As a result of the current global financial crisis, EMEs, including India, witnessed unexpectedly sharp reversals of earlier inflows on account of deleveraging and increased risk aversion on the part of global investors, which put local financial systems under considerable stress. According to the World Economic Outlook of the IMF, April 2010, net financial flows to emerging and developing economies have increased from an average of US$ 74.7 billion in 1999–2001, to a peak of US$ 692.4 billion in 2007 before declining to US$ 170.8 billion in 2009 under the impact of the global recession. A noticeable trend in recent times, and quite contrary to theoretical expectations, has been the flow of capital from EMEs to developed economies, where the return on capital has been low. This particular phenomenon has contributed to the growth of a bipolar view on the issue of global imbalances. Countries with current account surplus have been accused of perpetuating imbalances by not acting against the 'savings glut', while countries with current account deficit have been blamed for fuelling excessive consumption.

With feeble signs of recovery in EMEs, in the fourth wave, these economies have started attracting capital inflows since mid-2009, clearly endorsing the disconnect between the business cycles of developed and EMEs. Although inflows have boosted confidence in the performance of these economies, it is interfering with the domestic monetary policy operations. The exit from monetary stimulus, which has become essential with traces of inflation and asset price increases in the economy, has been made difficult by the influx of capital. In response, many economies have imposed capital controls and firmed up their prudential measures to safeguard financial stability instead of raising interest rates, which may encourage further capital inflows.

Large capital inflows are considered to be one of the key contributing factors for many financial crises in the EMEs in the past. It has become increasingly clear that whether the crisis originates in emerging economies or advanced economies, capital flows generally reverse from EMEs during the crisis. EMEs have experienced large swings in capital flows in recent years. It has been observed that periods of large capital inflows were followed by sudden drying up of capital inflows which adversely affected the financial markets. In fact, during the recent crisis, it has been proved that 'sudden stops' were largely due to failures and shortcomings in the functioning of international capital markets rather than a lack of sound policy framework in EMEs. However, with the return of some normalcy in the international financial markets and signs of recovery in major economies, there has been a strong revival in capital inflows to EMEs in 2009. This sudden switch from large capital outflows in the second half of 2008–9 to large inflows thereafter could be attributed to the strong growth potential, sound financial system, and higher returns in the EMEs as opposed to nascent economic recovery, lingering weaknesses in the financial system, and persistence of significantly low interest rates in the advanced economies. Thus, the search for lucrative yields and improved risk perception of the EMEs by the global investors has been the major driver of large capital inflows.

IMPACT OF RECENT CRISIS ON GLOBAL CAPITAL FLOWS

Capital flows to developing and EMEs were very large before the crisis, especially during 2002–7. Almost one-quarter of the total domestic capital formation of the developing countries was funded by foreign capital in the years immediately preceding the crisis. The pace, magnitude, direction, and composition of international capital flows have crucial implications for the recipient countries. Historically, most emerging market crises of the 1980s and 1990s were associated with reversals in gross private capital inflows that reflected a loss of confidence in emerging market policies. While in the past, official flows dominated capital flows to the developing economies, at present the bulk of capital flows come from private (bond and equity) sources. Thus, even though most developing countries maintain better policies and have stronger institutions than they did during the previous crises, many of them are nevertheless vulnerable to external disruptions. Emerging market equities and investments have always been sensitive to the global economic cycle, but the recent crisis has severely impacted the developing countries.

Total capital flows to developing countries declined from around US$ 1.2 trillion during 2007 to US$ 780 billion during 2008, mainly on account of sharp declines in portfolio equity and debt flows. On the other hand, FDI flows continued to grow, albeit at a decelerated pace. Capital inflows to EMEs slowed down, while capital outflows increased during the crisis, partly on account of growing financial integration. Driven by ample liquidity and a desire to diversify their assets, investors and multinational companies in developing countries have acquired assets and invested in debt markets abroad, in both developed and developing countries. Net equity outflows reached US$ 244 billion (1.5 per cent of GDP) in 2008, up from US$ 190 billion (1.4 per cent of GDP) in 2007. As part of deleveraging and also to meet domestic redemption pressures, advanced countries sharply cut their investments in emerging markets.

While FDI investment remained relatively stable, portfolio and other investments, including those through the banking channel, witnessed sharp reversals. Disruptions in emerging market portfolio flows became more widespread following the collapse of Lehman Brothers in mid-September 2008. The reversal in portfolio equity inflows, notably in Asia, led to the weakening of emerging market currencies, widening of spreads on international sovereign bonds, and a sharp rise in domestic bond yields in many EMEs. However, since the second quarter of 2009, there are indications of a revival in portfolio flows to EMEs in line with the recovery in major EME stock exchanges and prospects about growth in EMEs recovering faster than that of advanced economies.

In the international debt markets, primary issuance froze and secondary trading of emerging market bonds was greatly reduced in September and October 2008, even for highly rated corporations and sovereigns with relatively sound fiscal positions (for example, Brazil, Malaysia, and South Africa). External bond issuance and bank borrowing by corporations in developing countries had risen from US$ 81 billion in 2002 to US$ 423 billion in 2007, mainly driven by Europe and Central Asia where corporate borrowings increased sharply from

US$ 19 billion to US$ 197 billion over the same period. However, such borrowings fell to US$ 271 billion in 2008 with the deepening of the global financial turmoil. As against net borrowings of US$ 28 billion during the first three quarters of 2008, the last quarter saw net repayments by EMEs of US$27 billion as many emerging market corporate borrowers lost their access to international capital markets. Overall, emerging market bond issuance declined sharply from US$ 186 billion, in 2007, to US$ 106 billion, in 2008.

The collapse in trade during the crisis was partly attributed to the shortage of credit to exporters and importers. With the deepening of the global financial crisis, especially after the collapse of Lehman Brothers in September 2008, many international banks either did not allow rollover of credit or cancelled funded overdraft facilities without warning. According to the IMF, the combination of higher cost of funds, liquidity premiums, and higher risk resulted in a sharp increase in the price of short-term trade finance. Many exporters also restricted the credit they were willing to provide their customers as a result of reduced access to capital and heightened concerns about customer creditworthiness. Realizing that the higher cost along with declining availability of finance had the potential to undermine the efforts undertaken to stimulate domestic economies, coordinated global initiatives were announced to support trade finance. For instance, the G-20 agreed to ensure availability of at least US$ 250 billion over a two year period to support trade finance.

THE INDIAN CONTEXT

Recently, the external sector in India has been marked by strong capital flows. Capital flows to India, which were earlier mainly confined to small official concessional finance, gained momentum from the 1990s with the initiation of economic reforms. Apart from increase in size, capital flows to India have undergone a compositional shift from predominantly official and private debt flows to non-debt creating flows in the post-reform period. Private debt flows have begun to increase again in the more recent period. Though capital flows are generally seen to be beneficial to an economy, a large surge in flows over a short span of time, in excess of the domestic absorptive capacity, can, however, be a source of stress to the economy giving rise to upward pressures on the exchange rate, overheating of the economy, and possible asset price bubbles.

The far reaching economic reforms in India, in the 1990s, resulted in a sharp increase in capital inflows as a result of capital account liberalization in India and a gradual decrease in home bias in asset allocation in advanced economies. During 1990–1, it was clear that the country was heading for a balance of payment crisis due to deficit financed fiscal expansion of the 1980s and the trigger of oil price spike caused by the Gulf War. The balance of payments crisis of 1991 led to the initiation of reform process. The broad approach to reform in the external sector was based on the recommendations made in the Report of the High Level Committee chaired by C. Rangarajan on Balance of Payments in 1993. The objectives of reform in the external sector were conditioned by the need to correct the deficiencies that led to payment imbalances in the 1991. Recognizing that an inappropriate exchange rate regime, unsustainable current account deficit, and a rise in short term debt in relation to the official reserves were amongst the key contributing factors to the crisis, a series of reform measures were put in place. The measures included a swift transition to a market determined exchange rate regime, dismantling of trade restrictions, moving towards current account convertibility, and gradual opening up of the capital account. While liberalizing the private capital inflows, the Committee recommended, inter alia, a compositional shift in capital flows away from debt to non-debt creating flows, strict regulation of external commercial borrowings, especially short term debt, discouraging volatile element of flows from non-resident Indians, and gradual liberalization of outflows.

Magnitude and Composition of Capital Flows

Since the introduction of the reform process in the early 1990s, India has witnessed a significant increase in cross border capital flows, a trend that represents a clear break from the previous two decades. India has one of the highest net capital flows among the EMEs.

India has experienced both 'floods' and 'sudden stops' of capital flows. Net capital flows to India increased from as low as US$ 7 billion in 1990–1 to US$ 46 billion in 2006–7, and further to US$ 108 billion during 2007–8, the year just before the crisis (Figure 6.1).

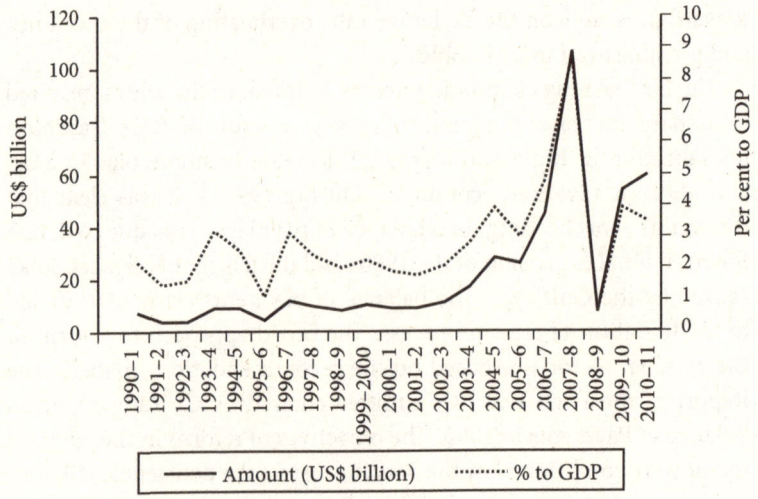

Figure 6.1   Capital Flows to India
Source: Reserve Bank of India.

At the height of the crisis in 2008–9, capital inflows dropped to as low as US$ 9 billion. During 2009–10, however, there was a revival in capital inflows to India, particularly foreign investments, which has been reflected in a turnaround of the capital account to a positive balance of US$ 53.6 billion. Net inward FDI (US$ 34.2 billion) and NRI inflows (US$ 2.9 billion) continued to be buoyant during 2009–10 reflecting the relatively better investment climate in India and various policy measures undertaken in response to the global financial crisis. The sharp increase in FII inflows during 2009–10 (net inflows of US$ 29.0 billion from net outflows of US$ 15.0 billion during the previous year) could be attributed to the recovery of the domestic stock market and comparatively better growth prospects of the Indian economy.

As regards the composition of capital flows, the thrust of the policy reform in India in the aftermath of the balance of payment crisis was to encourage non-debt creating flows and discourage short-term debt flows. Accordingly, the composition of capital inflows to India clearly reflects a shift towards non-debt creating flows (Table 6.1).

Although non-debt flows, particularly private foreign investments have gained importance, there is also a significant rise in the debt creating flows in the last two years mainly on account of rise in external commercial borrowings by Indian corporates (Table 6.2).

Table 6.1 External Financing in India

	1990–1	2000–1	2006–7	2007–8	2008–9	2009–10	2010–11
Current Account Balance	−9,680	−2,666	−9,565	−15,737	−27,915	−38,383	−44,282
As a percentage of GDP	−3.1	−0.6	−1.0	−1.3	−2.3	−2.8	−2.6
Net Capital Flows	7,056	8,840	45,203	1,06,585	6,768	53,397	59,738
of which							
1. Foreign Direct Investment							
Inflows	107	4,101	23,590	37,321	38,940	38,500	32,941
Outflows	10	829	15,897	21,429	19,124	19,729	25,804
Net	97	3,272	7,693	15,893	19,816	18,771	7,138
2. Foreign Portfolio Investment							
Inflows	6	13,619	1,09,620	2,33,800	1,28,654	1,60,169	2,53,952
Outflows	0	11,029	1,02,560	2,06,367	1,42,685	1,27,773	2,23,660
Net	6	2,590	7,060	27,433	−14,031	32,396	30,293
3. External Assistance							
Inflows	3,397	2,941	3,767	4,241	5,232	5,898	7,881
Outflows	1,193	2,531	1,992	2,126	2,791	3,005	2,941
Net	2,204	410	1,775	2,114	2,441	2,893	4,939
4. External Commercial Borrowings							
Inflows	4,282	9,621	20,883	30,293	15,223	14,954	23,089
Outflows	2,028	5,318	4,780	7,684	7,361	12,146	11,164
Net	2,254	4,303	16,103	22,609	7,862	2,808	11,925
5. NRI Deposits							
Inflows	7,348	8,988	19,914	29,400	37,147	41,356	49,252
Outflows	5,811	6,672	15,593	29,222	32,858	38,432	46,014
Net	1,537	2,316	4,321	179	4,290	2,924	3,238

Source: Reserve Bank of India.

Table 6.2 Composition of Capital Inflows to India

Item	1990–1	2000–1	2006–7	2007–8	2008–9	2009–10	2010–11
1	2	3	4	5	6	7	8
Net Capital Inflows (US$ Million)	7,056.0	8,840.0	45,203.0	1,06,585.0	6,768.0	53,397.0	59,738.0
of which: (in per cent)							
1. Non- Debt Creating Inflows	1.5	76.8	65.8	58.2	351.9	122.7	91.8
(a) Foreign Direct Investment	1.4	45.6	50.3	32.6	556.6	62.0	39.1
(b) Portfolio Investment	0.1	31.2	15.5	25.6	-204.7	60.6	52.7
2. Debt Creating Inflows	83.3	79.0	64.2	38.2	172.0	31.8	51.4
(a) External Assistance	31.3	4.8	4.0	1.9	41.1	6.1	8.3
(b) External Commercial Borrowings #	31.9	48.7	36.4	21.2	98.2	6.3	19.4
(c) Short term Credits	15.2	6.2	14.6	14.9	-29.3	14.2	18.4
(d) NRI Deposits	21.8	26.2	9.6	0.2	63.4	5.5	5.4
(e) Rupee Debt Service	-16.9	-7.0	-0.4	-0.1	-1.5	-0.2	-0.1
3. Other Capital @	15.2	-55.8	-30.0	3.6	-423.9	-54.5	-43.2
Total (1 to 3)	100.0	100.0	100.0	100.0	100.0	100.0	100.0

Source: Reserve Bank of India.

Notes: #Refers to medium and long-term borrowings.@ Includes leads and lags in exports (difference between the customs and the banking channel data), Indian Investment abroad and India's subscription to International Institution and quota.

Equity flows under FDI and foreign portfolio investments constitute the major forms of non-debt creating capital flows to India. There has been a marked increase in the magnitude of FDI inflows to India since the early 1990s, reflecting the liberal policy regime and growing investor confidence (Figure 6.2).

Impact of Recent Crisis on Capital Flows to India

The Indian economy, like other EMEs, got rapidly integrated with the global economy, particularly with advanced countries through increasing financial flows during the 1990s and the 2000s. The turmoil in financial markets in the advanced countries during the later part of 2007 spilled over to India through financial channels, through deceleration or reversals in capital inflows, especially portfolio investments. During the crisis, global financial institutions, as part of substantial global deleveraging, withdrew significant portfolio investments from India, like they did from other EMEs during 2008–9, despite strong macroeconomic fundamentals. With international financial markets stabilizing and signs of early recovery in India becoming prominent, portfolio inflows resumed in the aftermath of the crisis with net inflows during 2009–10. On the other hand, FDI in India remained almost

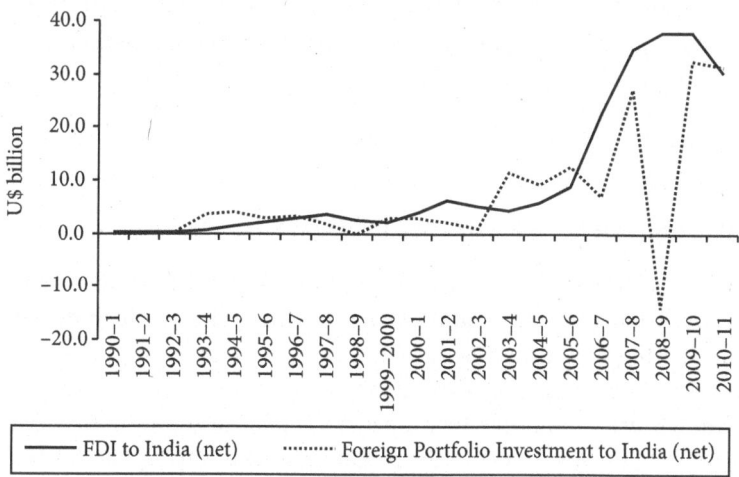

Figure 6.2 Foreign Investment Flows to India
Source: Reserve Bank of India.

unscathed from the ongoing global financial crisis. The continued buoyancy in FDI inflows during 2008–9 and 2009–10 reflected the relatively strong macroeconomic fundamentals of the Indian economy and recognition of India as a long-term investment destination. Interestingly, outbound FDI also remained strong during recent periods on account of Indian firms establishing their production, marketing, and distribution networks overseas to achieve a global scale along with accessing new technology and natural resources. Overseas investment by Indian corporates has surged considerably in recent years.

Commercial borrowings by Indian corporates have also declined sharply since the first half 2008–9 and, during the year, gross commercial borrowing disbursements in India were almost half of the disbursements in 2007–8. The short-term trade credit to India decelerated in the first half, but the decline was accentuated during the second half of 2008–9. On the other hand, Indian corporates were finding it difficult to roll over the existing trade credit and, hence, repayments of short-term credit escalated sharply, resulting in net outflows in the second half of 2008–9. Thus, gross disbursement of short-term trade credit to India declined sharply in 2008–9; repayments, however, increased significantly, mainly due to problems in rollover. With stabilization in global financial markets and revival in domestic growth, trade credit disbursements increased since the beginning of 2009–10 and resulted in net inflows during the second quarter of 2009–10 and subsequently. Indian banks' access to international capital markets was also significantly affected during the crisis on account of risk aversion towards the financial sector and the significant risk in re-pricing of EMEs assets.

MANAGEMENT OF CAPITAL INFLOWS TO INDIA

With the current account balance of India in deficit, unlike in many other Asian EMEs, capital flows are needed to finance such deficits. Capital flows in excess of such financing needs posed risks for the markets and the economy and, hence, called for effective management through use of multiple instruments available at the disposal of the RBI and the Government. The recent episode of capital flows, which has occurred in the backdrop of current account surplus in most of the emerging Asian economies, highlights the importance of absorption of capital flows. The absorption of capital flows is limited by the extant magnitude of the current account deficit, which has traditionally been low in India, and seldom above 2 per cent of GDP. However, since the crisis year 2008–9, the current account deficit has crossed 2 per cent of GDP. In 2009–10, it stood at 2.9 per cent of GDP. In India, with a view to neutralizing the impact of excess forex flows on account of large capital account surplus, the central bank has intervened in the foreign exchange market at regular intervals. But unsterilized forex market intervention can result in inflation, loss of competitiveness, and attenuation of monetary control. The loss of monetary control could be steep if such flows are large. Therefore, it is essential that the monetary authorities take measures to offset the impact of such foreign exchange market intervention, partly or wholly, so as to retain the intent of monetary policy through such intervention. The RBI of India has so far successfully modulated liquidity and interest rate conditions in the economy amidst the challenges posed by large capital flows. It has multiple instruments of liquidity and monetary management at its disposal.

In order to sterilize the impact of additional liquidity in the system generated through large capital inflows, RBI undertakes open market operations (OMOs), that is, outright sales of Government securities through repo and reverse repo auctions. Open market operations have been supplemented by daily liquidity adjustment facility (LAF). Since 2004, RBI has instituted additional instruments of sterilization namely the market stabilization scheme (MSS). Under this, the RBI has been empowered to issue Government Treasury Bills and medium-term dated securities for the purpose of liquidity absorption. Since its inception, MSS has served as a useful instrument for medium-term monetary and liquidity management. It has been unwound at times of low capital flows and built up when excess capital inflows translate into excess domestic liquidity. As and when necessary, RBI has also used traditional instruments like CRR and statutory liquidity ratio (SLR) to absorb excess liquidity in the system. However, the cost of the adjustment may be borne by different entities in the case of each of these instruments.

Greater flexibility in exchange rate movements, liberalization of capital outflows, prepayment of external debt obligations, and modulation of interest rate ceilings on non-resident deposits have also been used to manage capital account inflows from time to time. Given the availability of multiple instruments at its command, the RBI has the flexibility to use these instruments and modulate the liquidity and interest rate conditions amidst large capital flows. The use of specific instrument is contextual depending not only on the nature and size of flows but also domestic considerations.

For instance, during 2007–8, just prior to the crisis, capital flows to India (US$ 108 billion) were at its peak. During that year, capital flows in excess of the current account deficit (US$ 16 billion) were absorbed in the reserves which increased by US$ 92 billion (excluding valuation). To deal with such large inflows, a multi-pronged approach was followed. First, the resultant increase in liquidity due to large purchases of foreign exchange by the RBI (around US$ 78 billion) was partly sterilized by issuance of MSS bonds (US$ 26 billion) and increase in CRR (around US$ 12 billion). Second, in addition to LAF, OMO, and MSS operations, excess liquidity was also absorbed through building up of surplus balances of the Government with the RBI. Third, other measures undertaken during the year included: foreign exchange swaps, liberalization of capital outflows, pre-payment of external debt, lowering of interest rates on NRI deposits, and modulating debt creating flows, depending on the financing needs of the corporate sector. Fourth, as the capital inflows were in excess, the exchange rate also appreciated by 9 per cent from Rs 43.60 per US dollar at end March 2007 to Rs 40.00 per US dollar at end-March 2008.

During the crisis year 2008–9, the capital flows ebbed to a low of US$ 9 billion. The volatility in capital flows also translated into sharp volatility in the exchange rate of the rupee, which depreciated by 21.5 per cent during 2008–9. As the forex liquidity dried up in the market, along with forex sales (US$ 35 billion) in the foreign exchange market to meet the demand for forex liquidity, several measures were undertaken by the RBI to ease the forex liquidity situation:

(i) a rupee–dollar swap facility for Indian banks was introduced
(ii) Special Market Operations to meet the forex requirements of public sector oil marking companies (OMCs) was continued
(iii) measures to ease forex liquidity also included those aimed at encouraging capital inflows, such as an upward adjustment of the interest rate ceiling on NRI deposits, relaxation in

external commercial borrowings (ECBs), and short-term trade credits.

In addition, a series of domestic liquidity enhancing measures (OMO, special repos, buyback of MSS securities, special refinance facilities) including sharp and swift reduction in policy rates were undertaken. Thus, a notable feature of monetary operations during the second half of 2008–9 was the substitution of foreign assets by domestic assets.

The capital flows resumed in 2009–10, though not at the same pace as in 2007–8. The capital inflows increased to around US$ 53 billion in 2009–10, which was higher than the current account deficit of around US$ 39 billion, leading to net accretion in reserves of around US$ 14 billion. With the revival in capital inflows, the depreciation in exchange rate was halted and the rupee appreciated by around 13 per cent in nominal terms during the year. As the inflation in India continued to be high as compared to the trading partners, the rupee appreciated by around 19 per cent (end-March 2010 over end-March 2009) in terms of the six currency, real effective exchange rate (REER). As a result of the extraordinary monetary easing by the Reserve Bank, the banking system was awash with liquidity since November 2008 reflected in LAF being under the absorption mode during most of 2009–10. The large market borrowing by the central and state governments (5.1 lakh crore) was managed without any disruption due to active liquidity management by the RBI by way of unwinding of MSS securities and supported by subdued credit demand. The bulk of capital flows during 2009–10 were absorbed by higher current account deficit reflecting increasing absorptive capacity of the Indian economy. Managing the remaining capital flows did not pose any problem during the year.

Thus, various instruments have differential impact on the balance sheets of the central bank, government, and the financial sector. For example, in the case of OMO sales, the differential between the yield on government securities and return on foreign exchange assets is the cost to the RBI. The repo operations under LAF entail a direct cost to the RBI. In the context of an increase in CRR, the cost is borne mainly by the banking sector. The extent of capital flows to be sterilized and the choice of instruments, thus, also depend upon the impact on the balance sheets of these entities. In our case, the cost of sterilization in India is shared by the central government (the cost of

MSS), RBI (sterilization under LAF), and the banking system (in case of increase in the reserve requirements). Since surpluses of the RBI are transferred to the central government on a combined balance sheet basis, the relative burden of cost between the Government and RBI is not of great relevance. However, the direct cost borne by the Government is transparently shown in its budget accounts. Owing to the difference between international and Indian interest rates, there is a positive cost of sterilization, but the cost has to be traded off with the benefits associated with market stability, export competitiveness, and possible crisis avoidance in the external sector. Sterilized interventions and interest rate policy are generally consistent with overall monetary policy stance that is primarily framed on the basis of the domestic macroeconomic outlook.

CAPITAL FLOWS AND EXCHANGE RATE MANAGEMENT

The capital inflows and outflows have implications for the conduct of domestic monetary policy and exchange rate management. How such flows impact domestic monetary policy depends largely on the kind of exchange rate regime that the authorities follow. In a fixed exchange rate regime, excess forex inflows, resulting from current and capital account surpluses or net surpluses, would perforce need to be taken to forex reserves to maintain the desired exchange rate parity. In a fully floating exchange rate regime, the exchange rate would itself adjust according to demand and supply conditions in the foreign exchange market and there would be no need to take such inflows into the forex reserves. In many countries, intervention remains important even after moving to managed and independently floating exchange rates from various forms of pegs (Bubula and Otker-Robe 2002; Reinhart and Rogoff 2003).

Where the exchange rate is essentially market determined, but the authorities intervene in order to contain volatility and reduce risks to the market participants and for the economy as a whole, some difficult choices need to be made, including:

(i)   rules versus discretion (Should central bank intervention be rules based or discretionary?)

(ii)   amount and timing (When, and in what amounts, should a central bank intervene in the foreign exchange market?)

(iii) degree of transparency (Should interventions be announced or kept secret? What are the pros and cons of each?)
(iv) Markets and counterparties (In which currency pairs, instruments, and trading locations should intervention take place? With whom should the central bank trade and how should it approach them?)

Addressing these questions requires a comprehensive set of policies and guidelines on a wide range of policy, technical, and administrative issues.

TOOLS AND CHANNELS OF INTERVENTION

Despite the controversy surrounding it, interventions in the foreign exchange market remain an important tool for central banks, particularly in developing and emerging economies. Central bank interventions usually aim to correct exchange rate misalignment, moderate exchange rate volatility, accumulate reserves, and supply foreign exchange to the market. But most interventions are directed at the exchange rate, whether it is to fix it, to realign it, or to reduce its volatility.

Reflecting the orderly global financial environment in the years preceding the recent financial crisis, a declining frequency of intervention was observed in advanced economies. For example, the Bank of Canada actively intervened for many years but has not intervened since 1998. The Reserve Bank of New Zealand did not intervene since 1985. With the exception of the Bank of Japan, the central banks for the major international reserve currencies—the US Federal Reserve and the European Central Bank—seldom intervene. However, in sharp contrast, many developing economies continued to intervene actively in the spot foreign exchange market. The prevalence of intervention by emerging market countries had become necessary, primarily because of the importance of capital flows in determining exchange rate movements as against trade balances and economic growth which were important in the earlier days.

In recent times, there has been a large increase in international capital movements. Developing countries had been reaping handsome rewards from the surging capital flows for quite some time but after a certain stage started to experience the not so desirable impact of the continued capital inflows. These types of inflows were regarded as less welcome, having destabilizing side effects, including a tendency for the local currency to gain in value, undermining the competitiveness of the export oriented industries in the absence of intervention, or potentially giving rise to inflation in case the central banks in 'managed float economies' choose to intervene (unsterilized) in the forex markets to arrest the appreciation of the domestic currency. The surge in the capital flows till 2007–8 had coincided mostly with a faster pace of financial liberalization, particularly a shift to a more open economy. Moreover, the higher interest rates prevailing in the emerging market economies had led to a wider interest rate differential in favour of the domestic markets, which stimulated a further surge of capital flows. In EMEs particularly, these capital flows are very volatile and largely sentiment driven, and expose financial markets to large risks. In order to reduce the risks, authorities intervene to curb volatility.

Direct forex intervention or the unsterilized intervention involves using the country's forex reserves to intervene in the market and, consequently, results in an increase in the money supply in the economy. However, sterilized intervention occurs when a central bank counters direct intervention in the forex market with a simultaneous offsetting transaction in the bond market. The operation generally involves a two step process. In the first step, the monetary authority buys foreign currency assets by crediting cash to commercial banks' accounts. This increases bank reserves beyond the normal settlement cash and compulsory reserve requirements, if any, that banks are required to keep with the central bank, temporarily raising the monetary base. In the second stage, the central bank sells domestic assets (assumed to be government bonds) from its portfolio through the OMOs, and banks use their excess deposits to settle securities purchases from the central bank. This restores bank reserves and monetary base to the original equilibrium, preventing an unwarranted easing of monetary policy. Thus, the intended purpose of sterilized intervention is to cause a change in the exchange rate while at the same time leave the money supply unaffected. Most of the economies that implement inflation targeting follow sterilized intervention to resist exchange rate pressures, since unsterilized intervention creates a surge in domestic liquidity that impacts the domestic money supply and, in turn, exerts upward pressure on inflation.

In the literature, several instruments have been prescribed for sterilization purposes. Such tools include OMOs, tightening the access of banks at the discount window, adjusting reserve requirements or the placement of government deposits, using a foreign exchange swap facility, easing restrictions on capital outflows, pre-payment of external debt, and promoting investment through absorption of capital flows for growth purposes. In theory, each of these expedients holds out the prospect of achieving the same effect as OMOs. In practice, each has both advantages and disadvantages, which have been discussed extensively in literature.

The vast literature on foreign exchange intervention focuses on three main channels of influence: signalling, portfolio balancing, and market microstructure.

- Intervention can be effective through the signalling channel if it is perceived as a credible signal on the future stance of monetary policy. To the extent that intervention, even when sterilized, influences expectations on future money supply, then it can influence the exchange rate.
- According to the portfolio balance channel, domestic and foreign currency denominated bonds assets are imperfect substitutes (and therefore, the 'riskier' bond pays a risk premium) and intervention can be effective by modifying the currency composition of agents' asset portfolios. Sterilized intervention alters the relative supply of domestic versus foreign currency bonds, leading agents to re-balance their portfolios to equalize risk adjusted returns, which causes a change in the exchange rate.
- The microstructure approach emphasizes the effects of order flow, market participants, information asymmetries, and price discovery in the foreign exchange market. Central bank trades are assumed to emit information to the market, which modifies exchange rate expectations and ignites a tide of foreign exchange orders, magnified in part by trend chasing traders (Lyons 2001). Intervention induced order flows, in turn, tend to increase the short-term exchange rate volatility.

EFFECTIVENESS OF INTERVENTIONS

Central banks have an overriding interest in the effectiveness of intervention since it exposes them to reputational and financial risks.

Furthermore, interventions can be costly and may not achieve the desired results. Institutional and policy credibility is an important determinant of the effectiveness of intervention. Credibility enhances the effectiveness of intervention and may even obviate the need for it. Furthermore, efficient foreign exchange markets can help minimize instances of misalignment and disorderly markets and, hence, the need for intervention.

Intervention is not an independent policy tool. It cannot generate permanent changes in exchange rate levels when targeted levels are inconsistent with macroeconomic policies. A monetary authority not only has to coordinate intervention with monetary policy, but also may have to conduct sterilized intervention on a sustained basis. At least three major impediments come to the fore:

(i) On the one hand, intervention to prevent depreciation will deplete reserves and, at some stage, will make an interest rate increase inevitable. On the other hand, resisting currency appreciation would prevent the domestic money market interest rates from falling, attract more inflows, and, thus, continuously increase the need for sterilization. Eventually, the cost of sterilization would rise to high levels either making interest rates fall or the exchange rate to appreciate.

(ii) The demand for domestic assets gets affected by the nature of the forex inflow that gives rise to the forex intervention. Where financial markets are thin or the scale of intervention is very large, difference between the assets supplied by the central bank in the sterilization and the assets demanded can affect relative asset prices. Assume that the central bank sells domestic bonds to sterilize; the authorities have to pay higher interest on the sterilization bonds to create demand for the bonds.

(iii) The large cost of issuing high yield local currency debt to acquire low yielding reserves can exacerbate fiscal deficits and, therefore, threaten macroeconomic stability. This can be particularly serious in countries that already have large public sector debts.

The sterilization of prolonged or very large intervention could eventually have the following consequences:

(i) Risk of monetary imbalance: short term sterilization debts expose the central bank and the government to roll over risks. Not only do they necessitate future liquidity draining operations, but they would also raise future costs should domestic interest rates rise. Interest payments on the sterilization debt fuels bank reserves and the risk of inflation rises, adding to the challenges for the central bank's monetary management.

(ii) Risk to financial sector: intervention could accentuate financial imbalances. Increased bank lending resulting from ineffective sterilization could finance excessive investments in certain sectors such as equity and property markets, and a large overhang of excess liquidity might make banks too willing to accommodate demand for riskier credit.

(iii) Cost of intervention: in the case of EMEs facing large inflows, intervention may entail large running costs if the domestic assets have higher yields than the corresponding return on the forex reserves.

(iv) While in practice in all countries, the central banks do intervene in the forex markets there are some features in emerging markets where a more intensive approach to intervention may be warranted in the context of large inflows. In emerging markets, capital flows are often relatively more volatile and sentiment driven, not necessarily being related to the fundamentals in these markets. Such volatility imposes substantial risks on the market agents, which they may not be able to sustain or manage.

Forex Intervention

As observed during the episodic analysis of exchange rates in India, the RBI has been intervening to curb volatility arising due to demand–supply mismatch in the domestic foreign exchange market (Table 6.3).

Sales in the foreign exchange market are generally guided by excess demand conditions that may arise due to several factors. Similarly, the RBI purchases dollars from the market when there is an excess supply pressure in market due to capital inflows. Demand–supply

Table 6.3   Reserve Bank's Intervention in the Foreign Exchange Market

(US$ billion)

	Purchase	Sale	Net	Outstanding Net Forward Sales/Purchase (end-March)
1995–6	3.6	3.9	–0.3	—
1996–7	11.2	3.4	7.8	—
1997–8	15.1	11.2	3.8	–1.8
1998–9	28.7	26.9	1.8	–0.8
1999–2000	24.1	20.8	3.2	–0.7
2000–1	28.2	25.8	2.4	–1.3
2001–2	22.8	15.8	7.1	–0.4
2002–3	30.6	14.9	15.7	2.4
2003–4	55.4	24.9	30.5	1.4
2004–5	31.4	10.6	20.8	0
2005–6	15.2	7.1	8.1	0
2006–7	26.8	0.0	26.8	0
2007–8	79.7	1.5	78.2	14.7
2008–9	26.6	61.5	–34.9	2.0
2009–10	5.1	7.6	2.5	0.4
2010–11	2.5	0.8	1.7	0

Source: Reserve Bank of India.

mismatch proxied by the difference between the purchase and sale transactions in the merchant segment of the spot market reveals a strong co-movement between demand–supply gap and intervention by the RBI (Figure 6.3).[1]

Thus, the Reserve Bank has been prepared to make sales and purchases of foreign currency in order to even out lumpy demand and supply in the relatively thin foreign exchange market and to smooth jerky movements. However, such intervention is generally not governed by any predetermined target or band around the exchange rate (Jalan 1999).

The volatility of rupee–dollar exchange rate remained low compared to other major currencies as the RBI intervenes mostly through purchases/sales of the US dollar (Table 6.4).

Empirical evidence in the Indian case has generally suggested that in the present day managed float regime of India, intervention

---

[1] A positive correlation of 0.7 is also found in case of demand–supply mismatch and net RBI purchases.

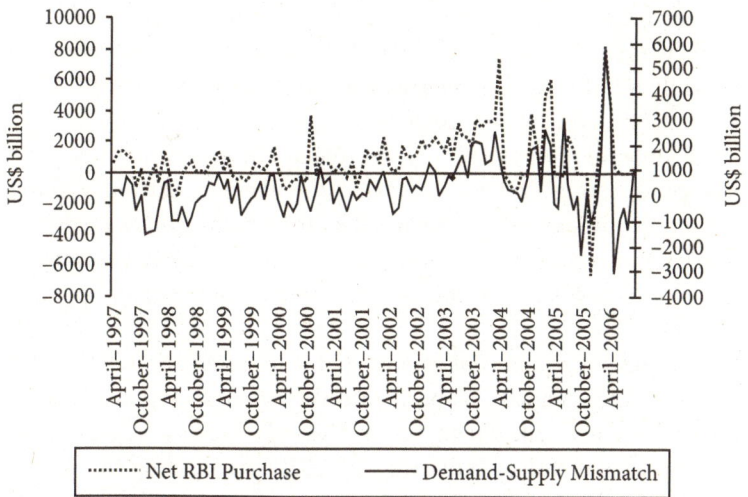

Figure 6.3 The Relationship between Market Mismatch and RBI Intervention
Source: Reserve Bank of India.

Table 6.4 Annualized Volatility of Indian Rupee vis-à-vis Major Currencies

(Per Cent)

Period/ Currency	US Dollar	Euro	Pound Sterling	Japanese Yen
1993	0.40	0.84	0.85	0.82
1994	0.02	0.57	0.72	0.66
1995	0.39	0.64	1.03	1.01
1996	0.47	0.64	0.88	0.75
1997	0.29	0.64	0.72	0.82
1998	0.34	0.54	0.68	1.18
1999	0.10	0.45	0.66	0.83
2000	0.14	0.58	0.88	0.61
2001	0.13	0.54	0.77	0.67
2002	0.08	0.43	2.56	0.65
2003	0.14	0.56	0.69	0.52
2004	0.32	0.65	0.71	0.61
2005	0.22	0.47	0.52	0.43
2006	0.26	0.47	0.46	0.49
2007	0.37	0.49	0.47	0.81
2008	0.68	1.03	0.96	1.36
2009	0.60	0.92	0.68	1.12
2010	0.52	0.65	0.65	0.92

Source: Reserve Bank of India.
Note: Volatility is the standard deviation of per cent changes in exchange rates of Indian rupee.

has served as a potent instrument in containing the magnitude of exchange rate volatility of the rupee. The intervention operations do not influence the level of the rupee much (Pattanaik and Sahoo 2001; Kohli 2000a; RBI 2002–3, 2005–6).

The intervention of RBI in order to neutralize the impact of excess foreign exchange inflows enhanced the Foreign Currency Assets (FCA) continuously. In order to offset the effect of increase in FCA on the monetary base, the RBI has been continuously mopping up the excess liquidity from the system through open market operation (Figure 6.4).

It is, however, pertinent to note that RBI's intervention in the foreign exchange market has been relatively small in terms of volume (less than 1 per cent during last few years). The largest gross intervention by the RBI of India was in 2003–4 accounting for about 4 per cent of the turnover in the foreign exchange market (Table 6.5). The extent of intervention by the RBI in the foreign exchange market also remains low when compared with other EMEs, suggesting the predominant role of market forces in determination of the external value of the rupee.

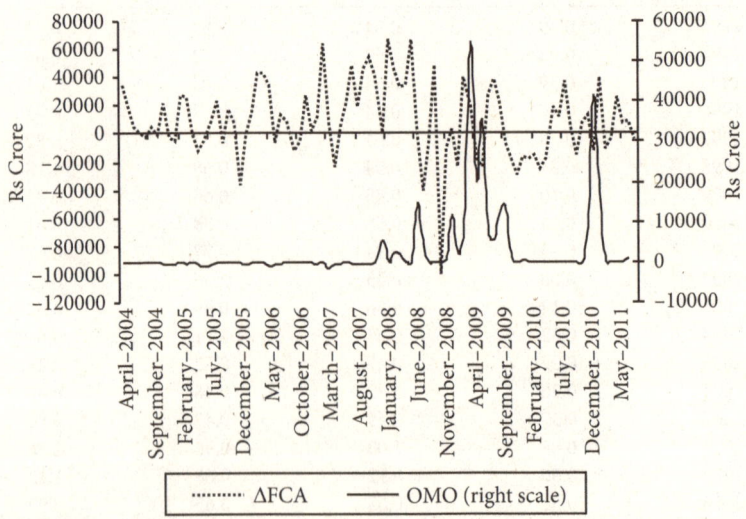

Figure 6.4   Sterilization Operation of the RBI
Source: Reserve Bank of India.

Table 6.5   Extent of RBI Intervention in Foreign Exchange Market

	RBI Intervention in Foreign Exchange Market (Purchase+Sale) ($ billion)	Foreign Exchange Market Turnover ($ billion)	Column 2 over 3 (in Per Cent)
1	2	3	4
2002–3	45.5	1,560	2.9
2003–4	80.3	2.118	3.9
2004–5	42	2,892	1.5
2005–6	22.3	4,413	0.4
2006–7	26.8	6,571	0.4
2007–8	81.2	12,249	0.7
2008–9	88.1	12,092	0.7
2009–10	12.7	10,355	0.1
2010–11	3.3	13,695	0.0

Source: Reserve Bank of India.

Another important feature associated with management of exchange rate is the adoption of prudent foreign exchange reserve management policies. Any change in the level of forex reserves is largely the outcome of the RBI's intervention in the foreign exchange market to smoothen excessive exchange rate volatility and the valuation changes that result from movements in the exchange rate of the US dollar against other currencies. Large capital flows witnessed in the current decade are reflected in large accumulation of foreign exchange reserves (Table 6.6).

During 2008–9, widening of the current account deficit coupled with net capital outflows resulted in the drawdown of foreign exchange reserves of US$ 57.7 billion (including valuation), but the reserves increased by US$ 27.1 billion during 2009–10 to reach the level of US$ 279.1 billion as at end-March 2010. The substantial decline in reserves during 2008–9 created some pressure on the foreign exchange market, but India continued to be one of the leading holders of foreign exchange reserves among the major EMEs, which helped it deal with severe external shocks.

* * *

The return of capital flows to EMEs in the post-crisis period has also brought with it a number of familiar concerns. One is that strong capital inflows, combined with forex intervention to limit currency appreciation, could stimulate excessive credit expansion, leading to

Table 6.6   India's Foreign Exchange Reserves

(*US$ million*)

As at end March	FCA	GOLD	SDRs	RTP	Total Reserves
1	2	3	4	5	6
1990–1	2,236	3,496	102		5,834
1991–2	5,631	3,499	90		9,220
1992–3	6,434	3,380	18		9,832
1993–4	15,068	4,078	108		19,254
1994–5	20,809	4,370	7		25,186
1995–6	17,044	4,561	82		21,687
1996–7	22,367	4,054	2		26,423
1997–8	25975	3,391	1		29,367
1998–9	29,522	2,960	8		32,490
1999–2000	35,058	2,974	4		38,036
2000–1	39,554	2,725	2		42,281
2001–2	51,049	3,047	10		54,106
2002–3	71,,890	3,534	4	672	76,100
2003–4	1,07,448	4,198	2	1,311	1,12,959
2004–5	1,35,571	4,500	5	1,438	1,41514
2005–6	1,45,108	5,755	3	756	1,51,622
2006–7	1,91,924	6,784	2	469	1,99,179
2007–8	2,99,230	10,039	18	436	3,09,723
2008–9	2,41,426	9,577	1	981	2,51,985
2009–10	254,685	17,986	5,006	1,380	279,057
2010–11	274,330	22,972	4,569	2,947	304,818
2011–12*	284,319	25,349	4,595	2,963	317,226

Source: Reserve Bank of India.
Note: * As on 5 August 2011.

overshooting in asset prices and increasing financial fragility. Raising interest rates could attract more inflows. The authorities are taking a hard look at feasible tools for preventing capital inflows from stimulating excessive credit growth or leading to a build-up of risk exposures in the banking system. Many of these supplementary tools have been used by EMEs in the past as complements to monetary and exchange rate policy.

In the past, policies of EMEs have responded to capital inflows in a variety of ways. While some countries allowed exchange rate to appreciate, in many cases monetary authorities have intervened heavily in forex markets to resist currency appreciation. EMEs have sought to neutralize the monetary impact of intervention through sterilization. The instruments used for sterilized intervention operations include direct money market borrowings, repo operations, issuance of central bank notes or bonds, and forex swap operations. Sometimes administrative controls and lending guidance are issued to restrain credit growth. Some of the countries with a large current account surplus have set up stabilization funds or sovereign wealth funds to stabilize the fluctuations in foreign exchange flows. Sterilized intervention operations are often supplemented with steady removal of restrictions on capital outflows such as overseas direct and portfolio investments by domestic residents, personal capital transfer, etc. The restrictions have generally taken the form of unremunerated reserve requirements. Most of the EMEs, including India, have also strengthened prudential and regulatory measures to promote the soundness of the financial system, in general, and the banking system, in particular.

In the post-crisis period, some of the countries like Brazil, Taiwan, Korea, and Indonesia have taken measures like capital controls on inflows and it is expected that some other countries may soon follow them. Opponents of controls have argued that capital controls are distortionary, difficult to implement, easy to evade, and that they become ineffective fairly quickly and entail negative externalities. On the other hand, supporters of capital controls contend that controls are desirable because they preserve monetary policy autonomy, save sterilization costs, tilt the composition of foreign liabilities toward long-term maturities, and ensure macroeconomic and financial stability. The challenge for policymakers is to design and implement controls where the cost of compliance is lower than the cost of evasion.

Intervention is not an independent policy tool. Its success is conditional upon the consistency of targeted exchange rates with macroeconomic policies. Exchange rate misalignments and disorderly markets, the most common justifications for intervention, are extremely difficult to detect, underscoring the need for central banks to be parsimonious in their interventions. Determining the timing and amount of intervention is a matter of judgement and depends heavily on ever changing market conditions, hence, some degree of discretion is necessary. Exercising discretion judiciously and ensuring transparency in intervention policies and objectives are likely to enhance the effectiveness of intervention while minimizing its risks. Traditionally, the policy approach has been microprudential (on a bank-by-bank basis in case of capital or loan-loss provisioning requirements, or loan-to-value ceilings) or monetary (for example, reserve requirements). More recently, there has been growing awareness that many such tools may serve financial stability objectives, the so-called 'macroprudential approach' designed to control systemic risk. The supplementary tools should not, however, be seen as a substitute for sound macroeconomic policies, in particular, sound fiscal and debt management policies, which are essential in limiting the consequences of volatile capital inflows in EMEs.

In India, capital flows have resumed on the promise of India's growth prospects. It is argued that if we tighten ahead of other economies, the wider interest rate differential will become a perverse incentive for even larger capital flows. In managing capital flows in excess of the current account deficit, the economy will have to pay a cost which will be a combination of exchange rate appreciation, larger systemic liquidity and fiscal costs of sterilization.

From the viewpoint of active management of the capital account, the quality of capital flows to India assumes critical importance. It is important that the public policy makes a conscious choice in terms of a hierarchy of capital flows by pitching for more stable components of capital flows. The judgement about excess volatility will depend not merely on the quantity of the flow, but also on the quality in terms of components of the capital flow. While the flows on account of equity, FDI into green field areas may be considered to be of a more permanent nature, flows on account of buy-outs, through channels that are only technically FDI, may not constitute a stable element. The market participants' views on what constitutes excess volatility would also be critical in this regard. Given the blurring of the nature of foreign investment flows, proper monitoring of the FDI flows may be desirable in terms of the nature of investing entry, the source of funds and the investment behaviour, and also the post investment performance of the investing entry and the investee company. Furthermore, long-term capital flows are generally preferred over short-term capital flows. However, greater reliance on long-term debt flows such as non-resident deposits and commercial borrowings can squeeze the comfort level of an economy.

In India, the capital account liberalization is not an event but a process. The RBI is consistently following a cautious and gradual approach to capital account management so as to ensure an orderly process of liberalization of the capital account. The extent of opening is contingent upon progress in other sectors. The policy framework encourages equity flows, especially direct investment flows but debt flows are subject to restrictions which are reviewed and fine tuned periodically. The exchange rate is largely market determined and the RBI intervenes in the foreign exchange market in times of excessive volatility.

7

Modelling and Forecasting the Exchange Rate

The exchange rate is a key financial variable that affects decisions made by foreign exchange investors, exporters, importers, bankers, businesses, financial institutions, policymakers, and tourists in the developed as well as developing world. Exchange rate fluctuations affect the value of international investment portfolios, competitiveness of exports and imports, value of international reserves, currency value of debt payments, and the cost to tourists in terms of the value of their currency. Movements in exchange rates, thus, have important implications for the economy's business cycle, trade and capital flows and are, therefore, crucial to understanding financial developments and changes in economic policy. Timely forecasts of exchange rates can, therefore, provide valuable information to decision makers and participants in the spheres of international finance, trade, and policymaking. Nevertheless, the empirical literature is sceptical about the possibility of accurately predicting exchange rates. The seminal paper by Meese and Rogoff (1983) showed that models based on economic fundamentals are unable to outperform a naïve random walk. Empirical research undertaken since then provides mixed evidence on the success of economic models to predict exchange rates.

This chapter is yet another attempt to gauge the forecasting ability of economic models with respect to exchange rates with the difference that this is done in the context of a developing country that follows a managed floating, as opposed to a flexible exchange rate regime. Starting from the naïve model, this chapter examines the forecasting performance of the monetary model and various extensions of it in the vector autoregressive (VAR) and Bayesian vector autoregressive (BVAR) framework. The focus is on the exchange rate of India vis-à-vis the US dollar, that is, the Rs/$ rate.

India has been operating on a managed flexible exchange rate regime since March 1993, marking the start of an era of a market determined exchange rate regime for the rupee with provision for timely intervention by the central bank. Prior to that, up to 1990, the exchange rate regime was an adjustable nominal peg to a basket of currencies of major trading partners with a band. In the early 1990s, India was faced with a severe balance of payments crisis due to the significant rise in oil prices, the suspension of remittances from the Gulf region and several other exogenous developments. Amongst the several measures taken to tide over the crisis was a devaluation of the rupee, in July 1991, to maintain the competitiveness of Indian exports. This initiated the move towards greater exchange rate flexibility. After a transitional 11-month period of dual exchange rates, a market determined exchange rate was established in March 1993. The current exchange rate policy relies on the underlying demand and supply factors to determine the exchange rate, with continuous monitoring and management by the central bank.

This chapter, thus, concentrates on the post March 1993 period and provides insights into forecasting exchange rates for developing countries, where the central bank intervenes periodically in the foreign exchange market. The alternative forecasting models are estimated using monthly data from July 1996[1] to December 2006 while out-of-sample forecasting performance is evaluated from January 2007 to June 2008.

Extensions of the monetary model considered in this chapter include variables such as forward premium, capital inflows, volatility of capital flows, order flows, and central bank intervention. The chapter, therefore, first examines whether the monetary model can beat a random walk. Second, it investigates if the forecasting performance of the monetary model can be improved by extending it. Third, the chapter evaluates the forecasting performance of a VAR model vs a BVAR model. Lastly, it considers if information on intervention by the central bank can improve forecast accuracy.

---

[1] The starting period is based on availability of data for all series.

ECONOMIC THEORY AND REVIEW OF LITERATURE

In the literature on international finance, various theoretical models are available to analyse exchange rate determination and behaviour. Most of the studies on exchange rate models prior to the 1970s were based on the fixed price assumption.[2] With the advent of the floating exchange rate regime amongst major industrialized countries in the early 1970s, an important advance was made with the development of the monetary approach to exchange rate determination. The dominant model was the flexible price monetary model that has been analysed in many early studies like Frenkel (1976), Mussa (1976, 1979), Frenkel and Johnson (1978), and more recently by Vitek (2005), Nwafor (2006), and Molodtsova and Papell (2007). Following this, the sticky price or overshooting model by Dornbusch (1976, 1980) evolved, which has been tested, amongst others, by Alquist and Chinn (2008) and Zita and Gupta (2007). The portfolio balance model also developed alongside,[3] which allowed for imperfect substitutability between domestic and foreign assets, and considered wealth effects of current account imbalances.

With liberalization and development of foreign exchange and assets markets, variables such as capital flows, volatility in capital flows, and forward premium have also became important in determining exchange rates. Further, with the growing development of foreign exchange markets and a rise in the trading volume in these markets, the micro level dynamics in foreign exchange markets became increasingly important in determining exchange rates. Agents in the foreign exchange market have access to private information about fundamentals or liquidity, which is reflected in the buying/selling transactions they undertake, that are termed as order flows (Medeiros 2005; Bjonnes and Rime 2005). Microstructure theory evolved in order to capture the micro level dynamics in the foreign exchange market (Evans and Lyons 2001, 2005, 2007). Another variable that is important in determining exchange rates is central bank intervention in the foreign exchange market.

---

[2] See Marshall (1923), Lerner (1936), Nurkse (1944), Harberger (1950), Mundell (1961, 1962, 1963), and Fleming (1962).

[3] See Dornbusch and Fischer (1980), Isard (1980), and Branson (1983, 1984).

Non-linear models have also been considered in the literature. Sarno (2003) and Altaville and Grauwe (2006) are some of the recent studies that have used non-linear models of the exchange rate.

Overall, forecasting the exchange rates has remained a challenge for both academicians as well as market participants. In fact, Meese and Rogoff's seminal study (1983) on the forecasting performance of the monetary models demonstrated that these failed to beat the random walk model. This has triggered a plethora of studies that test the superiority of theoretical and empirical models of exchange rate determination vis-à-vis a random walk.

Against this backdrop, various models of exchange rate determination are examined to derive the relevant macroeconomic fundamentals affecting exchange rates. The empirical literature on exchange rate determination is analysed next.

Exchange Rate Models: Theoretical Considerations

Theory: Purchasing Power Parity, Monetary, and Portfolio Balance Models

The earliest and simplest model of exchange rate determination, known as the Purchasing Power Parity (PPP) Theory, represented the application of the 'law of one price'. This states that arbitrage forces will lead to the equalization of goods prices internationally, once the prices are measured in the same currency. PPP theory provided a point of reference for the long-run exchange rate in many of the modern exchange rate theories. It was observed, initially, that there were deviations from PPP in the short-run, but in the long-run PPP holds in equilibrium. However, many of the recent studies like Jacobson et al. (2002) find deviations from PPP even in the long-run. Reasons for the failure of PPP have been attributed to heterogeneity in the basket of goods considered for construction of price indices in various countries, presence of transportation cost, imperfect competition in the goods market, and an increase in the volume of global capital flows during the last few decades, which led to sharp deviation from PPP.

The Harrod-Balassa-Samuelson model rationalized the long run deviations from PPP. According to this model, productivity differentials are important in explaining exchange rates. They relax PPP assumptions and allow real exchange rates to depend on relative price of non-tradables which are a function of productivity differentials. Chinn (1999) and Clostermann and Schnatz (2000) find that a model with productivity differential explains and forecasts exchange rate behaviour better.

The failure of PPP models gave way to the monetary models, which took into account the possibility of capital/bond market arbitrage apart from the goods market arbitrage assumed in the PPP theory. In the monetary models, it is the money supply in relation to money demand in both the home and foreign country, which determine the exchange rate. The prominent monetary models include the flexible and sticky-price monetary models of exchange rates, as well as the real interest differential model and Hooper-Morton's extension of the sticky-price model. In this class of asset market models, domestic and foreign bonds are assumed to be perfect substitutes.

The flexible-price monetary model (Frenkel 1976) assumes that prices are perfectly flexible. Consequently, changes in the nominal interest rate reflect changes in the expected inflation rate. A relative increase in the domestic interest rate compared to the foreign interest rate implies that the domestic currency is expected to depreciate through the effect of inflation, which causes the demand for the domestic currency to fall relative to the foreign currency. In addition to flexible prices, the model also assumes uncovered interest parity, continuous PPP, and the existence of stable money demand functions for the domestic and foreign economies.

The model further implies that an increase in the domestic money supply, relative to foreign money supply would lead to a rise in domestic prices and depreciation of the domestic currency to maintain PPP. Further, an increase in domestic output would lead to an appreciation of the domestic currency since an increase in real income creates an excess demand for money. This, in turn, causes a reduction in aggregate demand as agents try to increase their real money balances leading to a fall in prices until money market equilibrium is restored.

In the sticky-price monetary model (attributed originally to Dornbusch 1976), changes in the nominal interest rate reflect changes in the tightness of monetary policy. When the domestic interest rate rises relative to the foreign rate of interest, it is because there has been a contraction in the domestic money supply relative to the domestic money demand, without a matching fall in prices. The higher interest rate at home attracts a capital inflow, which causes the domestic currency to appreciate. This model retains the assumption of stability of the money demand function and uncovered interest parity, but replaces instantaneous purchasing power parity with a long-run version.

Since PPP holds only in the long-run, an increase in the money supply does not depreciate the exchange rate proportionately in the short-run. In the short-run, because of sticky prices, a monetary expansion leads to a fall in interest rates resulting in capital outflow. This causes the exchange rate to depreciate instantaneously and over-shoot its equilibrium level to give rise to an anticipation of appreciation in order to satisfy the uncovered interest parity condition. The above analysis assumes full employment so that real output is fixed. If, instead, output responds to aggregate demand, the exchange rate and interest rate changes will be dampened.

Frankel (1979) argued that a drawback of the Dornbusch (1976) formulation of the sticky-price monetary model was that it did not allow a role for differences in secular rates of inflation. He develops a model that emphasizes the role of expectation and rapid adjustment in capital markets. The innovation is that it combines the assumption of sticky prices with that of flexible prices with the assumption that there are secular rates of inflation. This yields the real interest differential model.

Hooper and Morton (1982) extend the sticky-price formulation by incorporating changes in the long-run real exchange rate. The change in the long-run exchange rate is assumed to be correlated with unanticipated shocks to the trade balance. They, therefore, introduce the trade balance in the exchange rate determination equation. A domestic (foreign) trade balance surplus (deficit) indicates an appreciation (depreciation) of the exchange rate.

The four models discussed above can be derived from the following equation specified in logs with starred variables denoting foreign counterparts:

$$e_t = \gamma + \delta(m_t - m_t^*) + \phi(y_t - y_t^*) + \alpha(i_t - i_t^*) + \beta(\pi_t - \pi_t^*) + \eta(tb_t - tb_t^*) + \mu_t$$

where e = price of foreign currency in domestic currency
   m = money supply
   y = real output
   i = nominal interest rate

π = inflation

tb = trade balance

The alternative testable hypotheses are as follows:

Flexible-price model:	$\delta>0, \alpha>0, \phi<0, \beta=\eta=0$
Sticky price model:	$\delta>0, \alpha<0, \phi<0, \beta=\eta=0$
Real interest differential model:	$\delta>0, \alpha<0, \phi<0, \beta>0, \eta=0$
Hooper-Morton model:	$\delta>0, \alpha<0, \phi<0, \beta>0, \eta<0$

These models can be further extended to incorporate portfolio choice between domestic and foreign assets. The portfolio balance model assumes imperfect substitutability between domestic and foreign assets. It is a dynamic model of exchange rate determination that allows for the interaction between the exchange rate, current account, and the level of wealth. For instance, an increase in the money supply is expected to lead to a rise in domestic prices. The change in prices, in turn, can affect net exports and, thus, imply changes in the current account of the balance of payments. This, in turn, affects the level of wealth (via changes in the capital account) and, consequently, asset market and exchange rate behaviour. Under freely floating exchange rates, a current account deficit (surplus) is compensated by accommodating transactions in the capital account, that is, capital account surplus (deficit). This has implications for the demand and supply of currency in the foreign exchange market, which can lead to appreciation (depreciation) of the exchange rate. Thus, the coefficient of the current account differential in the exchange rate model is hypothesized to have a positive sign. The portfolio approach, thus, introduces current account in the exchange rate equation. The theoretical model can be expressed (as a hybrid model) as follows:

$$e_t = \gamma + \delta(m_t - m_t^*) + \phi(y_t - y_t^*) + \alpha(i_t - i_t^*) + \beta(\pi_t - \pi_t^*) + \eta(tb_t - tb_t^*) + \theta(ca_t - ca_t^*) + \mu_t$$

where ca denotes current account balance and $\theta > 0$

Theory: Capital Flows, Forward Premium

With an increase in liberalization and opening up of capital accounts the world over, capital flows have become important in determining exchange rate behaviour. The relation between capital flows and exchange rates is hypothesized to be negative (with the exchange rate defined as the price of foreign currency in domestic currency). This is because capital inflow implies purchase of domestic assets by foreigners and capital outflow as purchase of foreign assets by residents. Since the exchange rate is determined by the supply and demand for foreign and domestic assets, the purchase of foreign assets drives up the price of foreign currency. Likewise, the purchase of domestic assets drives up the price of domestic currency. Thus, an increase in capital inflows leads to appreciation of the domestic currency, when there is no government intervention in the foreign exchange market, or if there is persistent sterilized intervention. In the case of unsterilized government intervention, the potential of capital inflows to influence exchange rates decreases to a great extent.

Dua and Sen (2009) developed a model which examines the relationship between the real exchange rate, level of capital flows, volatility of the flows, fiscal and monetary policy indicators, and the current account surplus, and found that an increase in capital inflows and their volatility leads to an appreciation of the exchange rate. The theoretical sign on volatility can, however, be positive or negative.

The forward premium measured by the difference between the forward and spot exchange rates can provide useful information about future exchange rates. According to covered interest parity, the interest differential between two countries equals the premium on forward contracts. Thus, if domestic interest rates rise, the forward premium on the foreign currency will rise and the foreign currency is expected to appreciate. The exchange rate defined as the price of foreign currency in domestic currency and the forward premium are, therefore, expected to be positively related.

Theory: Microstructure Framework

The microstructure theory of exchange rates provides an alternative view to the determination of exchange rates. Unlike macroeconomic models that are based on public information, micro-based models suggest that some agents may have access to private information about fundamentals or liquidity that can be exploited in the short-run. In microeconomic models of asset prices, transactions play a causal role in price determination (Evans and Lyons 2001, 2007). The causal role arises because transactions convey information that is not common knowledge. These models assume that information is dispersed and heterogeneous agents have different information sets. The trading process in foreign exchange markets is not transparent and features bid-ask spreads that reflect the costs to market makers/dealers of processing orders and managing inventories. Thus, a distinctive feature of the microstructure models is the central role played by transactions volume or order flows in determining nominal exchange rate changes (Medeiros 2005; Bjonnes and Rime 2003).

Order flow is the cumulative flow of transactions, with positive or negative sign depending on whether the initiator of the transaction is buying or selling. Order flow takes positive values if the agent purchases foreign currency from the dealer and takes negative values if he sells at the dealer's bid. Conventionally, order flow is taken as purchase minus sales of foreign currency. Hence, an increase in order flow (that is, an increase in the volume of positively signed transactions) will generate forces in the foreign exchange market such that there is pressure on the domestic exchange rate to depreciate. Hence, the order flow and the exchange rate are positively related. The explanatory power or information content of order flow depends on the factors that cause it. Order flow is most informative when it is caused due to dispersion of private information amongst agents with respect to macroeconomic fundamentals (Evans and Lyons 2005). Order flow is less informative when it is caused due to management of inventories by the foreign exchange dealers in response to liquidity shocks.

If the dealers of foreign exchange are heterogeneous and have different information sets, then there is information asymmetry in the foreign exchange market. In this case, order flow will capture the reaction of the market (obtained from aggregating the different reactions of the dealers having different information sets) to changes in macroeconomic fundamentals and news related to changes in economic conditions. As macroeconomic fundamentals change, future expectations of the dealers of foreign exchange also change and so they adjust their portfolio of foreign currency accordingly, leading to a change in exchange rates. Another aspect of microstructure theory that has drawn attention, is the liquidity effect of order flow. Studies in the literature have empirically tested whether the relationship between order flow and exchange rates is due to liquidity effects that are temporary in nature such as the herding behaviour of foreign exchange dealers (Breedon and Vitale 2004).

Theory: Intervention

Intervention by the central bank in the foreign exchange market also plays an important role in influencing exchange rates in countries that have managed the floating rate regime. With the growing importance of capital flows in determining exchange rate movements in most emerging market economies, intervention in foreign exchange markets by central banks has become necessary from time to time to contain volatility in foreign exchange markets.

The motive of central bank intervention may be to align the current movement of exchange rates with the long-run equilibrium value of exchange rates, to maintain export competitiveness, to reduce volatility, and to protect the currency from speculative attacks. Many studies in the literature including Edison (1993), Dominguez and Frankel (1993), Almekinders (1995) and, more recently, Sarno and Taylor (2001) and Neely (2005) survey the literature on modelling the reaction function of the central bank and assessing the effectiveness of intervention.

Intervention is of two types—sterilized and non-sterilized. Intervention is sterilized if the sale or purchase of foreign currency is accompanied by expansionary or contractionary open market operations so that domestic money supply is insulated from the effects of foreign exchange sale/purchase. Intervention is unsterilized if the sale or purchase of foreign currency is not accompanied by offsetting open market operations. The impact of sterilized and unsterilized intervention on exchange rates can be quite different.

In the case of non-sterilized intervention, say, purchase of foreign exchange (to prevent appreciation), money supply increases which reduces the rate of interest and increases demand. This leads to capital outflow, on the one hand, and an increase in import demand, on the other. All this leads to an increase in the demand for foreign currency and, hence, the exchange rate depreciates. Thus, non-sterilized intervention and exchange rates are positively related.

While non-sterilized intervention directly influences the exchange rate through the monetary channel, sterilized intervention also influences exchange rate through different channels by changing the portfolio balance, through the signalling channel where sterilised purchase of foreign currency will lead to a depreciation of the exchange rate if the foreign currency purchase is assumed to signal a more expansionary domestic monetary policy and, more recently, the noise trading channel, according to which, a central bank can use sterilized interventions to induce noise traders to buy or sell currency. Hence, the overall effect of sterilized intervention on exchange rates is ambiguous.

Kletzer and Kohli (2001) have developed a theoretical model in which they discuss the role of financial repression in exchange rate management in the Indian context. They find that policy instruments of financial repression can be used as tools for exchange rate intervention under a managed float.

Recognizing the importance of both monetary models as well as micro structure theory in determining exchange rates, the paper uses a combination of both the models. Exchange rate is determined by monetary variables as well as order flows. The theory has been further expanded to include forward premia, capital inflows, volatility of capital flows, and central bank intervention as determining the exchange rate behaviour. The theoretical model so generated can be expressed as follows:

$$e_t = \gamma + \delta(m_t - m_t^*) + \phi(y_t - y_t^*) + \alpha(i_t - i_t^*) + \beta(\pi_t - \pi_t^*) + \eta(tb_t - tb_t^*) + \theta(ca_t - ca_t^*) + \nu cap_t + \rho vol_t + \omega fdpm_t + \psi of_t + \xi\, int_t + \mu_t$$

where cap_t = capital inflow
vol_t = volatility of capital flows
$fdpm_t$ = 3-month forward premia
of_t = order flow
int_t = central bank intervention

The additional signs are as follows: $\theta>0$; $\nu<0$; $\rho>$or<0; $\omega>0$; $\psi>$or<0; and $\xi>$or<0. The expected signs can be summarized in Box 7.1:

Exchange Rate Models: Empirical Results

The previous section discusses, sequentially, the theoretical models that potentially determine exchange rate behaviour. The empirical performance of these theoretical models in forecasting and explaining exchange rate behaviour is crucial in determining the superiority of one theory over the other. A caveat, of course, is that if a theory can explain the behaviour of the exchange rate better than others, it

Box 7.1   Expected Signs of Independent Variables
Dependent Variable: e_t
(Price of Foreign Currency in Terms of Domestic Currency)

Variables	Expected Sign
$i_t\text{-}i_t^*$	+/-
$y_t\text{-}y_t^*$	-
$m_t\text{-}m_t^*$	+
$\pi_t\text{-}\pi_t^*$	+
tb-tb*	-
ca-ca*	+
$fdpm_t$	+
cap_t	-
vol_t	+/-
of_t	+/-
int_t	+/-

does not necessarily imply that it can also forecast exchange rates with relatively greater accuracy, and vice versa.

Some of the empirical findings for the various theoretical frameworks are given below. An extensive survey of literature is also available in Dornbusch (1990), Frankel and Rose (1995), Taylor (1995), Cuthbertson (1996), Sarno and Taylor (2002), Gandolfo (2006), and Schmidt (2006). The main conclusions drawn from the survey of literature are summarized as under.

Empirics: Purchasing Power Parity, Monetary, and Portfolio Balance Models

Frenkel (1976) suggests that PPP holds in the long-run but not in short-run because of price stickiness in the goods market. However, stationarity of the variables is not tested and the fact that exchange rate and prices are endogenous is not taken into account.

Recent studies that overcome these shortcomings like Johnson (1990), Kong (2000), Lothian and Mc Carthy (2001), Kleijn and Dijk (2001), Bahrumshah et al. (2003), and Diaz (2003), also find that PPP is a long-run phenomenon. Reitz (2002) studied the performance of PPP during periods of central bank intervention and found that PPP is not strengthened during intervention. On the other hand, many other studies like Jacobson et al. (2002), Cheung, Chinn, and Pascual

(2004) find that PPP is not a common phenomenon even in the long-run. Hence, the evidence in favour of PPP theory is mixed. In another strand of work on modelling the exchange rate, Apte et al. (1996) characterize the equilibrium exchange rate in a general equilibrium economy and show that standard regressions or co-integration tests of PPP suffer from missing variable biases and ignore variations in risk aversion across countries and over time.

Earlier studies, which modelled exchange rates using the flexible price monetary model such as Frenkel (1976), Bilson (1978), Hodrick (1978), Putnam and Woodbury (1980), and Dornbusch (1984), support the performance of the flexible price monetary model in modelling and forecasting exchange rates. Subsequent, studies by Frankel (1979), Driskill and Sheffrin (1981), and Taylor (1995), however, fail to support the performance of the flexible price monetary model and real interest differential model in terms of explaining the exchange rate behaviour.

Empirical studies on the sticky-price version of the monetary model show mixed results and suggest weak performance in explaining exchange rate movements. On the one hand, studies like Driskill (1981) show that the sticky-price monetary model explains exchange rates well, while studies such as Backus (1984) show that the sticky price monetary model fails to explain exchange rate behaviour.

Buiter and Miller (1981) proposed an extended version of the sticky price monetary model, which included trend inflation, which was put to test by Barr (1989), and Smith and Wickens (1986, 1990). These studies support the extended version of the model in terms of forecasting exchange rates.

The empirical literature suggests that there is no consensus among economists on the appropriate monetary model that explains exchange rates well. It is also observed that the in-sample predictive performance of monetary models was good in the years following the breakdown of the Bretton Woods system (see, for example, Frenkel 1976; Bilson 1978), but their performance collapsed in the 1980s.

Meese and Rogoff (1983) recognized the limitations of testing the in-sample predictive accuracy (that simply tell us that the model fits the data reasonably well), and examined the out-of-sample predictive performance of the monetary models vis-à-vis the simple random walk model. They observed that the forecasts using models based on economic fundamentals were, in all cases, worse than a random walk model. In response to this study, some of the studies tried to improve the forecasting performance of the monetary models using advanced techniques. Some other studies gave up the monetary model and tried to improve the forecasting performance of exchange rates using pure technical time series techniques. There were also studies that tried to explain the movement of the exchange rate through a suitable economy-wide macroeconometric model capable of capturing all complex associations between exchange rate and other variables. For example, using an economy-wide macroeconometric model for Italy, Gandolfo and Padaon (1990) and Gandolfo (2006) have shown that an economy-wide model beats the random walk (which in turn outperformed the traditional structural models) in out-of-sample forecasts of the exchange rate. There were also many studies which investigated the reasons for the failure of monetary models.

Meese (1990) attributed the failure of monetary models to weaknesses in their underlying relationships such as the PPP condition, the instability found in money demand functions, and expectations that agents' forecasts do not obey the axioms of rational expectations. Meese and Rose (1991) observed that the non-linearity in money demand functions is not responsible for the failure of monetary models in explaining and forecasting exchange rates. This is because the statistical performance of the monetary model could not be improved using a non-linear money demand function.

Flood and Rose (1995) compare the volatility in the exchange rate and in economic fundamentals for periods of fixed and floating rates. While exchange rates exhibit substantial volatility in the floating rate periods, a corresponding increase in volatility was not observed in the economic fundamentals. This led Flood and Rose to speculate that it is unlikely that any exchange rate model based only on economic fundamentals will prove adequate. This view is also supported by Baxter and Stockman (1989), who further explain that there are speculative forces in the foreign exchange market that are important in determining exchange rates, which are not reflected in the behaviour of macroeconomic variables.

Studies by MacDonald and Taylor (1991, 1993, 1994), Choudhry and Lawler (1997), Diamandis et al. (1998), Mark and Sul (2001) attributed monetary models to be long-run equilibrium phenomena.

Empirical literature (for example, Chinn and Meese 1995; Taylor 1995; Neely and Sarno 2002; Sarno and Taylor 2002) suggest that over short horizons of one to three years, monetary fundamentals generally do not predict changes in the spot rate. However, over longer horizons of four to five years, fundamentals do provide predictive power for some currencies (Kim and Mo, 1995; Mark, 1995; Chinn and Meese 1995). These studies examine the predictive power of structural exchange rate models using parametric and non-parametric techniques, and find that the random walk model outperforms monetary models in forecasting exchange rates in the short run. But in the long run, the monetary model outperforms the random walk model.

Some of the recent empirical studies on the monetary model performance have also exhibited mixed results. Studies have shown that inclusion of exchange rate expectations and the degree of openness in the Dornbusch sticky-price monetary model, improves forecast ability of the monetary model (Zita and Gupta 2007). While models involving the Taylor rule interest rate reaction functions forecast well when there is exchange rate targeting, the random walk, however, remains unbeaten in terms of forecasting ability (Molodtsova and Papell 2007). Alquist and Chinn (2008), however, report that structural models do not perform as poorly as suggested by earlier studies.

Recognizing the fact that monetary models do work in the long-run, studies have also attempted to obtain a combined forecast of all the monetary models and compared them with the benchmark obtained by the random walk model and the historical average return. Empirical results so obtained suggest the superiority of combined forecasts over benchmarks and generally yield better results than a single model (Lam et al. 2008).

For the portfolio balance model (PBM) of exchange rate determination, not much empirical literature is available because of data limitations which restricts its empirical application. The earlier studies that estimated the log-linear version of the reduced form portfolio balance model such as Branson et al. (1977), Bisignano and Hoover (1982), and Dooley and Isard (1982) find dismal performance of the PBM in explaining exchange rate behaviour. Studies by Frankel (1982a, 1982b) and Rogoff (1984) did not find any support in favour of the model. On the other hand, some empirical support for the PBM is provided by Backus (1984), Lewis (1988), and Dominguez and Frenkel (1993).

Empirics: Capital Flows, Forward Premium, Central Bank Intervention

Dua and Sen (2009) find that an increase in both net capital inflows and their volatility lead to an appreciation of the exchange rate, and that they jointly explain a large part of the variations in exchange rate in the Indian economy. Kohli (2001) analyses the effect of capital flows in the Indian context and finds that inflow of foreign capital results in a real appreciation of the exchange rate. Calvo et al. (1993) and Edwards (1999a) analysed the impact of capital flows on the exchange rate for Latin American and Asian countries and found that an increase in capital flows causes the exchange rate to appreciate. However, the degree of appreciation or the strength of the relation between capital flows and exchange rate may vary across countries and over time.

Clarida and Taylor (1997) examine the ability of forward exchange rate in forecasting exchange rates and argued that failure of the forward exchange rate in predicting future spot rates does not imply that forward exchange rates do not contain valuable information for forecasting exchange rates. Using the linear vector error correction model (VECM), they extract information from the term structure of forward premia and produce out-of-sample forecasts that outperform the forecasts from the random walk model. Clarida et al. (2003) used the markov switching intercept heteroscedastic VECM model for the term structure of forward premia and found that this model outperforms the linear VECM and the random walk model in terms of its forecasting performance. More recently, Della Corte et al. (2007) examined the predictive ability of exchange rate models based on lagged values of the forward premium and other macroeconomic variables, as compared to the random walk model. The study found that the predictive ability of forward exchange rate premia has substantial economic value in predicting exchange rates compared to a random walk model.

With respect to the effect of intervention, Dominguez and Frenkel (1993) examined its impact on exchange rates using primary survey data along with secondary intervention data. They found that intervention has a significant effect on exchange rates. Neely (2000) surveyed central bankers who conduct intervention and reports that intervention is effective in changing exchange rates. Fatum and King (2005) analyse the effects of Canadian intervention and find that intervention does systematically affect exchange rates and is associated with reduced volatility in exchange rates.

Other recent studies that use high frequency data (see, for example, Payne and Vitale 2003; Dominguez 2003a, 2003b) form a consensus that intervention has significant effects on exchange rates, especially in the very short run. Reitz (2002) concludes that the predictive power of forecasting methods increases in the case of intervention in the foreign exchange market by the central bank, relative to cases when the central bank does not intervene.

Empirics: Microstructure Theory

The microstructure theory of exchange rates gained popularity since the late 1990s when it was empirically tested that information in order flows drives exchange rates (Evans and Lyons 1999; Luo 2001; Medeiros 2005). In a landmark study by Evans and Lyons (2001), three sources of exchange rate variation were identified, that is, direct effect of changes in macro fundamentals, indirect effects of changes in macro fundamentals via order flow and order flow not related to macro news. The use of a pseudo GARCH model with high frequency hourly data reveals that the news of intervention increases the effect of order flow on the exchange rate (Scalia 2006). Recognizing that news effects are not common knowledge and are not impounded in exchange rates directly, Evans and Lyons (2007), have tried to quantify the effect of news on exchange rates. They observe that two-thirds of the effect of macro news on exchange rates is transmitted via order flow.

Bjonnes and Rime (2003) find that private information plays an important role in the foreign exchange market and has a permanent effect on exchange rates. Order flows carrying this private information are, hence, important in determining exchange rates. Marsh and Rourke (2005) find that order flows from profit seeking financial institutions are positively correlated with exchange rate and flows from non-financial corporates are negatively correlated. They also find that the impact of order flow on exchange rate increases as probability of flow from the informed source increases. These views are also supported by Menkhoff and Schmeling (2006) who find that order flows coming from centres of political and financial decision-making, influence exchange rates permanently.

Mizuno et al. (2004) find that traders in the foreign exchange market use past information on exchange rates to carry out transactions. This feedback of information from traders is responsible for autocorrelation in exchange rate changes and volatility.

The survey of literature based on microstructure theory by Sager and Taylor (2006) critically examines the role of order flows in forecasting exchange rates. They indicate that inter-dealer order flows can explain exchange rates contemporaneously, but cannot help to improve out-of-sample exchange rate forecasts. This is because order flow data comes with publication lags. These results cast doubt on the practical value of order flow data for traders in the foreign exchange market.

Another aspect of the asset market approach that has been empirically tested is whether there are systematic and meaningful effects of macroeconomic news on exchange rates. Love and Paynes (2002) find that the order flow is more informative around macroeconomic data releases. Additionally, recent studies like Galati and Ho (2003) and Andersen et al. (2003) report evidence of an asymmetric response of exchange rates to news. Markets respond differently to positive or negative news from the same category. This evidence once again contradicts the proposition of the asset market theory to exchange rate determination (Schmidt 2006). These results indicate that the response of traders in the foreign exchange market to macroeconomic announcements or data releases influence exchange rates via order flows.

Empirics: Time Series and Non-Linear Models

The general failure of structural models in explaining movements in the spot exchange rate has led researchers to consider time series and non-linear models. Vector autoregression models, vector error correction models, and BVAR formulations of the monetary models of exchange rate determination for developed countries are known to have produced forecasts which beat the random walk (see, for example, MacDonald and Taylor (1993, 1994) and Chaudhry and Lawler (1997) for VAR; Chen and Leung (2003) for BVAR and BVECM; Zita and Gupta (2007) for VAR, VECM, BVAR, and BVECM. Goldberg and Frydman (2001) maintain that the existing macroeconomic exchange rate models are able to explain monthly or quarterly movements of exchange rates for some sub-periods reasonably well, while for others their explanatory power completely disappears. This finding led them to suggest that empirical exchange rate models with fixed coefficients are unlikely to perform well either in-sample or out-of-sample. Analysing the relationship between exchange rates and fundamentals in a non-linear framework, De Grauwe and Vansteenkiste (2001) also find significant switches in the coefficients.

Sarno (2003) observes that a non-linear framework produces both better point forecasts and measure of uncertainty surrounding the forecasts. They further observe that the Markov switching intercept heteroscedastic (MSIH) VECM gives more accurate results than the random walk. Moreover, MSIH outperforms the linear VECM. Studies such as Cheung et al. (2004), have reported that model specifications/currency combinations that produce accurate forecasts at certain horizons may not do so at other horizons. Similarly, some models or specifications may forecast certain exchange rates well, but not others. In other words, there is no unique model or specification that may forecast well for all currencies and at all time horizons. It has also been empirically tested that while linear models outperform at short forecast horizons, non-linear models dominate at longer horizons (Altaville and Grauwe 2006).

Non-linear techniques like Artificial Neural Networks (ANN) and Chaos theory are being increasingly employed in the literature to predict exchange rates. Refenes et al. (1993), Verkooijen (1996), Plasmans et al. (1998), Zhang and Hu (1998), Hu et al. (1999), and Zhang and Berardi (2001) apply neural network models to forecast exchange rates. Panda and Narsimhan (2007) use an ANN model to predict the Indian rupee/US dollar exchange rate. Chen and Leung (2004) propose a hybrid approach which amalgamates the elements of artificial neural networks and multivariate econometric models to forecast exchange rates. Zhang (2003) suggests a methodology that combines autoregressive integrated moving average (ARIMA) models with ANN. Bajo-Rubio et al. (1992), Larsen and Lam (1992), De Grauwe and Dewatchter (1993), Cao and Soofi (1999), Gilmore (2001), and Strozzi et al. (2002) apply Chaos theory techniques to forecast exchange rates. Lisi and Schiavo (1999) compare the performance of neural network models and chaotic models in forecasting exchange rates. They find that ANN models outperform the chaotic models according to mean square error (MSE) criteria although they are equivalent on the basis of significance of forecasts.

Many studies like Diebold et al. (1994), Hock and Tan (1996), and Trapletti et al. (2002) analyse the dynamics of the foreign exchange market to see whether there is co-movement between different exchange rates. They report that observing the trading strategy in the foreign exchange market for a particular currency may provide additional information about the movement of another currency and, thus, produce better out-of-sample forecasts. However, their forecast performance results are not encouraging.

The common conclusion of these studies is that time series methods can produce accurate forecasts only in the very short-run but not in the medium or long-run. On the other hand, studies that use fractional integration or fractional co-integration methods (for example, Baillie and Bollerslev 1994; Belkacem et al. 2005; Chortareas et al. 2007) support the view that different exchange rates may be tied to each other through a long memory process and that it is possible to predict one exchange rate, given the observations of the other.

The literature on modelling or forecasting exchange rate volatility uses ARCH, GARCH, FIGARCH, and E-GARCH models (for example, Martens 2001; Wang et al. 2001; Bauwens and Sucarat 2006; Chortareas et al. 2007). There is a consensus that using higher frequency data improves the forecast performance of exchange rate volatility over that of lower frequency data.

Summing up: Theory and Empirics

In sum, several exchange rate models available in the literature have been tested during the last two-and-a-half decades. No particular model seems to work best at all times/horizons. Monetary models based on the idea of fundamentals driven exchange rate behaviour work best in the long-run, but lose their predictability in the short run to naïve random walk forecasts. The volatility of exchange rates also substantially exceeds that of the volatility of macroeconomic fundamentals, thus, providing further evidence of weakening fundamentals-exchange rate link. A combination of the different monetary models, however, at times gives better results than the random walk. Order flows also play an important role in influencing the exchange rate. Keeping in view all the above results of the literature, this chapter attempts to develop a model for the rupee–dollar exchange rate taking into account all the different monetary models along with the microstructure models incorporating order flow as well as capital flows, forward premium, and central bank intervention.

MODELLING AND FORECASTING THE EXCHANGE RATE: ECONOMETRIC METHODOLOGY

This chapter employs VAR and BVAR models to estimate the monetary model of the exchange rate (Re/$) and its augmented variants. Tests for nonstationarity are conducted first, followed by tests for co-integration and Granger causality. Finally, the VAR and BVAR models are estimated and tested for out-of-sample forecast accuracy. This section briefly describes the tests for nonstationarity, VAR and BVAR modelling, co-integration and Granger causality, and tests for out-of-sample forecast accuracy.

Tests for Nonstationarity

The classical regression model requires that the dependent and independent variables in a regression be stationary in order to avoid the problem of what Granger and Newbold (1974) called 'spurious regression' characterized by a high R^2, significant t-statistics but results that are without economic meaning. A stationary series exhibits mean reversion, has a finite, time invariant variance, and a finite covariance between two values that depend only on their distance apart in time, not on their absolute location in time. If the characteristics of the stochastic process that generated a time series change overtime, that is, if the series is non-stationary, it becomes difficult to represent it over past and future intervals of time by a simple algebraic model. Thus, the first econometric exercise is to test if all the series are non-stationary or have a unit root.

A battery of unit root tests now exists to discern whether a time series exhibits I(1) (unit root) or I (0) (stationary) behaviour. In this chapter, we employ the augmented Dickey-Fuller (ADF) test (1979, 1981) and its more powerful variant, the Dickey-Fuller generalized least squares (DF-GLS) test proposed by Elliot et al. (1996). These two tests share the same null hypothesis of a unit root. An alternative test Kwiatkowski-Phillips-Schmidt-Skin (KPSS) is that proposed by Kwiatkowski et al. (1992), which has a null hypothesis of stationarity. If two of these three tests indicate nonstationarity for any series, we conclude that the series has a unit root. The KPSS test is also often used in conjunction with these tests to investigate the possibility that a series is fractionally integrated (that is, neither I [1] nor I [0]), although this is not explored in this chapter.

To test if a sequence y_t contains a unit root using the ADF procedure, three different regression equations are considered.

$$\Delta y_t = \alpha + \gamma y_{t-1} + \theta t + \sum_{i=2}^{p} \beta_i \Delta y_{t-i+1} + \varepsilon_t \tag{7.1}$$

$$\Delta y_t = \alpha + \gamma y_{t-1} + \sum_{i=2}^{p} \beta_i \Delta y_{t-i+1} + \varepsilon_t \tag{7.2}$$

$$\Delta y_t = \gamma y_{t-1} + \sum_{i=2}^{p} \beta_i \Delta y_{t-i+1} + \varepsilon_t \tag{7.3}$$

The most general form of the D-F test (equation 7.1) allows for both a drift term and a deterministic trend; the second excludes the deterministic trend; and the third does not contain either an intercept or a trend term. In all three equations, the parameter of interest is γ. If $\gamma=0$, the y_t sequence has a unit root. The null is therefore $\gamma=0$ against the alternative $\gamma \neq 0$. The estimated t-statistic is compared with the appropriate critical value in the Dickey-Fuller tables to determine if the null hypothesis is valid. The critical values are denoted by τ_τ, τ_μ, and τ for equations (7.1), (7.2), and (7.3), respectively. The DF test presumes the existence of white noise errors in the regression, hence, lags of the dependent variable are added to the regressions to whiten the errors.

Following Doldado et al. (1990), a sequential procedure is used to test for the presence of a unit root when the form of the data generating process is unknown. This involves testing the most general model (equation 7.1) first and following various tests, moving to the most parsimonious model (equation 7.3). Such a procedure is necessary since including the intercept and trend term reduces the degrees of freedom and the power of the test, implying that we may conclude that a unit root is present when, in fact, this is not true. Further, additional regressors increase the absolute value of the critical value, making it harder to reject the null hypothesis. On the other hand, inappropriately omitting the deterministic terms can cause the power of the test to go to zero (Campbell and Perron 1991).

Compared to the ADF test, the DF-GLS test has substantially improved power when an unknown mean or trend is present (Elliot et al. 1996). The DF-GLS procedure relies on demeaning and/or detrending a series prior to the implementation of the auxiliary ADF regression as follows:

$$y^d_t = y_t - \varphi'z_t \tag{7.4}$$

For detrending, $z_t = (1, t)'$ and φ_0 and φ_1 are estimated by regressing $[y_1, (1-\bar{\rho}L)y_2, \ldots\ldots (1-\bar{\rho}L)y_T]$ on $[z_1, (1-\bar{\rho}L)z_2, \ldots\ldots (1-\bar{\rho}L)z_T]$, where $\bar{\rho} = 1 + (\bar{c}/T)$ with $\bar{c} = -13.5$, and L is the lag operator. For demeaning, $z_t = (1)'$ and the same regression is run with $\bar{c} = -7.0$. (See Elliott et al. 1996 for details). The ADF regression is then computed using the y^d_t series:

$$\Delta y^d_t = \alpha + \gamma\, y^d_{t-1} + \theta t + \sum_{i=2}^{p} \beta_i \Delta y^d_{t-i+1} + \varepsilon_t \tag{7.5}$$

Critical values for the GLS detrended test are taken from Elliott et al. (1996). Critical values for the GLS demeaned test are the same as those applicable to the no-constant, no-trend ADF test.

In contrast to the ADF and DF-GLS tests, the KPSS (Kwiatkowski et al. 1992) semi-parametric procedure tests the null hypothesis of level (with test statistic-η_μ) or trend stationarity (with test statistic η_τ) against the unit root alternative. The KPSS test starts with the following model:

$$y_t = \beta t + r_t + \varepsilon_t \tag{7.6}$$

where ε_t is a stationary process, r_t is a random walk given by $r_t = r_{t-1} + \mu_t$ and $\mu_t \sim N(0, \sigma^2_\mu)$. The initial value of r_t, r_0, is assumed fixed and, therefore, serves as the intercept. The null hypothesis of stationarity is $\sigma^2_\mu = 0$ (or r_t is a constant). Under the null hypothesis, $\beta=0$ implies y_t is level stationary and $\beta \neq 0$ means that it is trend-stationary (namely, stationary around a level r_0). The test statistic is as follows:

$$\eta_\mu \, (\eta_t) = T^{-2} \sum_{t=1}^{T} S^2_t / s^2(l)$$

This is derived from the residuals obtained from the regression of y_t on a constant (a constant and trend), e_t, $t = 1, 2, \ldots, T$. The partial sum process of the residuals is defined as:

$$S_t = \sum_{t=1}^{T} e_t \qquad \text{for } t = (1, \ldots T)$$

The long run variance of the partial error process is defined by KPSS as

$$\sigma^2 = \lim_{T \to \infty} T^{-1} E(S^2_T).$$

A consistent estimator of σ^2, $s^2(l)$, can be constructed from the residuals e_t as

$$s^2(l) = T^{-1} \sum_{t=1}^{T} e^2_t + 2T^{-1} \sum_{s=1}^{l} w(s,l) \sum_{t=s+1}^{T} e_t e_{t-s}$$

where $w(s, l)$ is an optional lag window that corresponds to the selection of a spectral window. KPSS employ the Bartlett window, $w(s, l) = 1 - s/(l+1)$ as in Newey and West (1987), which ensures the non-negativity of $s^2(l)$. The lag truncation parameter l corrects for residual serial correlation. If the residual series are independently and identically distributed, a choice of $l = 0$ is appropriate.

VAR and BVAR Modelling

In this chapter, we employ multivariate forecasting models in the VAR and BVAR. A VAR model does not require specification of the projected values of the exogenous variables as in a simultaneous equations model. It uses regularities in the historical data on the forecasted variables. Economic theory only selects the economic variables to include in the model. An unrestricted VAR model (Sims 1980) is written as follows:

$$y_t = C + A(L)y_t + \varepsilon_t,$$

where y: (nx1) vector of variables being forecast; A(L): (nxn) polynomial matrix in the back-shift operator L with lag length p, that is, $A(L) = A_1 L + A_2 L^2 + \ldots \ldots + A_p L^p$; C: (nx1) vector of constant terms; and ε: (nx1) vector of white noise error terms.

The model uses the same lag length for all variables. A serious drawback of the VAR model, however, is that overparameterization produces multicollinearity and loss of degrees of freedom that can lead to inefficient estimates and large out-of-sample forecasting errors. A possible solution is to exclude insignificant variables and/or lags based on statistical tests.

An alternative approach to overcome over-parameterization uses a BVAR model as described in Litterman (1981, 1982), Doan et al. (1984), Todd (1984), Litterman (1986), and Spencer (1993). Instead of eliminating longer lags and/or less important variables, the Bayesian technique imposes restrictions on these coefficients on the assumption that these are more likely to be near zero than the coefficients on shorter lags and/or more important variables. If, however, strong effects do occur from longer lags and/or less important variables, the data can override this assumption. Thus, the Bayesian model imposes prior beliefs on the relationships between different variables as well as between own lags of a particular variable. If these beliefs (restrictions) are appropriate, the forecasting ability of the model should improve. The Bayesian approach to forecasting therefore provides a scientific way of imposing prior or judgemental beliefs on a statistical model. Several prior beliefs can be imposed so that the set of beliefs that produces the best forecasts is selected for making forecasts. The selection of the Bayesian prior, of course, depends on the expertise of the forecaster.

The restrictions on the coefficients specify normal prior distributions with means zero and small standard deviations for all coefficients with decreasing standard deviations on increasing lags, except for the coefficient on the first own lag of a variable that is given a mean of unity. This so-called 'Minnesota prior' was developed at the Federal Reserve Bank of Minneapolis and the University of Minnesota.

The standard deviation of the prior distribution for lag m of variable j in equation i for all i, j, and $m-S(i, j, m)$ can be expressed as function of a small number of hyperparameters: w, d, and a weighting matrix $f(i, j)$. This allows the forecaster to specify individual prior variances for a large number of coefficients based on only a few hyperparameters. The standard deviation is specified as follows:

$$S(i, j, m) = \{w \times g(m) \times f(i, j)\} s_i / s_j;$$

$$f(i, j) = 1, \qquad if\ i = j;$$

$$\qquad = k \qquad otherwise\ (0 < k < 1); and$$

$$g(m) = m^{-d}, d > 0.$$

The term s_i equals the standard error of a univariate autoregression for variable i. The ratio s_i/s_j scales the variables to account for differences in units of measurement and allows the specification of the prior without consideration of the magnitudes of the variables. The parameter w measures the standard deviation on the first own lag and describes the overall tightness of the prior. The tightness on lag m relative to lag 1 equals the function $g(m)$, assumed to have a harmonic shape with decay factor, d. The tightness of variable j relative to variable i in equation i equals the function $f(i, j)$. Examples of selection of hyperparameters are given in Dua and Ray (1995), Dua and Smyth (1995), Dua and Miller (1996), and Dua et al. (1999), Dua et al. (2003, 2008).

The BVAR method uses Theil's (1971) mixed estimation technique that supplements data with prior information on the distributions of the coefficients. With each restriction, the number of observations and degrees of freedom artificially increase by one. Thus, the loss of degrees of freedom due to overparameterization does not affect the BVAR model as severely.

Another advantage of the BVAR model is that empirical evidence on comparative out-of-sample forecasting performance generally shows that the BVAR model outperforms the unrestricted VAR model. A few examples are Holden and Broomhead (1990), Artis and Zhang (1990),

Dua and Ray (1995), Dua and Miller (1996), Dua et al. (1999), Dua and Miller (2006), Dua et al. (2003, 2008).

The above description of the BVAR models assumes that the variables are stationary. If the variables are nonstationary, they can continue to be specified in levels in a BVAR model because as pointed out by Sims et al. (1990: 136) '... the Bayesian approach is entirely based on the likelihood function, which has the same Gaussian shape regardless of the presence of nonstationarity, [hence] Bayesian inference need take no special account of nonstationarity'. Furthermore, Dua and Ray (1995) show that the Minnesota prior is appropriate even when the variables are cointegrated.

In the case of a VAR, Sims (1980) and others, for example, Doan (1992), recommend estimating the VAR in levels even if the variables contain a unit root. The argument against differencing is that it discards information relating to comovements between the variables such as cointegrating relationships. The standard practice in the presence of a cointegrating relationship between the variables in a VAR is to estimate the VAR in levels or to estimate its error correction representation, the VECM. If the variables are nonstationary but not cointegrated, the VAR can be estimated in first differences.

Cointegration and Granger Causality

The possibility of a cointegrating relationship between the variables is tested using the Johansen and Juselius (1990, 1992) methodology. Since the Johansen procedure is well known in the time series literature, a detailed explanation is not presented here.

If the presence of cointegration is established, the concept of Granger causality can also be tested in the VECM framework. For example, if two variables are cointegrated, that is, they have a common stochastic trend, causality in the Granger (temporal) sense must exist in at least one direction (Granger 1986, 1988). Since Granger causality is also a test of whether one variable can improve the forecasting performance of another, it is important to test for it to evaluate the predictive ability of a model.

Granger-causality with respect to a particular variable can be tested by a joint test of statistical significance of the lagged error correction term and the lags of that explanatory variable.

Evaluation of Forecasting Models

Evaluation of the forecasting models is based on root mean square error (RMSE), Theil's U (Theil 1966), and the Diebold-Mariano (1995) test. The models are initially estimated using monthly data over the period July 1996 to December 2006 and tested for out-of-sample forecast accuracy from January 2007 to June 2008. Recursive forecasts are generated from one- through twelve-months-ahead and out-of-sample forecast accuracy of monetary model and its augmented variants is assessed. The overall average of the Theil U-statistic and the RMSE for up to 12 months ahead is also calculated to gauge the accuracy of a model. The forecast accuracy of the VAR technique vs the BVAR method is also evaluated.

To test for accuracy, the Theil coefficient that implicitly incorporates the naïve forecasts as the benchmark is used. If A_{t+n} denotes the actual value of a variable in period (t+n), and $_tF_{t+n}$ the forecast made in period t for (t+n), then for T observations, the Theil U-statistic is defined as follows:

$$U = [\Sigma(A_{t+n} - {}_tF_{t+n})^2 / \Sigma(A_{t+n} - A_t)^2]^{0.5}.$$

The U-statistic measures the ratio of the RMSE of the model forecasts to the RMSE of naive, no-change forecasts (forecasts such that $_tF_{t+n} = A_t$). The RMSE is given by the following formula:

$$RMSE = [\Sigma(A_{t+n} - {}_tF_{t+n})^2 / T]^{0.5}.$$

A comparison with the naïve model is, therefore, implicit in the U-statistic. A U-statistic of 1 indicates that the model forecasts match the performance of naïve, no-change forecasts. A U-statistic >1 shows that the naïve forecasts outperform the model forecasts. If U is < 1, the forecasts from the model outperform the naïve forecasts. The U-statistic is, therefore, a relative measure of accuracy and is unit-free.

Since the U-statistic is a relative measure, it is affected by the accuracy of the naïve forecasts. Extremely inaccurate naïve forecasts can yield U <1, falsely implying that the model forecasts are accurate. This problem is especially applicable to series with trend. The RMSE, therefore, provides a check on the U-statistic and is also reported.

The Diebold-Mariano test compares the forecast performance of alternative models, that is, it tests the null hypothesis of no difference in the accuracy of two competing forecasts. Let $\hat{Y}_{1t}$ and $\hat{Y}_{2t}$, where $t=1, 2\ldots n$, be a pair of h-step ahead forecasts of and e_{1t} and e_{2t} be the associated forecast errors. If $g(e)$ be a function (for example, mean square error) of the forecasts errors, then the null hypothesis of equality of expected forecast performance is: $E[g(e_{1t})-g(e_{2t})] = 0$. Define $d_t = g(e_{1t})-g(e_{2t})$; $t = 1, 2,\ldots n$. For optimal h-step ahead forecasts, the sequence of forecasts errors follows a moving average process of order $h-1$. Therefore, it is assumed that for h-step ahead forecasts, all autocorrelations of order h or higher of the sequence d_t are zero.

Then the variance of $\bar{d}\, (=n^{-1}\sum_{t=1}^{n} d_t)$ is, asymtotically,

$$V(\bar{d}) \overset{a}{\approx} n^{-1}\left[\gamma_o + 2\sum_{k=1}^{h-1}\gamma_k\right],$$

where γ_k is the kth autocovariance of d_t. This autocovariance can be estimated by

$$\hat{y}_k = n^{-1}\sum_{t=k+1}^{n}(d_t - \bar{d})(d_{t-k} - \bar{d}).$$

The Diebold-Mariano test statistic is given by

$$S_1 = \left[\hat{V}(\bar{d})\right]^{-1/2}\bar{d}$$

where $\hat{V}(\bar{d})$ is the estimated variance of $\bar{d}$. Under the null hypothesis, Diebold-Mariano test statistic has an asymptotic standard normal distribution.

Harvey et al. (1997) note that the Diebold-Mariano test could be seriously over-sized as the prediction horizon, h, increases. They, therefore, provide a modified Diebold-Mariano test statistic:

$$S_1^* = \left[\frac{n+1-2h+n^{-1}h(h-1)}{n}\right]^{-1/2} S_1$$

Harvey et al. also recommend a further modification of comparing the statistics with critical values from the Student's t distribution with (n–1) degrees of freedom, rather than from the standard normal distribution.

Summary of Steps in Econometric Estimation

In sum, the chapter proceeds as follows: First, the series are tested for the presence of a unit root using the augmented Dickey-Fuller, DF-GLS and KPSS tests.

Second, multivariate models (Models 2 through 4), described in the previous section on theoretical models, are estimated using the VAR and BVAR techniques. Since Model 2 is the monetary model, Models 3 and 4 examine if the forecast performance of the monetary model can be improved by including additional variables. To estimate VAR models, if all the variables are nonstationary and integrated of the same order, the Johansen test is conducted for the presence of cointegration. If a cointegrating relationship exists, the VAR model can be estimated in levels. Tests for Granger causality are also conducted in the VECM framework to evaluate the forecasting ability of the model. Lastly, BVAR models are estimated that impose prior beliefs on the relationships between different variables as well as between own lags of a particular variable. If these beliefs (restrictions) are appropriate, the forecasting ability of the model should improve. Thus, the performance of the VAR models against the corresponding BVAR versions is also assessed.

ESTIMATION AND EVALUATION OF ALTERNATIVE FORECASTING MODELS

The models discussed in the earlier sections have been estimated and evaluated in this section. The alternative models are estimated from July 1996 through December 2006. The out-of-sample forecasting performance of the alternative models is evaluated over January 2007 to June 2008 and also over the sub-period January 2007 to January 2008 to take into account the turning point in January 2008. Figure 7.1 shows the movements in the Re/$ rate in the period under study: July 1996 through June 2008. Table 7.1 reports the summary statistics of the exchange rate over the full period and sub-periods. These statistics, along with the plot indicate turning points in May 2002

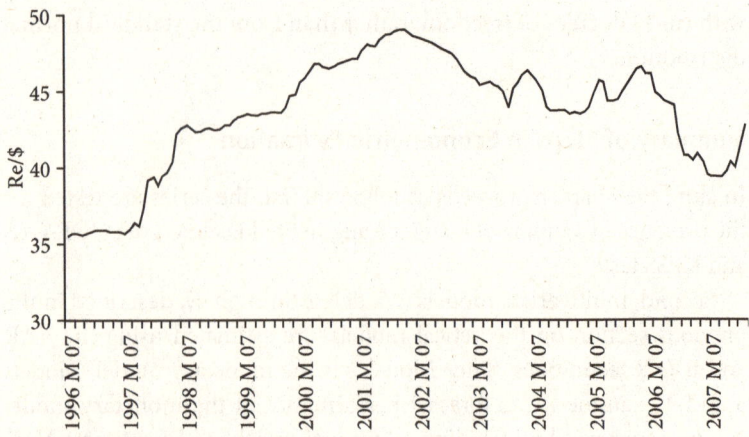

Figure 7.1   Exchange Rate: Re/$
Source: Authors' own.

(maximum of Rs 49/$), January 2007 (maximum of Rs 44.33/$), and January 2008 (minimum of Rs 39.37).

Table 7.1   Summary Statistics for Exchange Rate

Time Period	Mean	Maximum	Minimum	Standard Deviation
Jul 1996–Jun 2008	43.52	49.00 (May 2002)	35.51 (Jul 1996)	3.73
Jul 1996–Dec 2006	43.86	49.00 (May 2002)	35.51 (Jul 1996)	3.82
Jan 2007–Jun 2008	41.12	44.33 (Jan 2007)	39.37 (Jan 2008)	1.69
Jan 2007–Jan 2008	41.20	44.33 (Jan 2007)	39.37 (Jan 2008)	1.86
Feb 2008–Jun 2008	40.90	42.82 (Jun 2008)	39.73 (Feb 2008)	1.28

Source: Authors' calculation.

The various models estimated in the VAR and BVAR framework are summarized below:

Theoretical Models

Model 1: Naïve forecast

$$_t e_{t+n} = e_t$$

Model 2: Monetary Model

$$e_t = f[(i_t - i_t^*), (y_t - y_t^*), (m_t - m_t^*)]$$

Model 3:[4] Model 2 + other variables (inflation differential + trade balance differential + forward premium + volatility of capital inflows + order flow)

$$e_t = f((i_t - i_t^*), (y_t - y_t^*), (m_t - m_t^*), (\pi_t - \pi_t^*), (tb - tb^*), fdpm_t, vol_t, of_t)$$

Model 4: Model 3 + central bank intervention

$$e_t = f((i_t - i_t^*), (y_t - y_t^*), (m_t - m_t^*), (\pi_t - \pi_t^*), (tb - tb^*), fdpm_t, vol_t, of_t, int_t)$$

Box 7.2 Expected Signs of Variables—Dependent Variable: e_t	
Variables	Expected Sign
$i_t - i_t^*$	+/-
$y_t - y_t^*$	-
$m_t - m_t^*$	+
$\pi_t - \pi_t^*$	+
$tb - tb^*$	-
$fdpm_t$	+
vol_t	+/-
of_t	+/-
int_t	+

The expected signs are in Box 7.2 and notation is as follows:

e_t : Log of exchange rate of India (Re/$)

$i_t - i_t^*$: Difference between Indian (domestic) and US (foreign) Treasury bill rate

$y_t - y_t^*$: Difference between log of Indian and US index of industrial production

$m_t - m_t^*$: Difference between log of Indian and US money supply

$\pi_t - \pi_t^*$: Difference between inflation rate of India and US

$tb - tb^*$: Difference between trade balance of India and US

$fdpm_t$: 3-month forward premia

vol_t : Volatility of capital inflows

[4] Current account differential is not included due to its correlation with trade balance differential. Capital flows have not been included because of its correlation with volatility of these flows.

of$_t$:   Order Flow
int$_t$:   Government intervention in open market

Data definitions and sources are given in Annexure 1. Unit root tests are conducted on the above variables. Tests for the existence of a cointegrating relationship as well for Granger causality are also undertaken for the multivariate models given above. The models are then estimated in the VAR and BVAR framework.

Tests for Nonstationarity

The first step in the estimation of the alternative models is to test for nonstationarity. Three alternative tests are used, that is, the ADF test, the Dickey-Fuller Generalized Least Squares test, and the KPSS test. If at least two of the three tests show the existence of a unit root, the series is considered as nonstationary. The tests for nonstationarity are reported using monthly data from June 1996 to December 2006.

Table 7.2 reports the three tests with constant and trend.

Table 7.2   ADF, DF-GLS, and KPSS Tests (Constant and Trend)

VARIABLE	ADF	DF-GLS	KPSS (l = 8)
e_t	−1.1192	−0.4147	0.346
$i_t - i_t^*$	−2.5144	−2.2992	0.227
$y_t - y_t^*$	−3.0568	−0.5383	0.317
$m_t - m_t^*$	−0.77086	−0.2207	0.354
$\pi_t - \pi_t^*$	−2.6037	−2.9580	0.116
tb–tb*	−2.5620	−3.1571	0.108
fdpm$_t$	−2.6281	−3.3942	0.054
vol$_t$	−3.1237	−0.7189	0.239
Δof$_t$	−2.5657	−8.0816	0.107
int$_t$	−24.184	−8.6548	0.122
		Critical Value	
10%	−3.13	−3.55	0.119
5%	−3.41	−3.01	0.146
1%	−3.96	−2.72	0.216

Source: Authors' calculation.

The inference at the 5 per cent significance level is given in Table 7.3. This shows that apart from order flow and intervention, all other variables are nonstationary. Testing for differences of each variable confirms that all the variables are integrated of order one.

Table 7.3   Unit Root Test Summary: July 1996 to December 2006

Variables	ADF	DF-GLS	KPSS	Inference
e_t	I(1)	I(1)	I(1)	I(1)
$i_t-i_t^*$	I(1)	I(1)	I(1)	I(1)
$y_t-y_t^*$	I(1)	I(1)	I(1)	I(1)
$m_t-m_t^*$	I(1)	I(1)	I(1)	I(1)
$\pi_t-\pi_t^*$	I(1)	I(1)	I(0)	I(1)
$tb-tb^*$	I(1)	I(1)	I(0)	I(1)
$fdpm_t$	I(1)	I(1)[a]	I(0)	I(1)
vol_t	I(1)	I(1)	I(1)	I(1)
Δof_t	I(1)	I(0)	I(0)	I(0)
int_t	I(0)	I(0)	I(0)[b]	I(0)

Source: Authors' calculation.

Notes: a. Null hypothesis of unit root not rejected at 1 per cent.
b. Null hypothesis of no unit root not rejected at 1 per cent but rejected at 5 per cent. This does not affect overall inference.

Tests for Cointegration and Granger Causality

Various specifications of the theoretical Model 3 were estimated using the cointegration approach. The final model was selected based on diagnostic checking and signs of the coefficients. The empirical models selected are given below and their cointegration equations are reported in Table 7.4.

Empirical Models (based on overall fit)

Model 1: Naïve forecast

$$_te_{t+n} = e_t$$

Model 2: Monetary Model

$$e_t = f((i_t-i_t^*), (y_t-y_t^*), (m_t-m_t^*))$$

Model 3': Model 2 + other variables (forward premium + volatility of capital inflows + order flow)

$$e_t = f((i_t-i_t^*), (y_t-y_t^*), (m_t-m_t^*), fdpm_t, vol_t, \Delta of_t)$$

Model 4': *Model 3 + central bank intervention*

$$e_t = f((i_t-i_t^*), (y_t-y_t^*), (m_t-m_t^*), fdpm_t, vol_t, \Delta of_t, \Delta int_t)$$

Table 7.4   Cointegrating Equations (Dependent Variable: e_t): July 1996 to December 2006

Variable	Model 2	Model 3	Model 4
$i_t - i_t^*$	−0.097	−0.126	−0.185
$y_t - y_t^*$	−1.061	−3.277	−4.228
$m_t - m_t^*$	2.283	5.585	6.401
$fdpm_t$	—	0.070	0.0833
vol_t	—	−2.102	−1.999

Source: Authors' calculation.

Models 1 and 2 above are the same as the theoretical versions. Model 3' has fewer independent variables compared to its theoretical counterpart. This directly feeds into Model 4'. Since the order flow and intervention variables are stationary, their sign and significance is determined in the framework of an error correction model. The empirical signs of all the variables conform to economic theory and are given below in Box 7.3:

Box 7.3   Empirical Signs of Variables: Model 4' Dependent Variable: e_t

Variables	Estimated Sign
$i_t - i_t^*$	−
$y_t - y_t^*$	−
$m_t - m_t^*$	+
$fdpm_t$	+
vol_t	−
Δof_t	+
Δint_t	+

The Granger causality tests for Models 2–4 are reported in Tables 7.5 through 7.7. Apart from the intervention variable, all other variables, Granger cause the exchange rate.[5] This result, thus, justifies the inclusion of all the variables that Granger cause the exchange rate since these variables can potentially improve the predictive performance of the model.

[5] The null hypothesis of no causality is tested up to 15 per cent level of significance.

Models 2 through 4 are estimated both in the VAR and BVAR frameworks and their predictive ability is evaluated over two out-of-sample periods taking into account the turning point in January 2008: January 2007 through January 2008 and January 2007 through June 2008.

Table 7.5   Model 2: Granger Causality Tests: July 1996 to December 2006

Null Hypothesis	Number of Lags	χ^2 [p-value]	Conclusion
e_t is not Granger caused by i_t-i_t^*	2	4.2082[.122]	Reject H_0
e_t is not Granger caused by y_t-y_t^*	2	6.6321[.036]	Reject H_0
e_t is not Granger caused by m_t-m_t^*	2	5.2722[.072]	Reject H_0

Souce: Authors' calculation.

Table 7.6   Model 3: Granger Causality Tests: July 1996 to December 2006

Null Hypothesis	Number of Lags	χ^2 [p-value]	Conclusion
e_t is not Granger caused by i_t-i_t^*	2	4.8623[.088]	Reject H_0
e_t is not Granger caused by y_t-y_t^*	2	5.9908[.050]	Reject H_0
e_t is not Granger caused by m_t-m_t^*	2	6.1741[.046]	Reject H_0
e_t is not Granger caused by $fdpm_t$	2	4.8883[.087]	Reject H_0
e_t is not Granger caused by vol_t	2	5.7506[.056]	Reject H_0
e_t is not Granger caused by Δof_t	2	2.5585[.012]*	Reject H_0

Souce: Authors' calculation.
Note: * t-statistic is from the error correction model where Δof_t has a positive sign.

Table 7.7   Model 4: Causality Tests: July 1996 to December 2006

Null Hypothesis	Number of Lags	χ^2 [p-value]	Conclusion
e_t is not Granger caused by i_t-i_t^*	2	5.2473[.073]	Reject H_0
e_t is not Granger caused by y_t-y_t^*	2	6.4220[.040]	Reject H_0
e_t is not Granger caused by m_t-m_t^*	2	6.5762[.037]	Reject H_0
e_t is not Granger caused by $fdpm_t$	2	5.2624[.072]	Reject H_0
e_t is not Granger caused by vol_t	2	6.1058[.047]	Reject H_0
e_t is not Granger caused by Δof_t	2	2.4236[.017]**	Reject H_0
e_t is not Granger Caused by Δint_t	2	0.48722[.627]**	Do not reject H_0

Souce: Authors' calculation.
Note: ** t-statistic from the error correction model where Δint_t has a positive sign.

Empirical Results: Out-of-sample Forecasts: January 2007 to January 2008

VAR Models: January 2007 to January 2008

The forecast accuracy results for the VAR models are reported in Table 7.8. The main results are summarized below:

(i) Model 2 performs consistently better than Model 1. This implies that the monetary model outperforms the random walk model.

(ii) Model 3' performs better than Model 2. Thus, forecast accuracy can be improved by extending the monetary model to include forward premium, volatility of capital inflows, and order flow.

(iii) Model 4' performs better than Model 3', especially for longer term forecasts. Information on intervention by the central bank thus helps to improve forecasts at the longer end.

BVAR Models: January 2007 to January 2008

The forecast accuracy statistics for the BVAR models are reported in Table 7.9. Overall, the results are generally similar to those obtained for VAR models.

(i) Model 2 (monetary model) performs consistently better than Model 1 (random walk).

(ii) Model 3' performs consistently better than Model 2.

(iii) Model 4' performs better than Model 3', especially for longer term forecasts implying that information on central bank intervention produces more accurate forecasts at the longer end.

VAR vs BVAR Models: January 2007 to January 2008

The Diebold Mariano test results for the comparison of VAR and BVAR models for Models 3 and 4 are reported in Table 7.10.

(i) BVAR Model 3' performs almost consistently better than the corresponding VAR model.

(ii) BVAR Model 4' performs almost consistently better than the corresponding VAR model.

The above results show that BVAR models yield more accurate forecasts than the VAR models.

Table 7.8 VAR Models: Out-of-Sample Forecast Accuracy: January 2007 to 2008

Months ahead	No of Obs	RMSE								Theil U2					
		Model 1 3 month average	average	Model 2 3 month average	average	Model 3' 3 month average	average	Model 4 3 month average	average	Model 2 3 month average	average	Model 3' 3 month average	average	Model 4 3 month average	average
1	13	0.722		0.508		0.447		0.446		0.704		0.619		0.618	
2	12	1.275		0.945		0.877		0.877		0.741		0.688		0.688	
3	11	1.756	1.251	1.344	0.932	1.325	0.883	1.318	0.880	0.765	0.737	0.754	0.687	0.751	0.685
4	10	2.252		1.694		1.719		1.712		0.752		0.763		0.760	
5	9	2.617		1.919		1.940		1.931		0.733		0.741		0.738	
6	8	2.888	2.586	2.017	1.876	1.931	1.863	1.909	1.851	0.698	0.728	0.669	0.724	0.661	0.720
7	7	3.302		2.189		1.900		1.870		0.663		0.576		0.566	
8	6	3.709		2.444		2.069		2.001		0.659		0.558		0.539	
9	5	4.307	3.773	2.910	2.514	2.566	2.178	2.472	2.114	0.676	0.666	0.596	0.576	0.574	0.560
10	4	4.852		3.407		3.242		3.132		0.702		0.668		0.645	
11	3	4.962		3.765		3.784		3.654		0.759		0.763		0.736	
12	2	5.079	4.964	3.657	3.609	3.803	3.610	3.746	3.511	0.720	0.727	0.749	0.727	0.738	0.706
Average		3.143		2.233		2.134		2.089		0.714		0.679		0.668	

Souce: Authors' calculation.

Notes: 1. Accuracy measures are calculated using antilog of forecast and actual values although the models are estimated using logs.

2. For Model 1 (naïve forecast), Theil U2, by definition, equals one.

3. Optimal number of lags for all VAR models is 2.

Table 7.9 BVAR Models: Out-of-Sample Forecast Accuracy: January 2007 to 2008

Months ahead	No of Obs	RMSE								Theil U2					
		Model 1	3 month average	Model 2	3 month average	Model 3´	3 month average	Model 4	3 month average	Model 2	3 month average	Model 3´	3 month average	Model 4´	3 month average
1	13	0.722		0.528		0.467		0.465		0.731		0.647		0.644	
2	12	1.275		0.958		0.858		0.851		0.752		0.673		0.668	
3	11	1.756	1.251	1.320	0.935	1.231	0.852	1.217	0.845	0.752	0.745	0.701	0.674	0.693	0.668
4	10	2.252		1.634		1.540		1.526		0.725		0.684		0.678	
5	9	2.617		1.829		1.694		1.679		0.699		0.647		0.642	
6	8	2.888	2.586	1.905	1.789	1.610	1.615	1.585	1.597	0.660	0.695	0.557	0.630	0.549	0.623
7	7	3.302		2.103		1.504		1.472		0.637		0.455		0.446	
8	6	3.709		2.379		1.699		1.631		0.641		0.458		0.440	
9	5	4.307	3.773	2.830	2.437	2.124	1.776	2.047	1.717	0.657	0.645	0.493	0.469	0.475	0.454
10	4	4.852		3.321		2.673		2.592		0.684		0.551		0.534	
11	3	4.962		3.661		3.107		3.016		0.738		0.626		0.608	
12	2	5.079	4.964	3.654	3.546	3.198	2.993	3.166	2.925	0.720	0.714	0.630	0.602	0.623	0.588
Average		3.143		2.177		1.809		1.771		0.700		0.594		0.583	

Source: Authors' calculation.

Notes: 1. Accuracy measures are calculated using antilog of forecast and actual values although the models are estimated using logs.
2. For Model 1 (naïve forecast), Theil U2, by definition, equals one.
3. Optimal hyperparameters for all BVAR models are as follows: w=.2, d=1, k=7.
4. Optimal number of lags is 3 for Model 2 and 2 for Models 3 and 4.

Table 7.10   DM Test for VAR vs BVAR Models Out-of-Sample Period: January 2007 to 2008

Model 3′		Model 4′	
Month Ahead	VAR vs BVAR	Month Ahead	VAR vs BVAR
1	VAR better than BVAR[b]	1	VAR better than BVAR[b]
2	Indifferent	2	Indifferent
3	BVAR better than VAR[c]	3	BVAR better than VAR[c]
4	BVAR better than VAR[b]	4	BVAR better than VAR[b]
5	BVAR better than VAR[a]	5	BVAR better than VAR[a]
6	BVAR better than VAR[a]	6	BVAR better than VAR[a]
7	BVAR better than VAR[a]	7	BVAR better than VAR[a]
8	BVAR better than VAR[a]	8	BVAR better than VAR[b]
9	BVAR better than VAR[a]	9	BVAR better than VAR[b]
10	BVAR better than VAR[a]	10	BVAR better than VAR[a]
11	BVAR better than VAR[a]	11	BVAR better than VAR[a]
12	BVAR better than VAR[a]	12	BVAR better than VAR[a]

Notes: 1. 'Better' implies 'yields more accurate forecasts'.
2. *a*: significant at 1%; *b*: significant at 5%; *c*: significant at 10%; *d*: significant at 15%; *e*: significant at 20%.

Observations: January 2007 to January 2008

(a)   The monetary model outperforms the naïve forecast model.

(b)   Information on the forward premium, volatility of capital inflows and order flows improve the accuracy of forecasts. It is thus possible to beat the monetary model.

(c)   Including data on central bank intervention (Model 4′) helps to improve forecast accuracy further.

(d)   BVAR models yield more accurate forecasts than their VAR counterparts.

Empirical Results: Out-of-sample Forecasts— January 2007 to June 2008

VAR vs BVAR Models: January 2007 to June 2008

The out-of-sample forecast accuracy statistics for the VAR model are reported in Table 7.11. The corresponding table for the BVAR model is 7.12. A comparison of VAR and BVAR models is reported in Table 7.13.

Table 7.11 VAR Models: Out-of-Sample Forecast Accuracy: January 2007 to June 2008

Months ahead	No of Obs	RMSE								Theil U2					
		Model 1	3 month average	Model 2	3 month average	Model 3'	3 month average	Model 4	3 month average	Model 2	3 month average	Model 3'	3 month average	Model 4'	3 month average
1	18	0.795		0.617		0.520		0.519		0.777		0.654		0.652	
2	17	1.328		1.168		1.013		1.016		0.879		0.763		0.765	
3	16	1.673	1.266	1.569	1.118	1.434	0.989	1.433	0.989	0.938	0.864	0.857	0.758	0.856	0.758
4	15	2.104		1.933		1.761		1.756		0.919		0.837		0.835	
5	14	2.384		2.223		1.985		1.973		0.932		0.833		0.828	
6	13	2.545	2.345	2.363	2.173	2.051	1.932	2.021	1.917	0.928	0.926	0.806	0.825	0.794	0.819
7	12	2.782		2.497		2.080		2.046		0.898		0.748		0.736	
8	11	2.966		2.568		2.122		2.101		0.866		0.716		0.708	
9	10	3.177	2.975	2.587	2.551	2.155	2.119	2.122	2.089	0.814	0.859	0.678	0.714	0.668	0.704
10	9	3.435		2.534		2.365		2.304		0.738		0.689		0.671	
11	8	3.581		2.449		2.440		2.377		0.684		0.681		0.664	
12	7	3.666	3.561	2.573	2.519	2.541	2.449	2.469	2.383	0.702	0.708	0.693	0.688	0.673	0.669
Average		2.536		2.090		1.872		1.845		0.840		0.746		0.737	

Source: Authors' calculation.

Notes: 1. Accuracy measures are calculated using antilog of forecast and actual values although the models were estimated using logs.

2. For Model 1 (naïve forecast), Theil U2, by definition, equals one.

3. Optimal number of lags for all VAR models is 2.

Table 7.12 BVAR Models: Out-of-Sample Forecast Accuracy: January 2007 to June 2008

Months ahead	No of Obs	RMSE Model 1	3 month average	Model 2	3 month average	Model 3'	3 month average	Model 4	3 month average	Theil U2 Model 2	3 month average	Model 3'	3 month average	Model 4'	3 month average
1	18	0.795		0.646		0.550		0.548		0.813		0.692		0.689	
2	17	1.328		1.218		1.039		1.039		0.917		0.783		0.782	
3	16	1.673	1.266	1.642	1.169	1.435	1.008	1.430	1.005	0.982	0.904	0.858	0.777	0.854	0.775
4	15	2.104		2.032		1.750		1.742		0.966		0.832		0.828	
5	14	2.384		2.347		1.952		1.941		0.985		0.819		0.814	
6	13	2.545	2.345	2.518	2.299	1.984	1.895	1.957	1.880	0.989	0.980	0.779	0.810	0.769	0.804
7	12	2.782		2.659		1.979		1.951		0.956		0.711		0.701	
8	11	2.966		2.698		1.945		1.924		0.910		0.656		0.649	
9	10	3.177	2.975	2.683	2.680	1.905	1.943	1.856	1.910	0.845	0.903	0.600	0.656	0.584	0.645
10	9	3.435		2.613		2.081		1.990		0.761		0.606		0.579	
11	8	3.581		2.566		2.110		2.020		0.717		0.589		0.564	
12	7	3.666	3.561	2.771	2.650	2.226	2.139	2.129	2.046	0.756	0.744	0.607	0.601	0.581	0.575
Average		2.536		2.199		1.746		1.710		0.883		0.711		0.700	

Source: Authors' calculation.

Notes: 1. Accuracy measures are calculated using antilog of forecast and actual values, although the models were estimated using logs.
2. For Model 1 (naïve forecast), Theil U2, by definition, equals one.
3. Optimal hyperparameters for all BVAR models are as follows: w=.2, d=1, k=.7.
4. Optimal number of lags is 3 for Model 2 and 2 for Models 3 and 4.

Table 7.13   DM Test for VAR vs BVAR Models—Out-of-Sample Period: January 2007 to June 2008

Model 3′		Model 4′	
Month Ahead	VAR vs BVAR	Month Ahead	VAR vs BVAR
1	VAR better than BVAR[a]	1	VAR better than BVAR[a]
2	VAR better than BVAR[e]	2	Indifferent
3	Indifferent	3	Indifferent
4	Indifferent	4	Indifferent
5	Indifferent	5	Indifferent
6	Indifferent	6	Indifferent
7	Indifferent	7	Indifferent
8	BVAR better than VAR[d]	8	BVAR better than VAR[d]
9	BVAR better than VAR[c]	9	BVAR better than VAR[c]
10	BVAR better than VAR[c]	10	BVAR better than VAR[c]
11	BVAR better than VAR[c]	11	BVAR better than VAR[b]
12	BVAR better than VAR[d]	12	BVAR better than VAR[c]

Notes: 1. 'Better' implies 'yields more accurate forecasts'.
2. *a* : significant at 1%; *b* : significant at 5%; *c* : significant at 10%; *d* : significant at 15%; *e* : significant at 20%.

This period includes a turning point in January 2008. Possibly due to this, the empirical results are not as sharp as those obtained in the shorter period, although the main results stand as before.

Figures 7.2a through 7.2d illustrate the 3, 6, 9, and 12 month-ahead out-of-sample forecasts made using both the VAR and BVAR versions of Model 3′. Likewise, Figures 7.3a through 7.3d report the same on the basis of Model 4′. It is clear from these figures that the VAR and BVAR forecasts move in tandem. Further, the differences between the directions of forecasts made using Model 3′ vs Model 4′ are not obvious from the graphs. The two sets of graphs look similar. Therefore, the benefit of including intervention data is not apparent by examining the graphs.

We also examine the direction of forecasts made around a turning point. This is illustrated by using Model 4′ to forecast in February 2008 up to June 2008. The forecasts are shown in Figure 7.4 and highlight the problem common to forecasting models—that forecasters tend to miss the turning point. The forecasts exhibit a downward trend while the series has moved upwards.

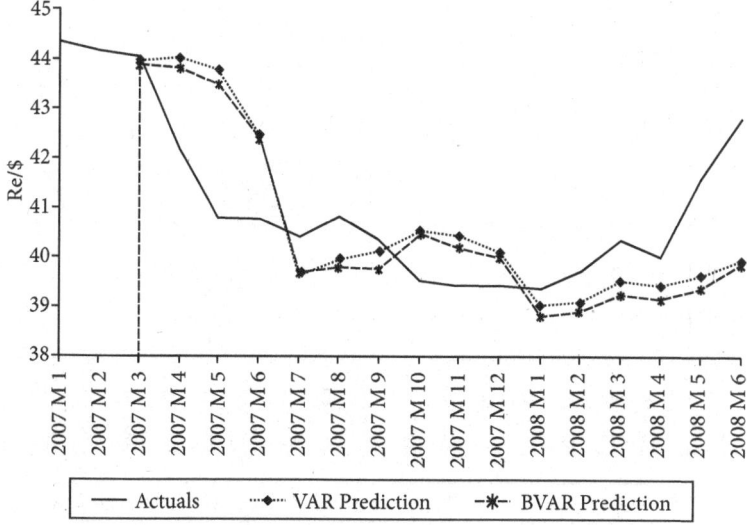

Figure 7.2a 3-Month Ahead Forecast for Model 3'
Source: Authors' own.

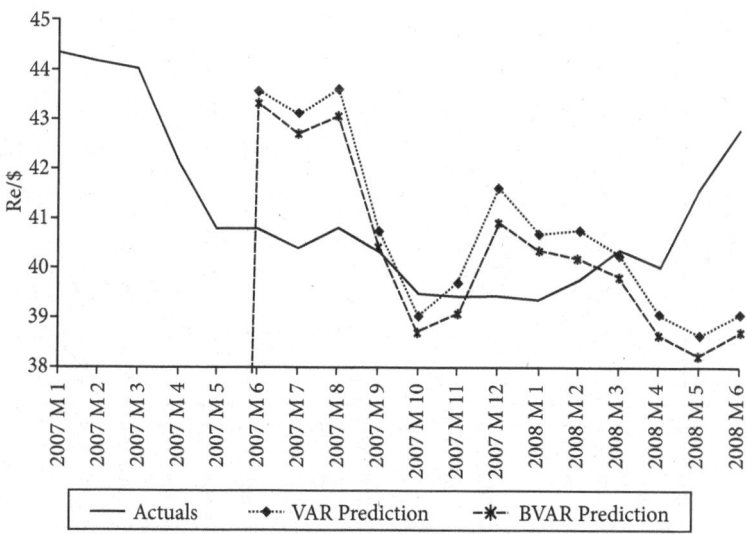

Figure 7.2b 6-Month Ahead Forecast for Model 3'
Source: Authors' own.

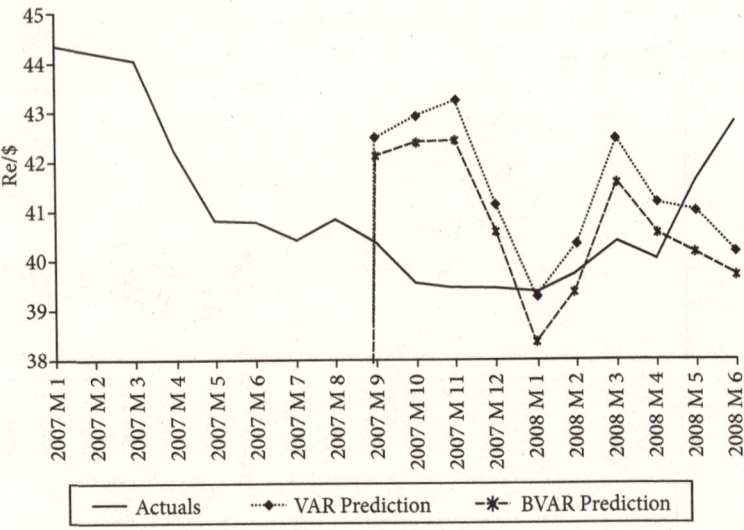

Figure 7.2c 9-Month Ahead Forecast for Model 3'
Source: Authors' own.

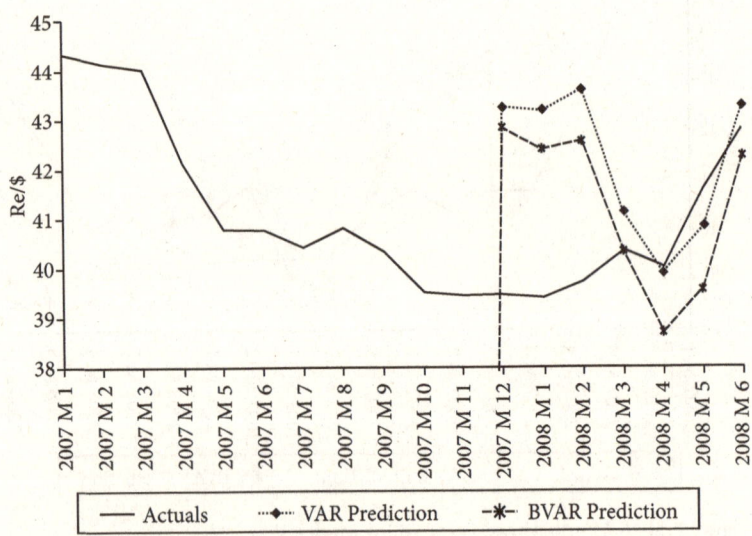

Figure 7.2d 12-Month Ahead Forecast for Model 3'
Source: Authors' own.

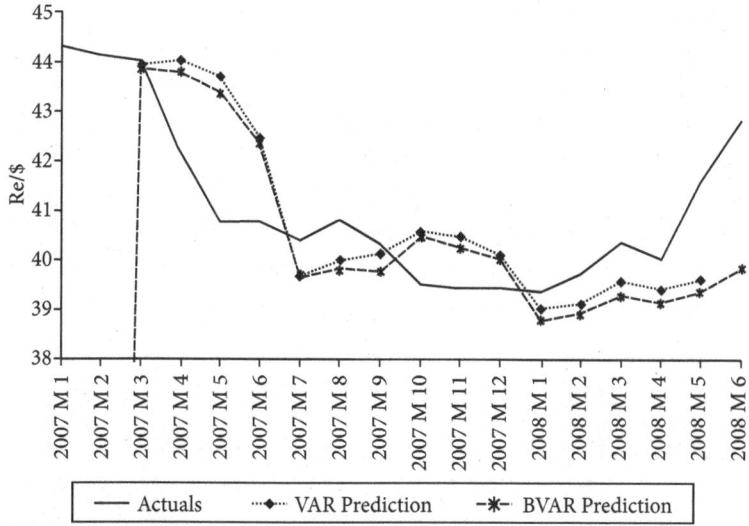

Figure 7.3a 3-Month Ahead Forecast
Source: Authors' own.

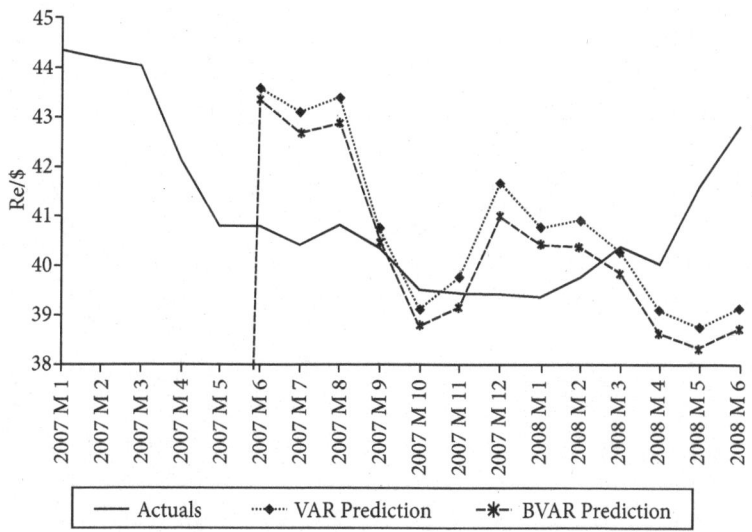

Figure 7.3b 6-Month Ahead Forecast
Source: Authors' own.

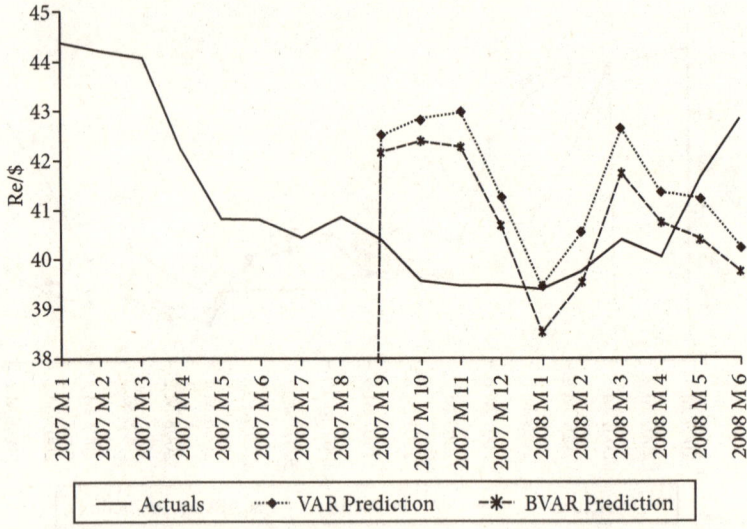

Figure 7.3c 9-Month Ahead Forecast
Source: Authors' own.

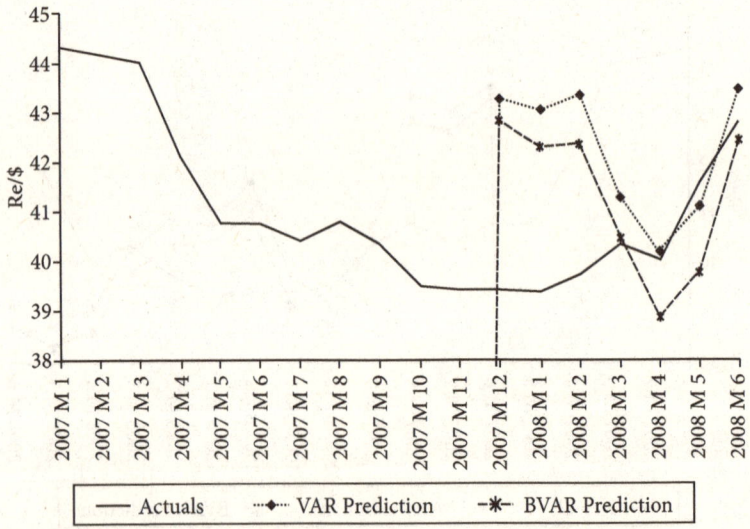

Figure 7.3d 12-Month Ahead Forecast
Source: Authors' own.

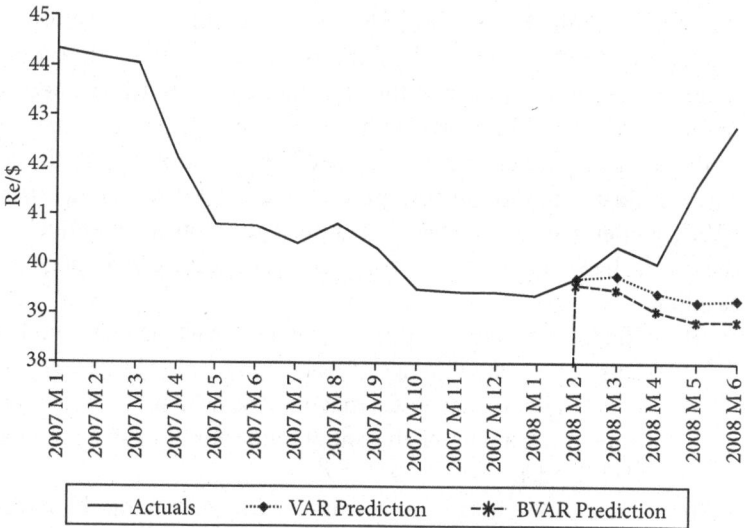

Figure 7.4   Model 4'—Multi-period Forecasts made in February 2008
Source: Authors' own.

Observations: January 2007 to June 2008

(i)   The monetary model beats the naïve forecast.

(ii)   Information on the forward premium, volatility of capital inflows, and order flows improve the accuracy of forecasts. It is, thus, possible to beat the monetary model.

(iii) Including data on central bank intervention (Model 4') helps to improve forecast accuracy further, especially at the longer end.

(iv)   BVAR models yield more accurate forecasts than their VAR counterparts, especially at longer forecast horizons.

* * *

This study attempts to gauge the forecasting ability of economic models with respect to exchange rates with the difference that this is done in the context of a developing country that follows a managed floating (as opposed to flexible) exchange rate regime. Starting from the naïve model, this study examines the forecasting performance of the monetary model and various extensions of it in the VAR and BVAR framework. Extensions of the monetary model considered in this study include the forward premium, capital inflows, volatility of capital flows, order flows, and central bank intervention. The study, therefore, examines, first, whether the monetary model can beat a random walk. Second, it investigates if the forecasting performance of the monetary model can be improved by extending it. Third, the study evaluates the forecasting performance of a VAR model vs a BVAR model. Lastly, it considers if information on intervention by the central bank can improve forecast accuracy. The main findings are as follows:

(i) The monetary model generally outperforms the naïve model. This negates the findings of the seminal paper by Meese and Rogoff (1983) that finds that models which are based on economic fundamentals cannot outperform a naïve random walk model.

(ii) Forecast accuracy can be improved by extending the monetary model to include forward premium, volatility of capital inflows, and order flow.

(iii) Information on intervention by the central bank helps to improve forecasts at the longer end.

(iv) Bayesian vector autoregressive models generally outperform their corresponding VAR variants.

(v) Turning points are difficult to predict as illustrated using Model 4' with predictions made in February 2008.

Thus, availability of information on certain key variables at regular intervals that affect the exchange rate can lead to a more informed view about the behaviour of the future exchange rates by the market participants, which may allow them to plan their foreign exchange exposure better by hedging them appropriately. Such key variables could include past data on exchange rates, forward premia, capital flows, turnover, and intervention by central banks, etc. As regards availability of data on key variables relating to the Indian foreign exchange market, most of the data are available in the public domain and can easily be accessed by market participants, academicians, and professional researchers. Using these variables skilfully will help them to gain sound insight into future exchange rate movements.

In this context, it is important to recognize that the Indian approach in recent years has been guided by the broad principles of careful monitoring and management of exchange rates with flexibility, without a fixed target or a pre-announced target or a band, coupled with the ability to intervene, if and when necessary, while allowing the underlying demand and supply conditions to determine the exchange rate movements over a period in an orderly way. Subject to this predominant objective, the exchange rate policy is guided by the need to reduce excess volatility, prevent the emergence of establishing speculative activities, help maintain adequate level of reserves, and develop an orderly foreign exchange market. The Indian market, like markets of other developing countries, is not yet very deep and broad and can, sometimes, be characterized by uneven flow of demand and supply over different periods. In this situation, the central bank (RBI) has been prepared to make sales and purchases of foreign currency in order to even out lumpy demand and supply in the relatively thin forex market and to smoothen out jerky movements.

8
Epilogue

The exchange rate is a key financial variable that affects decisions made by foreign exchange investors, exporters, importers, bankers, businesses, financial institutions, policymakers, and tourists in the developed as well as developing world. Exchange rate fluctuations affect the value of international investment portfolios, competitiveness of exports and imports, value of international reserves, currency value of debt payments, and the cost to tourists in terms of the value of their currency. Movements in exchange rates, thus, have important implications for the economy's business cycle, trade and capital flows, and are, therefore, crucial for understanding financial developments and changes in economic policy.

This book attempts to develop a model for the rupee–dollar exchange rate, taking into account variables from monetary and micro structure models as well as other variables, including intervention by the central bank. The focus is on the exchange rate of the Indian rupee vis-à-vis the US dollar, that is, the Re/$ rate. To model the exchange rate, the monetary model is expanded to include variables that may have been important in determining exchange rate movements in India such as forward premia, capital flows, order flows, and central bank intervention. Accordingly, the book analyses India's exchange rate story and discusses the exchange rate regime, structure of the foreign exchange market in India in terms of participants, instruments and trading platform, as also turnover in the Indian foreign exchange market, and forward premia. The Indian foreign exchange market has evolved over time as a deep, liquid, and efficient market, as against a highly regulated market prior to the 1990s. The market participants have become sophisticated, the range of instruments available for trading has increased, the turnover has also increased, while the bid–ask spreads have declined. This book also covers the exchange rate policy of India in the background of large capital flows.

India's exchange rate policy has evolved over time, in line with the gradual opening up of the economy, as part of the broader strategy of macroeconomic reforms and liberalization since the early 1990s. In the post-independence period, India's exchange rate policy has seen a shift from a par value system to a basket peg and, further, to a managed float exchange rate system. With the breakdown of the Bretton Woods System in 1971, the rupee was linked with the Pound Sterling. In order to overcome the weaknesses associated with a single currency peg and to ensure stability of the exchange rate, the rupee, with effect from September 1975, was pegged to a basket of currencies till the early 1990s.

The initiation of economic reforms saw, among other measures, a two step downward exchange rate adjustment by 9 per cent and 11 per cent between 1 and 3 July 1991 to counter the massive draw down in the foreign exchange reserves, to instill confidence in the investors, and to improve domestic competitiveness. The Liberalized Exchange Rate Management System (LERMS) was put in place in March 1992 involving the dual exchange rate system in the interim period. The dual exchange rate system was replaced by a unified exchange rate system in March 1993. The experience with a market determined exchange rate system in India, since 1993, is generally described as 'satisfactory' as orderliness prevailed in the Indian market during most of the period. Episodes of volatility were effectively managed through timely monetary and administrative measures.

An important aspect of the policy response in India to the various episodes of volatility has been market intervention combined with monetary and administrative measures to meet the threats to financial stability, while complementary or parallel recourse has been taken to communications through speeches and press releases. In line with the exchange rate policy, it has also been observed that the Indian rupee is moving along with the economic fundamentals in the post-reform period. Moving forward, as India progresses towards full capital account convertibility and gets more and more integrated with the rest of the world, managing periods of volatility is bound to pose greater challenges in view of the impossible trinity of independent monetary policy, open capital account, and exchange rate management. Preserving stability in the market would require more flexibility, adaptability, and innovations with regard to the strategy for liquidity management as well as exchange rate management. With the likely turnover in the foreign exchange market rising in future, further development of the foreign exchange market will be crucial to manage the associated risks.

While discussing different exchange rate regimes, it is noted that there is no consensus regarding an ideal exchange rate regime as it varies from country to country. The choice of the optimal exchange rate regime varies across countries and through time, depending upon circumstances. 'Optimal' exchange rate system is not an option but rather a decision determined by the failure of previous systems to deliver stability and sustained growth. Further, the optimal system may be imposed by exogenous developments such as the increased financial integration of the 1990s. Thus, the challenge confronting the policymakers is to pre-empt changes in the economic environment and to adjust the exchange rate and other policies consistently. Based on the experiences of various countries, consistency across policies, per se, is considered more important than the exchange rate system.

From the perspective of EMEs including India, a broad lesson of this crisis is that with increasing globalization of trade, finance, and labour, they are more strongly integrated with advanced economies than ever before. Consequently, any crisis that affects a major country, or group of countries, in the global economy or financial system will have implications for EMEs as well, sooner or later, depending on the nature and magnitude of the crisis. Thus, policymakers need to enhance their capacity to pre-empt the potential of such global shocks while formulating their policies. EMEs need to carry out their own due diligence to ensure that systemic risks are monitored within their countries. Large capital inflows are considered to be a key contributing factor in many financial crises in EMEs in the past. The recent experience of EMEs with capital flows seems to point towards the potential role for prudential measures to reduce systemic risk associated with large capital inflows. Recent experience suggests a cautious approach to the pace and scope of capital account liberalization as there is a strong linkage among capital account liberalization, domestic financial sector reform, and the design of monetary and exchange rate policy.

India's approach towards liberalizing the capital account has been one of gradualism, treating the liberalization as a continuous process rather than a single event. The lessons from the East Asian and other financial crises of 1990s have brought about a marked shift in the approach towards capital account liberalization, particularly among developing countries. Opening up of the capital account in India was an integral part of the well sequenced economic reforms programme initiated in 1991. Recognizing the macroeconomic implications of volatility and possibility of reversals associated with capital inflows, as experienced by many EMEs, India adopted a policy of managing the capital account with a preference for non-debt flows, de-emphasis on short-term debt flows, and adequate foreign exchange reserves which has ensured the sustainability of capital flows and minimized contagion that could have arisen from financial crises elsewhere. In retrospect, this calibrated approach has paid India rich dividends. India plans to continue its gradualist approach as it enables harmonization and synchronization with reforms in other sectors of the economy.

Prior to the 1990s, the Indian foreign exchange market, with a pegged exchange rate regime, was highly regulated with restrictions on transactions, participants, and use of instruments. The period since the early 1990s has witnessed a wide range of regulatory and institutional reforms, resulting in substantial development of the rupee exchange market as it is observed today. Market participants have become sophisticated and have acquired reasonable expertise in using various instruments and managing risks.

The foreign exchange market in India today is equipped with several derivative instruments. Various informal forms of derivatives contracts have existed since time immemorial though the formal introduction of a variety of instruments in the foreign exchange derivatives market started only in the post reform period, especially since the mid-1990s. These derivative instruments have been cautiously introduced as part of the reforms in a phased manner, both for product diversity and, more importantly, as a risk management tool. Recognizing the relatively nascent stage of the foreign exchange market then, with the lack of capabilities to handle massive speculation, the 'underlying exposure' criteria had been imposed as a prerequisite.

Trading volumes in the Indian foreign exchange market have grown significantly over the last few years. The daily average turnover has seen almost a 10-fold rise during the 10-year period from 1997–8 to 2007–8, from US$ 5 billion to US$ 48 billion. The pickup has been particularly sharp from 2003–4 onwards when there was a massive surge in capital inflows. It is noteworthy that the increase in foreign exchange market turnover in India between April 2004 and April 2007 was the highest amongst the 54 countries covered in the latest Triennial Central Bank Survey of Foreign Exchange and Derivatives Market Activity conducted by the BIS. According to the survey, daily average turnover in India jumped almost fivefold from US$ 7 billion in April 2004 to US$ 34 billion in April 2007; global turnover over the same period rose by only 66 per cent from US$ 2.4 trillion to US$ 4.0 trillion. Reflecting these trends, the share of India in global foreign exchange market turnover trebled from 0.3 per cent in April 2004 to 0.9 per cent in April 2007. With increasing integration of the Indian economy with the rest of the world, the efficiency in the foreign exchange market has improved as evident from low bid-ask spreads. It is found that the spread is almost flat and very low. In India, the normal spot market quote has a spread of 0.25 paisa to 0.01 paise, while swap quotes are available at 1 to 2 paise spread. Thus, the foreign exchange market has evolved over time as a deep, liquid, and efficient market as against a highly regulated market prior to the 1990s.

In the recent period, external sector developments in India have been marked by strong capital flows, which had led to an appreciating tendency in the exchange rate of the Indian rupee up to January 2008. The movement of the Indian rupee is largely influenced by the capital flow movements rather than traditional determinants like trade flows. Though capital flows are generally perceived to be beneficial to an economy, a large surge in flows over a short span of time in excess of the domestic absorptive capacity can, however, be a source of stress to the economy, giving rise to upward pressures on the exchange rate, overheating of the economy, and possible asset price bubbles.

In India, the liquidity impact of large capital inflows was traditionally managed mainly through the repo and reverse repo auctions under the day-to-day LAF. The LAF operations were supplemented by outright OMO, that is, outright sales of government securities to absorb liquidity on an enduring basis. In addition to LAF and OMO, excess liquidity from the financial system was also absorbed through the building up of surplus balances of the Government with the Reserve Bank, particularly by raising the notified amount of 91-day Treasury Bill auctions, and forex swaps. In view of the large capital flows during the past few years, relaxations were effected in regard to outflows, both under the current and capital accounts. In addition, changes in policies are made from time to time to modulate the debt creating capital flows, depending on the financing needs of the corporate sector and vulnerability of the domestic economy to external shocks.

In the face of large capital flows coupled with the declining stock of government securities, the Reserve Bank of India introduced a new instrument of sterilization, namely, the market stabilization scheme (MSS) to sustain market operations. Since its introduction in April 2004, the MSS has served as a very useful instrument for medium term monetary and liquidity management. The cost of sterilization in India is shared by the central government (the cost of MSS), Reserve Bank (sterilization under LAF), and the banking system (in case of increase in the reserve requirements).

With the surge in capital flows to EMEs, issues relating to management of those flows have assumed importance as they have bearings on the exchange rates. Large capital inflows create important challenges for policymakers because of their potential to generate overheating, loss of competitiveness, and increased vulnerability to crisis. Reflecting these concerns, policies in EMEs have responded to capital inflows in a variety of ways. While some countries have allowed the exchange rate to appreciate, in many cases monetary authorities have intervened heavily in forex markets to resist currency appreciation. EMEs have sought to neutralize the monetary impact of intervention through sterilization. Cross-country experiences reveal that in the recent period, most of the EMEs have adopted a more flexible exchange rate regime.

In view of the importance of capital flows, foreign exchange intervention, and turnover in determination of exchange rates, these variables are included in the modelling exercise undertaken to analyse the behaviour of the exchange rate.

MODELLING AND FORECASTING OF THE RE/$ EXCHANGE RATE

In the international finance literature, various theoretical models are available to analyse exchange rate determination and behaviour. Most of the studies on exchange rate models prior to the 1970s were based on the fixed price assumption.[1] With the advent of the floating exchange rate regime amongst major industrialized countries in the early 1970s, an important advance was made with the development of the monetary approach to exchange rate determination. The dominant model was the flexible-price monetary model that has been analysed in many early studies like Frenkel (1976), Mussa (1976, 1979), Frenkel and Johnson (1978), and more recently by Vitek (2005), Nwafor (2006), Molodtsova and Papell (2007). Following this, the sticky price or overshooting model by Dornbusch (1976, 1980) evolved, which has been tested, amongst others, by Alquist and Chinn (2008) and Zita and Gupta (2007). The portfolio balance model also developed alongside,[2] which allowed for imperfect substitutability between domestic and foreign assets, and considered wealth effects of current account imbalances.

With liberalization and development of foreign exchange and assets markets, variables such as capital flows, volatility in capital flows, and forward premium have also became important in determining exchange rates. Furthermore, with the growing development of foreign exchange markets and a rise in the trading volume in these markets, micro level dynamics in foreign exchange markets increasingly became important in determining exchange rates. Agents in the foreign exchange market have access to private information about fundamentals or liquidity, which is reflected in the buying/selling transactions they undertake, that are termed as order flows (Medeiros 2005; Bjonnes and Rime 2003). Microstructure theory evolved in order to capture micro level dynamics in the foreign exchange market (Evans and Lyons, 2001, 2005, 2007). Another variable that is important in determining exchange rates is central bank intervention in the foreign exchange market.

[1] See, for example, Marshall (1923), Lerner (1936), Nurkse (1944), Harberger (1950), Mundell (1961, 1962, 1963), and Fleming (1962).

[2] See, for example, Dornbusch and Fischer (1980), Isard (1980), and Branson (1983, 1984).

Non-linear models have also been considered in the literature. Sarno (2003) and Altaville and Grauwe (2006) are some of the recent studies that have used non-linear models of the exchange rate.

Overall, forecasting exchange rates have remained a challenge for both academicians as well as market participants. In fact, Meese and Rogoff's seminal book (1983) on the forecasting performance of the monetary models demonstrated that these failed to beat the random walk model. This has triggered a plethora of studies that test the superiority of theoretical and empirical models of exchange rate determination, vis-à-vis a random walk.

In sum, several exchange rate models available in the literature have been tested during the last two-and-a-half decades. No particular model seems to work best at all times/horizons. Monetary models, based on the idea of fundamentals' driven exchange rate behaviour, work best in the long-run but lose their predictability in the short-run to naïve random walk forecasts. The volatility of exchange rates also substantially exceeds that of the volatility of macroeconomic fundamentals, thus, providing further evidence of weakening 'fundamentals exchange rate link'. A combination of the different monetary models, however, at times gives better results than the random walk. Order flows also play an important role in influencing the exchange rate. Keeping in view all the above results in the literature, this book attempts to develop a model for the rupee–dollar exchange rate taking into account all the different monetary models along with the microstructure models incorporating order flow, as well as capital flows, forward premium, and central bank intervention.

This book attempts to gauge the forecasting ability of economic models with respect to exchange rates with the difference that this is done in the context of a developing country that follows a managed floating (as opposed to flexible) exchange rate regime. Starting from the naïve model, this book examines the forecasting performance of the monetary model and various extensions of it in the VAR and BVAR framework. Extensions of the monetary model considered in this book include the forward premium, capital inflows, volatility of capital flows, order flows, and central bank intervention. The book, therefore, examines first, whether the monetary model can beat a random walk. Second, it investigates if the forecasting performance of the monetary model can be improved by extending it. Third, the book evaluates the forecasting performance of a VAR model vs a BVAR model. Lastly, it considers if information on intervention by the central bank can improve forecast accuracy. The main findings are as follows:

(i) The monetary model generally outperforms the naïve model. This negates the findings of the seminal book by Meese and Rogoff (1983) that finds that models which are based on economic fundamentals cannot outperform a naïve random walk model.

(ii) The result that it is possible to beat the naïve model may be due to the fact that the intervention by the central bank may help to curb volatility arising due to demand-supply mismatch and stabilize the exchange rate. The exchange rate policy of the RBI is guided by the need to reduce excess volatility. The RBI has been prepared to make sales and purchases of foreign currency in order to even out lumpy demand and supply in the relatively thin foreign exchange market, and to smoothen out jerky movements.

(iii) Forecast accuracy can be improved by extending the monetary model to include forward premium, volatility of capital inflows, and order flow.

(iv) Information on intervention by the central bank helps to improve forecasts at the longer end.

(v) Bayesian vector autoregressive models generally outperform their corresponding VAR variants.

(vi) Turning points are difficult to predict as illustrated using Model 4' with predictions made in February 2008.

Thus, availability of information on certain key variables at regular intervals affects the exchange rate and can lead to a more informed view about the behaviour of the future exchange rates by the market participants, and this may allow them to plan their foreign exchange exposure better by hedging them appropriately. Such key variables could include past data on exchange rates, forward premia, capital flows, turnover, and intervention by central banks, etc. As regards availability of data on key variables relating to the Indian foreign exchange market, most of the data are available in the public domain and can be easily accessed by market participants, academicians, and professional researchers. Using these variables skilfully will help them to gain sound insight into future exchange rate movements.

In this context, it is important to recognize that the Indian approach in recent years has been guided by the broad principles of careful monitoring and management of exchange rates with flexibility, without a fixed target or a pre-announced target or a band, coupled with the ability to intervene if and when necessary, while allowing the underlying demand and supply conditions to determine the exchange rate movements over a period in an orderly way. Subject to this predominant objective, the exchange rate policy is guided by the need to reduce excess volatility, prevent the emergence of establishing speculative activities, help maintain adequate level of reserves, and develop an orderly foreign exchange market.

Annexures

ANNEXURE 1   MEASURES ANNOUNCED DURING 1995–6

October 1995   Imposition of interest surcharge on import finance.

Tightening of concessions in export credit for longer periods.

November 1995   Consequent upon tightness in liquidity conditions due to intervention, which led to soaring of call money rates, money market support was restored with an easing of CRR requirements on domestic as well as non-resident deposits from 15.0 per cent to 14.5 per cent, and further to 14 per cent in December 1995.

Ceiling interest rates on NRE term deposits (for 6 months to 3 years and above) raised from 10 to 12 per cent.

February 1996   With a view to discouraging the excessive use of bank credit for funding the demand for foreign exchange, interest rate surcharge on import finance was raised from 15 to 25 per cent.

The scheme for extending Post-Shipment Export Credit denominated in US dollar (PSCFC) was discontinued with effect from 8 February 1996 as it enabled exporters to earn a positive differential over the cost of funds simply by drawing credit and selling forward, thereby, receiving the premia.

Exporters were also cautioned to recognize their statutory obligation to release export proceeds within six months from shipment of goods, failing which they invite punitive action under FERA.

To curb excessive speculation in the forward market, cancellation of forward contracts booked by ADs, for amounts of US$ 100,000 and above was required to be reported to the Reserve Bank on a weekly basis.

ANNEXURE 2 POLICY MEASURES UNDERTAKEN IN THE WAKE OF THE ASIAN CRISIS

26 November 1997

Export Credit	Increase in interest rate on post-shipment rupee export credit on usance bills for period (comprising usance period of export bills, transit period as specified by Foreign Exchange Dealers Association of India (FEDAI), and grace period, wherever applicable) beyond 90 days and up to six months from the date of shipment to 15 per cent per annum.

28 November 1997

CRR	Deferment of a future programme of bringing about a reduction in CRR.
Repos	Introduction of fixed rate repos at 4.5 per cent to absorb surplus liquidity.
Export Credit	With effect from 15 December 1997, interest rate on post-shipment rupee export credit of 15 per cent was to be applicable from the date of advance. Exporters were expected to take advantage of the time gap available up to 15 December 1997 by expediting realizations of their export proceeds.
Forward Contracts	Reporting cancellations of forward contracts beyond US$ 500,000 and merchant sales of US$ 2 million and above.

1 December 1997

Forward Contracts	Ban on rebooking of cancelled forward contracts on non-trade transactions for the same underlying exposure (only roll over allowed).

2 December 1997

CRR	Increase in CRR by 0.5 percentage points to 10 per cent with effect from the fortnight beginning 6 December 1997.
Repos	The interest rate on fixed rate repos was raised to 5 per cent with effect from 3 December 1997.
Forward Contracts	The facility granted to ADs in April 1997 to offer forward contracts based on past performance and declaration of exposure was suspended and forward contracts were allowed based only on documents evidencing exposure.
Non-Resident Indian (NRI) Deposits	Abolition of 10 per cent incremental CRR on Non-Resident (External) Rupee Accounts NRE(R)A and Non-Resident (Non-Repatriable) Rupee Deposits NR(NR)RD schemes with effect from 6 December 1997.

4 December 1997

Repos | The interest rate on fixed rate repos was raised to 6.5 per cent.

11 December 1997

Repos | The interest rate on fixed rate repos was raised to 7.0 per cent.

17 December 1997

Export Credit | Imposition of interest rate of 20 per cent per annum (minimum) on overdue export bills from the date of advance. In case of demand bills and short term usance bills, the higher rate of interest was not applicable wherever the total period of credit, including the period of overdue, is less than one month from the date of bill/ negotiation.

Surcharge on Import Finance | Imposition of interest rate surcharge of 15 per cent of the lending rate (excluding interest tax) on import finance.

19 December 1997

Overseas Investments | Overnight investments from nostro accounts were included in the 15 per cent of unimpaired Tier I capital limit for overseas investments by ADs.

31 December 1997

Export Credit | The increase in the interest rate on post-shipment rupee export credit (measures undertaken on 26 and 28 November 1997) was rolled back. In other words, the rate of interest on post-shipment rupee export credit (other than against overdue export bills) for periods beyond 90 days and up to six months was to be 13 per cent per annum with effect from 1 January 1998. Hence, the position prevailing prior to 26 November 1997 was restored.

Export Credit | Imposition of interest rate of 20 per cent per annum on overdue export bills will only be applicable for the overdue period and not from the date of advance and this rate will not be applicable in respect of certain chronic cases (where even six months ago, the bills were overdue).

6 January 1998

Overnight Position Limits | The banks would have to square up their foreign exchange positions on a daily basis.

16 January 1998

CRR | Increase in CRR by 0.5 percentage points to 10.5 per cent with effect from the fortnight beginning 17 January 1997.

Repos Interest Rate | The interest rate on fixed rate repos was raised to 9.0 per cent from 7.0 per cent.

Reverse Repos	Reverse repos facility was made available to Primary Dealers in Government Securities market at Bank Rate on a discretionary basis and subject to a stipulation of conditions relating to their operations in the call money market.
Surcharge on Import Finance	The interest rate surcharge on import finance was increased from 15 per cent to 30 per cent.
Overnight Position Limits	It was decided to withdraw the across-the-board formal stipulation regarding square/near-square positions and to restore to banks the freedom to run exposure within the limits approved. Banks were, however, advised to use their overnight position limits for genuine transactions.
Overseas Investments	To meet genuine operational requirements in foreign exchange transactions, requests of individual banks would be considered with regard to limits on nostro account balances.
Bank Rate	Bank rate was increased from 9 per cent to 11 per cent with a corresponding increase in the interest rate on Export Credit Refinance as well as General Refinance.
Refinance	Export refinance limit was reduced from 100 to 50 per cent of the increase in outstanding export credit eligible for refinance over the level of such credit as on 16 February 1996.
Refinance	General refinance limit was reduced from 1 per cent to 0.25 per cent of the fortnightly average of outstanding aggregate deposits in 1996–7.

ANNEXURE 3   POLICY MEASURES UNDERTAKEN DURING 1999–2000

October 1999

It was decided to allow the ADs, who were permitted by the RBI to accept gold under the Gold Deposit Scheme to use exchange-traded and over-the-counter hedging products available overseas to manage their price risk arising out of the sale of gold. However, while using products involving options, ADs were to ensure that there was no net receipt of premium, either direct or implied.

November 1999

Simplifying the procedure for NRI/Overseas Corporate Body (OCB) investment in India, the RBI granted general permission to Indian companies for issuing non-convertible debentures to such investors on non-repatriation/repatriation basis, subject to certain conditions. Further, all portfolio investments made by NRIs and/or OCBs, on non-repatriation/repatriation basis in shares/debentures of Indian companies and other securities through designated branches of ADs, would not require specific permission from the RBI. Authorized dealers were permitted to grant loans and advances to NRIs and Persons of Indian Origin against the security of shares/debentures/immovable property held by them in India, according to their commercial judgement and subject to certain conditions.

With a view to minimizing the country's short-term external borrowing liabilities, the minimum maturity of FCNR(B) deposits was raised to one year from six months.

With a view to promoting FDI by Indian companies under the RBI Fast Track Route and Normal Route, the condition that the amount of investment should be repatriated in full by way of dividend, royalty, and so on within a period of five years was dispensed with.

It was decided that in the case of ECBs approved by the Government of India, ADs, designated by the borrowers, may allow the remittance towards prepayment/part-prepayment of ECBs to the extent such prepayment had been approved by the Government of India. In case of prepayment of ECBs approved by the RBI, the borrower had to submit an application through the designated AD to the RBI with the necessary documents.

March 2000

Expanding substantially the foreign investment under the Automatic Route of the Reserve Bank, the Union

Government granted general permission under FERA, 1973, for issue of shares to non-residents (which included FDI and NRI/OCB investment) subject to certain conditions.

June 2000

The limit for ECB approvals given by the RBI was increased to US$ 100 million under all windows. Even in cases of prepayments approved by the Government, the RBI was empowered to give all such approvals.

October 2000

State Bank of India was permitted to float a scheme called India Millennium Deposits.

March 2001

In respect of Indian investment abroad, Indian companies were allowed to acquire foreign companies or make direct investment in joint ventures/wholly owned subsidiaries abroad (i) up to US$ 50 million on an annual basis through the automatic route without the earlier three-year profitability condition and (ii) by utilizing the entire proceeds (from the earlier 50 per cent) of their ADR/GDR.

FIIs allowed to invest in a company under the portfolio investment route up to 24 per cent of the paid up capital of the company. This could be increased to 40 per cent with the approval of the General Body of shareholders by a special resolution. This limit was increased from 40 per cent to 49 per cent.

September 2001

Indian companies were permitted to raise the 24 per cent limit on FIIs investment to the sectoral cap/statutory ceiling as applicable.

February 2002

As announced in the Budget speech for 2002–3, FIIs' portfolio investments would not be subject to sectoral limits for FDI except in specified sectors.

March 2002

Corporates allowed to issue FCCBs up to US$ 50 million under the automatic route.

April 2002

Non-resident non-repatriable account and non-resident special rupee account schemes were discontinued with effect from 1 April 2002 in order to provide full convertibility on non-resident deposit schemes.

With a view to enabling corporates to manage their exposure efficiently, the facility to cancel and rebook forward contracts which was available in respect of export transactions only was extended to all forward contracts.

August 2002

An 'automatic route' for prepayment of external commercial borrowings, without prior permission of the RBI, was introduced.

January 2003   Listed Indian companies and mutual funds (MFs) were permitted to invest in companies listed on a recognized stock exchange abroad but with shareholding of at least 10 per cent in an Indian company listed on a recognized stock exchange in India, provided such investment did not exceed 25 per cent of the company's net worth. Resident individuals were also permitted to invest in these companies without any monetary limit.

ANNEXURE 4   POLICY MEASURES UNDERTAKEN DURING 2000

25 May 2000

Interest rate surcharge of 50 per cent of the lending rate was imposed on import finance, as a temporary measure, on all non-essential imports.

Banks were to charge interest at 25 per cent per annum (minimum) from the date that the bill fell due for payment, in respect of overdue export bills, in order to discourage any delay in realization of export proceeds.

It was indicated that the RBI would meet, partially or fully, the Government debt service payments directly, as considered necessary.

It was indicated that arrangements would be made to meet, partially or fully, the foreign exchange requirements for import of crude oil by the IOC.

The RBI would continue to sell US dollars through State Bank of India in order to augment supply in the market or intervene directly, as considered necessary, to meet any temporary demand supply imbalances.

ADs, acting on behalf of FIIs, could approach the RBI to procure foreign exchange at the prevailing market rate and the RBI would, depending on market conditions, either sell the foreign exchange directly or advise the concerned bank to buy it from the market.

Banks were advised to enter into transactions in the forex market only on the basis of genuine requirements and not for the purpose of building up speculative positions.

21 July 2000

Bank Rate was increased from 7 per cent to 8 per cent.

CRR was increased from 8 per cent to 8.5 per cent in two stages.

The limits available to banks for refinance facilities including the collateralized lending facility were reduced temporarily to the extent of 50 per cent of the eligible limits under two equal stages.

ANNEXURE 5 POLICY MEASURES UNDERTAKEN BY THE RBI TO TACKLE CONTAGION FROM THE GLOBAL FINANCIAL TURMOIL

29 July 2008

Repo Rate	Repo rate under the LAF increased by 50 basis points from 8.50 per cent to 9.00 per cent with immediate effect.
CRR	CRR of Scheduled Banks increased by 25 basis points of their net time and demand liabilities (NDTL) to 9.00 per cent with effect from 30 August 2008.

16 September 2008

(i) NRI deposits	Increase in interest rate ceiling on FCNR(B) deposits by 50 basis points, *that is*, to Libor/Euribor/Swap rates minus 25 basis points.
	Increase in interest rate ceiling on NR(E)RA deposits by 50 basis points, *that is*, to Libor/Euribor/Swap rates plus 50 basis points.
(ii) LAF	Scheduled banks were allowed to avail additional liquidity support under the LAF to the extent of up to 1 per cent of their net demand and time liabilities, and seek waiver of penal interest (against the practice of obtaining liquidity for securities in excess of the prescribed SLR).
(iii) SLAF	Second LAF to be conducted on a daily basis (as against the practice of reporting every Friday).

22 September 2008

ECB	The ECB limit of US$ 100 million was raised to US$ 500 million per financial year for the borrowers in the infrastructure sector for Rupee expenditure under the Approval Route. External commercial borrowings in excess of US$ 100 million for Rupee expenditure should have a minimum average maturity period of seven years. In view of widening credit spreads in the international financial markets, the all-in-cost ceiling for ECBs for (more than seven years) was revised upwards from 350 basis points to 450 basis points.

6 October 2008

CRR	Reduction in CRR by 50 basis points from 9 per cent to 8.5 per cent of NDTL with effect from the fortnight beginning 11 October 2008, resulting in the release of about Rs 20,000 crore into the system.

8 October 2008

ECB

As per ECB policy, Infrastructure included power, telecom, railways, roads (including bridges), seaports and airports, industrial parks, and urban infrastructure (water supply, sanitation and sewage projects). The definition of infrastructure was expanded to include mining, exploration, and refining firms.

10 October 2008

(i) CRR

Reduction in CRR by 150 basis points from 9 per cent to 7.5 per cent of NDTL with effect from the fortnight beginning 11 October 2008 (instead of the 50 basis points reduction announced on 6 October 2008) resulting in the release of Rs 60,000 crore into the system.

(ii) Communication

A statement by the Governor saying that Indian banking system is stable and sound and forex and money market are functioning orderly.

14 October 2008

(i) LAF

Special 14-day repo to be conducted at 9 per cent per annum for a notified amount of Rs 20,000 crore with a view to enabling banks to meet the liquidity requirements of MFs.

(ii) Lending to Mutual

Funds Banks and FIs were permitted to grant loans to mutual funds against Certificates of Deposits (CDs) as well as to buy back their own CDs before maturity for a period of 15 days.

15 October 2008

(i) CRR

Reduction in CRR by 100 basis points to 6.5 per cent of NDTL with effect from 11 October 2008, resulting in the release of additional liquidity of Rs 40,000 crore into the system.

(ii) LAF

Special 14-day repo to be conducted every day up to a cumulative amount of Rs 20,000 crore. Banks could avail of additional liquidity support exclusively for the purpose of meeting their liquidity requirements of MFs to the extent of up to 0.5 per cent of their NDTL. This accommodation was to be in addition to the permission given to banks on 16 September 2008 for availing additional liquidity support to the extent of up to 1 per cent of their NDTL. For any shortfall in maintenance of SLR arising out of availment of this additional liquidity support under LAF, the bank could apply to the RBI in writing with a request not to demand payment of the penal interest thereon.

(iii) Provision of Credit	Special Market Operations were instituted by RBI for public sector oil marketing companies in June–July 2008 taking into account the extraordinary situation then prevailing in the money and forex markets. RBI was to institute a similar facility when oil bonds become available.
	Under the Agricultural Debt Waiver and Debt Relief Scheme the government had agreed to provide to the commercial banks, regional rural banks (RRBs), and cooperative credit institutions a sum of Rs 25,000 crore as the first installment. At the request of the government, RBI agreed to provide the sum to the scheduled banks and NABARD, immediately.
(iv) NRI Deposits	Increase in interest rate ceiling on FCNR(B) deposits by 50 basis points, *that is*, to Libor/Euribor/Swap rates plus 25 basis points.
	Increase in interest rate ceiling on NR(E)RA deposits by 50 basis points, *that is*, to Libor/Euribor/Swap rates plus 100 basis points.
(v) Bank overseas borrowings	Banks permitted to borrow funds from their overseas branches and correspondent banks up to a limit of 50 per cent of their unimpaired Tier-I capital as at the close of the previous quarter or US$ 10 million, whichever is higher, as against the existing limit of 25 per cent.

16 October 2008

(i) LAF	A special fixed rate term repo conducted at 9 per cent per annum against eligible securities for Rs 16,300 crore on 16 October 2008, due for reversal on 31 October 2008, with a view to enabling banks to meet the liquidity requirements of mutual funds. Of this facility, Rs 2,270 crore was utilized by banks on 15 October 2008.
(ii) Ceiling rate on NRI Deposits	Ceiling rate on FCNR(B) deposits increased by 50 basis points to LIBOR/swap rates minus 25 basis points for the respective currency/corresponding maturities.
	Interest rate on NR(E)RA term deposits was increased by 50 basis points to LIBOR/swap rates plus 50 basis points for US dollar of corresponding maturities.
(iii) Forex intervention	RBI assured that it would sell foreign exchange through agent banks to augment supply in the domestic foreign exchange market or intervene directly to meet any demand–supply gaps.
(iv) LAF	Allow banks to borrow from RBI's LAF window to the tune of additional 1 per cent of their NDTL and seek waiver

of penal interest; second LAF window opened on a daily basis.

17 October 2008

LAF

A special fixed rate term repo at 9 per cent per annum against eligible securities for the balance amount, that is, Rs 14,030 crore, conducted on 17 October 2008, due for reversal on 31 October 2008, with a view to enabling banks to meet the liquidity requirements of mutual funds.

20 October 2008

Repo rate

The repo rate under the LAF was reduced by 100 basis points to 8.0 per cent from 9.0 per cent.

22 October 2008

ECB

External Commercial Borrowings up to US$ 500 million per borrower per financial year would be permitted for Rupee expenditure and/or foreign currency expenditure for permissible end uses under the Automatic Route. Accordingly, the requirement of minimum average maturity period of seven years for ECBs of more than US$ 100 million for Rupee capital expenditure by the borrowers in the infrastructure sector was dispensed with.

In order to further develop the telecom sector, payment for obtaining licence/permit for 3G Spectrum would be considered an eligible end use for the purpose of ECB.

Borrowers were extended the flexibility to either keep these funds off-shore or remit these funds to India for credit to their Rupee accounts with AD Category I banks in India, pending utilization for permissible end use.

In view of the tight liquidity conditions in the international financial markets, the all-in-cost ceilings on ECBs were revised upwards to 300 basis points for loans maturing between three to five years and to 500 basis points for loans with maturity above five years.

1 November 2008

(i) CRR

Reduction in CRR by 100 basis points from 6.5 per cent to 5.5 per cent of NDTL to be effected in two stages: by 50 basis points, retrospectively, with effect from the fortnight beginning 25 October and by a further 50 basis points, prospectively, with effect from the fortnight beginning 8 November 2008. This measure was expected to release around Rs 40,000 crore into the system.

(ii) Repo rate

Reduction in the repo rate by 50 basis points to 7.5 per cent with effect from 3 November 2008.

(iii) LAF	On 16 September 2008, the RBI had announced, as a temporary and ad hoc measure, that scheduled banks could avail additional liquidity support under the LAF to the extent of up to 1 per cent of their NDTL and seek waiver of penal interest. This measure was made permanent. Accordingly, SLR was reduced to 24 per cent of NDTL with effect from the fortnight beginning 8 November 2008.
	Banks allowed to avail liquidity support under the LAF through relaxation in the maintenance of SLR to the extent of up to 1.5 per cent of their NDTL, to be used exclusively for the purpose of meeting the funding requirements of MFs and NBFCs which could be apportioned between MFs and NBFCs flexibly.
(iv) Additional liquidity facility	In order to provide further comfort on liquidity and to impart flexibility in liquidity management for banks, it was decided to introduce a special refinance facility under Section 17(3B) of the Reserve Bank of India Act, 1934. Under this facility, all scheduled commercial banks (excluding RRBs) would be provided refinance from the RBI equivalent to up to 1.0 per cent of each bank's NDTL as on 24 October 2008 at the LAF repo rate up to a maximum period of 90 days. During this period, refinance could be flexibly drawn and repaid.
(v) Foreign currency borrowings by non-deposit taking NBFCs	It was decided, as a temporary measure, to permit Systemically Important Non-Deposit taking NBFCs to raise short-term foreign currency borrowings under the approval route, subject to their complying with the prudential norms on capital adequacy and exposure norms.
(vi) Buy back of MSS securities	In the context of forex outflows in the recent period, buy back of MSS dated securities was conducted so as to provide another avenue for injecting liquidity of a more durable nature into the system. This was calibrated with the market borrowing programme of the Government of India. On 7 November 2008, The Reserve Bank had announced to provide forex liquidity to Indian public and private sector banks having foreign branches or subsidiaries through forex swaps or tenors up to 3 months which was later extended up to June 2010.

28 November 2008

Export Credit	In view of the difficulties being faced by exporters on account of the weakening of external demand, it was decided to extend the period of entitlement of the first slab of post-shipment rupee export credit, currently available at

a concessional interest rate ceiling of the benchmark prime lending rate (BPLR) minus 2.5 percentage points, from 90 days to 180 days with effect from 1 December 2008.

6 December 2008

(i) Repo Rate

Reduced the repo rate under the LAF by 100 basis points from 7.5 per cent to 6.5 per cent and the reverse repo rate by 100 basis points from 6.0 per cent to 5.0 per cent, with effect from 8 December 2008.

(ii) Credit Delivery

In view of the need to enhance credit delivery to the employment intensive micro and small enterprises sector, it was decided to provide refinance of an amount of Rs 7,000 crore to the Small Industries Development Bank of India under the provisions of Section 17(4H) of the Reserve Bank of India Act, 1934.

The loans granted by banks to Housing Finance Companies (HFCs) for lending to individuals for purchase/construction of dwelling units was classified under priority sector, provided the housing loans granted by HFCs did exceed Rs 20 lakh per dwelling unit per family.

Extended exceptional/concessional treatment of retaining the asset classification of the restructured accounts in standard category to the commercial real estate exposures were restructured up to 30 June 2009.

As a one-time measure, the second restructuring of exposures done by banks (other than exposures to commercial real estate, capital market exposures and personal/consumer loans) up to 30 June 2009, were also to be eligible for exceptional regulatory treatment.

(iii) Export Credit

The prescribed interest rate, as applicable to post-shipment rupee export credit (not exceeding benchmark prime lending rate [BPLR] minus 2.5 percentage points), was also permitted to be extended to overdue bills up to 180 days from the date of advance.

(iv) FCCBs

Permitted ADs Category-I banks to consider applications for premature buyback of FCCBs from their customers.

11 December 2008

(i) Credit delivery

In order to provide liquidity support to the housing sector, and particularly to HFCs which had been adversely affected by the recent financial market developments, it was decided to provide a refinance facility of an amount of Rs 4,000 crore to the NHB under the provisions of Section 17(4DD) of the Reserve Bank of India Act, 1934.

| (ii) Refinance to EXIM Bank | With a view to mitigating the pressures on account of the recent developments on loan disbursements to Indian exporting companies and for honouring disbursements under export lines of credit extended at the behest of the Government of India to overseas financial institutions, sovereign governments, and other entities for financing imports from India, it was decided to provide a refinance facility to the EXIM Bank for an amount of Rs 5,000 crore under the provisions of Section 17(4J) of the Reserve Bank of India Act, 1934. |

2 January 2009

| (i) Repo Rate | Reduction in the repo rate under the LAF by 100 basis points from 6.5 per cent to 5.5 per cent and the reverse repo rate by 100 basis points from 5.0 per cent to 4.0 per cent, effective from 3 January 2009. |
| (ii) CRR | The CRR of scheduled banks was reduced by 50 basis points from 5.5 per cent to 5.0 per cent of NDTL with effect from the fortnight beginning 17 January 2009 releasing around Rs 20,000 crore into the system. |

Movements in Key Policy Rates in India

Effective Since	Reverse Repo Rate		Repo Rate		Cash Reserve Ratio	
21 April 2009	3.25	(−0.25)	4.75	(−0.25)	5.00	
13 February 2010	3.25		4.75		5.50	(+0.50)
27 February 2010	3.25		4.75		5.75	(+0.25)
19 March 2010	3.50	(+0.25)	5.00	(+0.25)	5.75	
20 April 2010	3.75	(+0.25)	5.25	(+0.25)	5.75	
24 April 2010	3.75		5.25		6.00	(+0.25)
2 July 2010	4.00	(+0.25)	5.50	(+0.25)	6.00	
27 July 2010	4.50	(+0.50)	5.75	(+0.25)	6.00	
16 September 2010	5.00	(+0.50)	6.00	(+0.25)	6.00	
2 November 2010	5.25	(+0.25)	6.25	(+0.25)	6.00	
25 January 2011	5.50	(+0.25)	6.50	(+0.25)	6.00	
17 March 2011	5.75	(+0.25)	6.75	(+0.25)	6.00	
3 May 2011	6.25	(+0.50)	7.25	(+0.50)	6.00	
16 June 2011	6.50	(+0.25)	7.50	(+0.25)	6.00	

Source: Reserve Bank of India.

Note: Figures in parentheses indicate change in policy rates in percentage points.

Data Definitions and Sources

Variable	Definition	Source
e	Rupee/US dollar Spot Exchange Rate	Handbook of Statistics on the Indian Economy and RBI Bulletin
i	Auctions of 91-day Government of India Treasury Bills	Handbook of Statistics on the Indian Economy and RBI Bulletin
i*	3-Month Treasury Bill of US, Secondary Market Rate	Board of Governors of the Federal Reserve System
y	Index of Industrial Production for India seasonally adjusted using Census X12.	Handbook of Statistics on the Indian Economy and RBI Bulletin
y*	Industrial Production Index for US (seasonally adjusted)	Board of Governors of the Federal Reserve System
π	Year-on-year Inflation Rate calculated from Consumer Price Index for Industrial Workers for India	Handbook of Statistics on the Indian Economy and RBI Bulletin
π*	Year-on-year Inflation Rate calculated from Consumer Price Index for All Urban Consumers; All Items for US	US Department of Labor: Bureau of Labor Statistics
m	Money supply (M3) for India, seasonally adjusted using Census X12	Handbook of Statistics on the Indian Economy and Weekly Statistical Supplement
m*	M2 for US, seasonally adjusted	Board of Governors of the Federal Reserve System
tb	Trade Balance of India in US$ Billion	RBI Bulletin
tb*	Trade Balance of US in US$ Billion	US Census Bureau of Economic Analysis

fdp	Three-month forward premium (% per annum)	Handbook of Statistics on the Indian Economy and Weekly Statistical Supplement
cap	Capital flows measured by Foreign Direct Investment plus Foreign Private Investment Inflows in India in US$ (Billion)	Handbook of Statistics on the Indian Economy and RBI Bulletin
vol	Volatility of capital inflows measured by three period moving average standard deviation of sum of FDI and FII:	Calculated

$$V_t = [(1/m)\sum_{i=1}^{m}(Z_{t+i-1} - Z_{t+i-2})^2]^{1/2}$$

where m=3 and Z is cap

of	Order flow—Turnover in foreign exchange market in US$ (Billion)	Handbook of Statistics on the Indian Economy and RBI Bulletin
int	Purchase minus Sale of US dollars by RBI	Handbook of Statistics on the Indian Economy and RBI Bulletin

Bibliography

Agosin, M.R. (1998). 'Capital Inflow and Investment Performance: Chile in the 1990s', in R. Ffrench-Davis and H. Reisen (eds), *Capital Inflows and Investment Performance: Lessons from Latin America*, Paris and Santiago: ECLAC/OECD Development.

Almekinders, G.J. (1995). *Foreign Exchange Intervention: Theory and Evidence*, Cheltanham: Edward Elgar Publishing.

Alquist, R. and M. Chinn (2008). 'Conventional and Unconventional Approaches to Exchange Rate Modelling and Assessment', *International Journal of Finance and Economics*, vol. 13, pp. 2–13.

Altavilla, C. and P. De Grauwe (2006). 'Forecasting and Combining Competing Models of Exchange Rate Determination', CESifo Working Paper No. 1747.

Andersen, T.G., T. Bollerslev, F.X. Diebold, and C. Vega (2003). 'Micro Effects of Macro Announcements: Real-Time Price Discovery in Foreign Exchange', *American Economic Review*, vol. 93, pp. 38–62.

Apte, P., P. Sercu, and R. Uppal (1996). 'The Equilibrium Approach to Exchange Rates: Theory and Tests', NBER Woking Paper Series, Working Paper No. 5748.

Ariyoshi, A., K.F. Habermeier, B. Laurens, I. Ötker, J.I. Canales K., and A. Kirilenko (2000). 'Capital Controls: Country Experiences with Their Use and Liberalization', IMF Occasional Paper No. 190.

Artis, M.J. and W. Zhang (1990). 'BVAR Forecasts for the G7', *International Journal of Forecasting*, vol. 6, pp. 349–62.

Backus, D. (1984). 'Empirical Models of the Exchange Rate: Separating the Wheat from the Chaff', *The Canadian Journal of Economics/Revue Canadienne d'Economique*, vol. 17, pp. 824–46.

Baharumshah, A.Z., L.K. Sen, and L.K. Ping (2003). 'Exchange Rates Forecasting Model: An Alternative Estimation Procedure', manuscript available at http://ideas.repec.org/p/wpa/wuwpif/0307005.html

Baillie, R.T. and T. Bollerslev (1994). 'Cointegration, Fractional Cointegration, and Exchange Rate Dynamics', *Journal of Finance*, vol. 49, pp. 737–45.

Bailliu, J. and E. Fujii (2004). 'Exchange Rate Pass-Through and the Inflation Environment in Industrialized Countries: An Empirical Investigation', Bank of Canada Working Paper No. 2004–21, Ottawa: Bank of Canada.

Bajo-Rubio, O., F. Fernandez-Rodriguez, and S. Sosvilla-Rivero (1992). 'Chaotic Behaviour in Exchange Rate Series: First Results for the Peseta-US Dollar Case', *Economic Letters*, vol. 39, pp. 207–11.

Bakker, Age and Bryan Chapple (2002). 'Advanced Country, Experiences with Capital Account Liberalization, IMF Occasional Paper No. 214, Washington: International Monetary Fund.

Barr, D.G. (1989). 'Exchange Rate Dynamics: An Empirical Analysis', in R. MacDonald and M.P. Taylor (eds). *Exchange Rate and Open Economy Macroeconomics*, pp. 109–29, Oxford: Blackwell.

Bauwens, L. and G. Sucarat (2006). 'General to Specific Modelling of Exchange Rate Volatility: A Forecast Evaluation', Core Discussion Paper, No. 2006/21.

Baxter, M. and A.C. Stockman (1989). 'Business Cycles and the Exchange Rate Regime: Some International Evidence', *Journal of Monetary Economics*, vol. 23, pp. 5–37.

Belkacem, L., Z.E. Meddeb, and H. Boubaker (2005). 'Foreign Exchange Market Efficiency: Fractional Cointegration Approach', *International Journal of Business*, vol. 10, pp. 285–302.

Bhagwati, J. (1998). 'The Capital Myth: The Difference between Trade in Widgets and Dollars', *Foreign Affairs*, vol. 77, pp. 7–12.

Bilson J.F.O. (1978). 'The Monetary Approach to the Exchange Rate: Some Em-pirical Evidence', Staff Papers, International Monetary Fund, 25, pp. 48–75.

Bank for International Settlements [BIS] (2007). 'The Triennial Central Bank Survey of Foreign Exchange and Derivatives Market Activity', available at http://www.bis.org/publ/rpfxf07t.html

Bisignano J. and K. Hoover (1982). 'Some Suggested Improvements to a Portfolio Balance of Exchange Rate Determination with Special Reference to US Dollar/Canadian Dollar Rate', *Weltwirtschaftliches Archiv*, vol. 118, pp. 1305–11.

Bjonnes, G.H. and D. Rime (2005). 'Dealer Behavior and Trading Systems in Foreign Exchange Markets', *Journal of Financial Economics*, vol. 75, pp. 571–605.

Branson, W.H. (1983). 'Macroeconomic Determinants of Real Exchange Risk', in R.J. Herring (ed.) *Managing Foreign Exchange Risk*, Cambridge: Cambridge University Press.

_____ (1984). 'A Model of Exchange Rate Determination with Policy Reaction: Evidence from Monthly Data', in P. Malgrange and P.A. Muet (eds). *Contemporary Macroeconomic Modelling*, Oxford: Basil Blackwell.

Branson, W.H., H. Halttunen, and P. Masson (1977). 'Exchange Rates in the Short Run: The Dollar-Deutschemark Rate', *European Economic Review*, vol. 10, pp. 303–24.

Breedon, F. and P. Vitale (2004). 'An Empirical Study of Liquidity and Information Effects of Order Flow on Exchange Rates', Centre for Economic Policy Research, Discussion Paper No. 4586, August.

Bubula, Andrea and Inci Otker-Robe (2002). 'The Evolution of Exchange Rate Regimes since 1990: Evidence from De Facto Policies', IMF Working Paper No. WP/02/155.

Buiter, W.H. and M. Miller (1981). 'Monetary Policy and International Competitiveness: The Problems of Adjustment', *Oxford Economic Papers*, vol. 33, Supplement, pp. 143–75.

Calvo, G.A. and C.M. Reinhart (2000). 'Fear of Floating', NBER Working Paper No. 7993.

Calvo, G.A. and F.S. Mishkin (2003). 'The Mirage of Exchange Rate Regimes for Emerging Market Countries', NBER Working Paper No. 9808.

Calvo, G.A., L. Leiderman, and C.M. Reinhart (1993). 'Capital Inflows and Real Exchange Rate Appreciation: The Role of External Factors', *International Monetary Fund Staff Papers*, vol. 40, pp. 108–51.

Campbell, J.Y. and P. Perron (1991). 'Pitfalls and Opportunities: What Macroeconomists Should Know About Unit Roots', *NBER Macroeconomic Annual*, University of Chicago Press, Illinois, vol. 6, pp. 141–220.

Cao, L. and A.S. Soofi (1999). 'Nonlinear Deterministic Forecasting of Daily Dollar Exchange Rates', *International Journal of Forecasting*, vol. 15, pp. 421–30.

Caramazza, F. and J. Aziz (1998). 'Fixed or Flexible? Getting the Exchange Rate Right in the 1990s', *IMF Economic Issues 13*.

Chen, A. and M.T. Leung (2003). 'A Bayesian Vector Error Correction Model for Forecasting Exchange Rates', *Computers and Operations Research*, vol. 30, pp. 887–900.

_____ (2004). 'Regression Neural Network for Error Correction in Foreign Exchange Forecasting and Trading', *Computers and Operations Research*, vol. 31, pp. 1049–68.

Cheung, Y., M. Chinn, and A.G. Pascual (2004). 'Empirical Exchange Rate Models of the Nineties: Are Any Fit to Survive?', IMF Working Paper No. WP/ 04/73.

Chinn, M.D. (1999). 'Measuring Misalignment—Purchasing Power Parity and East Asian Currencies in the 1990s', IMF Working Paper No. 99/120.

Chinn, M.D. and R.A. Meese (1995). 'Banking on Currency Forecasts: How Predictable is Change in Money?', *Journal of International Economics*, vol. 38, pp. 161–78.

Chortareas, G., J. Nankervis, and Y. Jiang (2007). 'Forecasting Exchange Rate Volatility at High Frequency Data: Is the Euro Different?', available at http://ideas.repec.org/p/mmf/mmfc06/79.html

Choudhry, T. and P. Lawler (1997). 'The Monetary Model of Exchange Rates: Evidence from the Canadian Float of the 1950s', *Journal of Macroeconomics*, vol. 19, pp. 349–62.

Clarida, R.H., and M.P. Taylor (1997). 'The Term Structure of Forward Exchange Premiums and Forecastability of Spot Exchange Rates: Correcting the Errors', *Review of Economics and Statistics*, vol. 70, pp. 508–11.

Clarida, R.H., L. Sarno, M.P. Taylor, and G. Valente (2003). 'The Out-of-Sample Success of Term Structure Models as Exchange Rate Predictors: A Step Beyond', *Journal of International Economics*, vol. 60, pp. 61–83.

Clostermann, J. and G. Schnatz (2000). 'The Determinants of the Euro Dollar Exchange Rates: Synthetic Fundamentals and Non-existing Currency', Discussion Paper No. 2/00, Economic Research Group of the Deutsche Bundesbank.

Committee on the Global Financial System (2009). *Report of the Working Group on Capital Flows to Emerging Market Economies*). Bank for International Settlements, Basel.

Cuthbertson, K. (1996). *Quantitative Financial Economics: Stocks, Bonds and Foreign Exchange*, Chichester: John Wiley and Sons.

De Grauwe, P. and H. Dewatchter (1993). 'A Chaotic Model of the Exchange Rate: The Role of Fundamentalists and Chartists', *Open Economy Review*, vol. 4, pp. 351–79.

De Grauwe, P. and I. Vansteenkiste (2001). 'Exchange Rates and Fundamentals: A Non-Linear Relationship?', CESifo Working Paper No. 577.

De Gregorio, J., S. Edwards, and R. Valdés (2000). 'Controls on Capital Inflows: Do They Work?', *Journal of Development Economics*, vol. 63, available at http:// ideas.repec.org/p/nbr/nberwo/7645.html

Della Corte, P., L. Sarno, and I. Tsiakas (2007). 'An Economic Evaluation of Empirical Exchange Rate Models', CEPR Discussion Paper No. 6598.

Diamandis, P.F., D.A. Georgoutsos, and G.P. Kouretas (1998). 'The Monetary Approach to the Exchange Rate: Long-Run Relationships, Identification and Temporal Stability', *Journal of Macroeconomics*, vol. 20, pp. 741–66.

Diaz, D.G. (2003). 'How Does the Monetary Model of Exchange Rate Determination Look When it Really Works?', Working Paper, Bank of Mexico.

Dickey, D.A. and W.A. Fuller (1981). 'Likelihood Ratio Statistics for Autoregressive Time Series with a Unit Root', *Econometrica* , vol. 49, pp. 1057–72.

_____ (1979). 'Distribution of the Estimators for Autoregressive Time Series with a Unit Root', *Journal of the American Statistical Association*, vol. 74, pp. 427–31.

Diebold, F.X., J. Gardeazabal, and K. Yilmaz (1994). 'On Cointegration and Exchange Rate Dynamics', *The Journal of Finance*, vol. 49, pp. 727–35.

Diebold, F.X. and R. Mariano (1995). 'Comparing Predictive Accuracy', *Journal of Business and Economic Statistics*, vol.13, pp. 253–62.

Doan, T.A. (1992). *RATS User's Manual*, III, Estimation.

Doan, T.A., R.B. Litterman, and C.A. Sims (1984). 'Forecasting and Conditional Projection Using Realistic Prior Distributions', *Econometric Reviews*, vol. 3, pp. 1–100.

Doldado, J., T. Jenkinson, and S. Sosvilla-Rivero (1990). 'Cointegration and Unit Roots', *Journal of Economic Surveys*, vol. 4, pp. 249–73.

Dominguez, K.M. (2003a). 'The Market Microstructure of Central Bank Intervention', *Journal of International Economics*, vol. 59, pp. 25–45.

_____ (2003b). 'When Do Central Bank Interventions Influence Intra-Daily and Longer-Term Exchange Rate Movements?' *Journal of International Money and Finance*, vol. 25, pp. 1051–71.

Dominguez, K.M. and J.A. Frenkel (1993) 'Does Foreign Exchange Intervention Matter? The Portfolio Balance Effect', *American Economic Review*, vol. 83, pp. 1356–69.

Dooley, M. and P. Isard (1982). 'A Portfolio Balance Rational Expectations Model of the Dollar Mark Exchange Rate', *Journal of International Economics*, vol. 12, pp. 257–76.

Dornbusch, R. (1976). ' Expectations and Exchange Rate Dynamics', *Journal of Political Economy*, vol. 84, pp. 1161–76.

_____ (1980). 'Exchange Rate Economics: Where Do We Stand?' *Brookings Papers on Economic Activity*, vol. 1, pp. 143–85.

_____ (1984). 'Monetary Policy under Exchange Rate Flexibility', in D. Bigman and T. Taya (eds) *Floating Exchange Rates and the State of World Trade Payments*, New York: Harper and Row, pp. 3–31.

_____ (1990). 'Real Exchange Rates and Macroeconomics: A Selective Survey', NBER Working Paper No. 2775, National Bureau of Economic Research.

Dornbusch, R. and F. Stanley (1980). 'Exchange Rates and the Current Account', *American Economic Review*, vol. 70, pp. 960–71.

Dornbusch, R. and S. Fischer (1980). 'Exchange Rates and the Current Account', *American Economic Review*, vol. 70, pp. 960–71.

Driskill, R.A. (1981). 'Exchange-Rate Dynamics: An Empirical Investigation', *Journal of Political Economy*, vol. 89, pp. 357–71.

Driskill, R.A. and S.M. Sheffrin (1981). 'On the Mark: Comment', *American Economic Review*, vol. 71, pp. 1068–74.

Dua, P. and D.J. Smyth (1995). 'Forecasting U.S. Home Sales Using BVAR Models and Survey Data on Households' Buying Attitudes for Homes', *Journal of Forecasting*, vol. 14, pp. 167–80.

Dua, P. and S.C. Ray (1995). 'A BVAR Model for the Connecticut Economy', *Journal of Forecasting*, vol. 14, pp. 217–27.

Dua, P. and S.M. Miller (1996). 'Forecasting Connecticut Home Sales in a BVAR Framework Using Coincident and Leading Indexes', *Journal of Real Estate Finance and Economics*, vol. 13, pp. 219–35.

Dua, P., S.M. Miller, and D.J. Smyth (1999). 'Using Leading Indicators to Forecast U.S. Home Sales in a Bayesian Vector Autoregressive Framework', *Journal of Real Estate Finance and Economics*, vol. 18, pp. 191–205.

Dua, P., N. Raje, and S. Sahoo (2003). 'Interest Rate Modelling and Forecasting in India', Reserve Bank of India Development Research Group, Study No. 24.

_____ (2008). 'Forecasting Interest Rates in India', *Margin—The Journal of Applied Economic Research*, vol. 2, pp. 1–41.

Dua, P. and P. Sen (2009). 'Capital Flow Volatility and Exchange Rates: The Case of India', in *Macroeconomic Management and Government Finances*, Asian Development Bank, New Delhi: Oxford University Press.

Edison, H. (1993). 'The Effectiveness of Central Bank Intervention: A Survey of the Literature after 1982', *Princeton Special Papers in International Economics*, No. 18, July.

Edison, H. and C. Reinhart (2001) 'Stopping Hot Money', *Journal of Development Economics*, vol. 66, pp. 533–53.

Edwards, S. (1999a). 'Capital Flows to Latin America', in Martin Feldstein (ed.) *International Capital Flows,* , Cambridge, Mass: National Bureau of Economic Research, pp. 5–42.

Edwards, S. (1999b). 'How Effective are Capital Controls?' *Journal of Economic Perspectives*, vol. 13, pp. 65–84.

_____ (2002). 'Capital Mobility, Capital Controls, and Globalisation in the 21st Century', *The Annals of the American Academy of Political and Social Science*, vol. 579, pp. 261–70.

Eichengreen, B. (1994). *International Monetary Arrangements for the 21st Century*, Washington DC: Brookings Institution.

Eichengreen, B., P. Masson, M. Savastano, and S. Sharma (1999). 'Transition Strategies and Nominal Anchors on the Road to Greater Exchange-rate Flexibility. Essays in International Finance', no. 213, Princeton University, Princeton, NJ.

Elliott, G., T.J. Rothenberg, and J.H. Stock (1996). 'Efficient Tests for an Autoregressive Unit Root', *Econometrica*, vol. 64, pp. 813–36.

European Central Bank (2007). 'The Impact of Short-Term Interest Rates on Bank Risk-taking', *Financial Stability Review*, December, pp. 163–7.

Evans, M.D.D. and R.K. Lyons (1999). 'Order Flow and Exchange Rate Dynamics', Cambridge Mass.: NBER, August.

_____ (2001). 'Why Order Flow Explains Exchange Rates', Cambridge Mass.: NBER, November.

_____ (2005). 'Meese-Rogoff Redux: Micro-Based Exchange Rate Forecasting', *American Economic Review*, vol. 95, pp. 405–14.

_____ (2007). 'How is Macro News Transmitted to Exchange Rates?', Cambridge Mass.: NBER, May 2007.

Fatum, R. and M.R. King (2005). 'Rules versus Discretion in Foreign Exchange Intervention: Evidence from Official Bank of Canada High-Frequency Data', Working Paper No. 04–24, Santa Cruz Center for International Economics.

Fischer, S. (1998). 'Capital Account Liberalization and the Role of the IMF', in *Should the IMF Pursue Capital-Account Convertibility?* Essays in International Finance, Princeton University, vol. 227, pp. 1–10.

_____ (2001). 'Distinguished Lecture on Economics in Government: Exchange Rate Regimes: Is the Bipolar View Correct?', *The Journal of Economic Perspectives*, vol. 15, no. 2, (Spring 2001), pp. 3–24.

Fleming, J.M. (1962). 'Domestic Financial Policies under Fixed and Floating Exchange Rates', IMF Staff Papers, vol. 9, pp. 369–80.

Flood, Robert P. and Andrew K. Rose (1995). 'Fixing Exchange Rates: A Virtual Quest for Fundamentals', *Journal of Monetary Economics*, vol. 36, pp. 3–37.

_____ (1995). 'Empirical Research on Nominal Exchange Rates', in G.M. Grossman and K. Rogoff (eds) *Handbook of International Economics*, vol. 3, Elsevier Science, pp. 1689–729.

Frankel, J.A. (1979). 'On the Mark: A Theory of Floating Exchange Rates Based on Real Interest Differentials', *American Economic Review*, vol. 69, pp. 610–22.

_____ (1982a). 'A Test of Perfect Substitutability in the Foreign Exchange Market', *Southern Economic Journal*, vol. 49, pp. 406–16.

_____ (1982b). 'In Search of the Exchange Risk Premium: A Six-Currency Test Assuming Mean-Variance Optimization', *Journal of International Money and Finance*, vol. 1, pp. 255–74.

_____ (1999a). 'Proposals Regarding Restrictions on Capital Flows', *The African Finance Journal*, vol. 1, part 1, pp. 92–104.

_____ (1999b). *No Single Currency Regime is Right for all Countries or at all Times, Essays in International Finances*, 215, Princeton, NJ: International Finance Section, Princeton University.

Frankel, J.A. and A.K. Rose (1995). 'An Empirical Characterization of Nominal Exchange Rates', in Gene Grossman and Kenneth Rogoff (eds), *The Handbook of International Economics*, vol. 3, Amsterdam: North-Holland Publishing Co.

Frenkel, J.A. (1976). 'A Monetary Approach to the Exchange Rate: Doctrinal Aspects and Empirical Evidence', *Scandinavian Journal of Economics*, vol. 78, Proceedings of a Conference on Flexible Exchange Rates and Stabilization Policy, pp. 200–24.

Frenkel, J.A. and H.A. Johnson (eds) (1978). 'The Economics of Exchange Rates: Selected Studies', Addison-Wesley.

Friedman, Milton (1953). 'Discussion of the Inflationary Gap', in Milton Friedman (ed.) *Essays in Positive Economics*, Chicago: University of Chicago Press, pp. 251–62

Galati, G. and C. Ho (2003). 'Macroeconomic News and the Euro/Dollar Exchange Rate', in *Economic Notes* by Banca Monte Dei Paschi Die Siena SpA, vol. 32, pp. 371–98.

Gandolfo, G. (2006). 'International Finance and Open Economy Macroeconomics', Springer.

Gandolfo, G. and P.C. Padoan (1990). 'The Italian Continuous Time Model: Theory and Empirical Results', *Economic Modelling*, Elsevier, vol. 7, pp. 91–132.

Gilbert, Irwin, and Vines (2000). 'Capital Account Convertibility and Risk management in India', Amadou N.R.Sy, IMF Working Paper No. WP/07/251 5, 'International Financial Architecture, Capital Account Convertibility and Poor Developing Countries'.

Gilmore, C.G. (2001). 'An Examination of Nonlinear Dependence in Exchange Rates using Recent Methods from Chaos Theory', *Global Finance Journal*, vol. 12, pp. 139–51.

Goldberg, Linda S. and Cedric Tille (2008). 'Vehicle Currency Use in International Trade', *Journal of International Economics*, vol. 76, pp. 177–92.

Goldberg, M.D. and R. Frydman (2001). 'Macroeconomic Fundamentals and the DM/Dollar Exchange Rate: Temporal Instability and the Monetary Model', *International Journal of Finance and Economics*, vol. 6, pp. 421–35.

Gourinchas, Pierre-Olivier and Olivier Jeanne (2002). 'On the Benefits of Capital Account Liberalization for Emerging Economics' (unpublished; Berkeley: University of California).

Government of India (1993). *High Level Committee on Balance of Payments*, Chairman: C. Rangarajan, Ministry of Finance.

_____ (2007). *Mid-Year Review 2007-8*, Government of India, New Delhi: Ministry of Finance.

Granger, C.W.J. (1986). 'Developments in the Study of Cointegrated Variables', *Oxford Bulletin of Economics and Statistics*, vol. 48, pp. 213–27.

_____ (1988). 'Some Recent Developments in the Concept of Causality', *Journal of Econometrics*, vol. 39, pp. 199–212.

Granger, C.W.J. and P. Newbold (1974). 'Spurious Regressions in Econometrics', *Journal of Econometrics*, vol. 2, pp. 111–20.

Greene, W. (1999). 'Marginal Effects in the Censored Regression Model'. *Economic Letters*, vol. 64, pp. 43–50.

Gruben, William C. and Darryl McLeod (2001). 'Capital Account Liberalization and disinflation in the 1990s', Center for Latin America Working Papers No. 0101, Federal Reserve Bank of Dallas.

Harberger, A.C. (1950). 'Currency Depreciation, Income and the Balance of Trade', *Journal of Political Economy*, vol. 58, pp. 47–60.

Harvey, D., S. Laybourne, and P. Newbold (1997). 'Testing the Equality of Prediction Mean Squared Errors', *International Journal of Forecasting*, vol. 13, pp. 281–91.

Henry, P.B. (2007). 'Capital Account Liberalization: Theory, Evidence, and Speculation', *Journal of Economic Literature*, vol. 45, pp. 887–935, December.

Hock, M.T.C. and R. Tan (1996). 'Forecasting Exchange Rates: An Econometric Illusion', Nanyang Business School, Nanyang Technological University, Singapore, Manuscript.

Hodrick, R.J. (1978). 'An Empirical Analysis of the Monetary Approach to the Determinants of the Exchange Rate', in Frenkel J.A. and H.A. Johnson (eds), *The Economics of Exchange Rates: Selected Studies*, pp. 97–116, Addison-Wesley.

Holden, K. and A. Broomhead, (1990). 'An Examination of Vector Autoregressive Forecasts for the U.K. Economy', *International Journal of Forecasting*, vol. 6, pp. 11–23.

Hooper, P. and J. Morton (1982). 'Fluctuations in the Dollar: A Model of Nominal and Real Exchange Rate Determination', *Journal of International Money and Finance*, vol. 1, pp. 39–56.

Hu, M.Y., G. Zhang, C.X. Jiang and B.E. Patuwo (1999). 'A Cross-Validation Analysis of Neural Network Out-of-Sample Performance in Exchange Rate Forecasting', *Decision Sciences*, vol. 30, pp. 197–216.

IMF (2005). *Report on the Evaluation of the IMF's Approach to Capital Account Liberalization*, Washington DC: IMF.

_____ (2008a). *Annual Report on Exchange Arrangements and Exchange Restrictions*, Washington DC: IMF.

_____ (2008b). *Global Financial Stability Report: Containing Systemic Risks and Restoring Financial Soundness*, Washington DC: IMF.

_____ (2008c). *World Economic Outlook Update: Rapidly Weakening Prospects Call for New Policy Stimulus, Data and Statistics*, Washington DC: IMF.

_____ (2008d). *World Economic Outlook: Financial Stress, Downturns and Recoveries*, Washington DC: IMF.

_____ (2010). *Annual Report on Exchange Arrangements and Exchange Restrictions 2010*, IMF.

Isard, P. (1980). 'Lessons from an Empirical Model of Exchange Rates', IMF Staff Papers, vol. 34, pp. 1–28.

Jacobson, T., J. Lyhagen, R. Larsson, and M. Nessén (2002). 'Inflation, Exchange Rates and PPP in a Multivariate Panel Cointegration Model', Sveriges Riksbank Working Paper Series No. 145.

Jalan, Bimal (1999). 'International Financial Architecture: Developing County's Perspective', RBI Bulletin.

_____ (2003). 'Exchange Rate Management an Emerging Consensus'. Address made at 14th National Assembly of the Forex Association of India on 14 August 2003.

Johansen, S. and K. Juselius (1990). 'Maximum Likelihood Estimation and Inference on Cointegration with Applications to the Demand for Money' *Oxford Bulletin of Economics and Statistics*, vol. 52, pp. 169–209.

_____ (1992). 'Testing Structural Hypothesis in a Multivariate Cointegration Analysis of PPP and the UIP for UK', *Journal of Econometrics*, vol. 53, pp. 211–44.

Johnson, D.R. (1990). 'Co-Integration, Error and Purchasing Power Parity between Canada and the United States', *Canadian Journal of Economics/Revue Canadienne d'Economique*, vol. 23, pp. 839–55.

Johnston, R.B., S.M. Darbar, and C. Echeverria (1999). 'Sequencing Capital Account Liberalization—Lessons from the Experiences in Chile, Indonesia, Korea, and Thailand', IMF Working Paper No. 97/157.

Kaminsky, G.L. and C.M. Reinhart (1999). 'The Twin Crises: The Causes of Banking and Balance of Payments Problems', *American Economic Review*, vol. 89, no. 3, pp. 473–500.

Kaplan, E. and D. Rodrik (2002). 'Did the Malaysian Capital Controls Work?', Working Paper No. 8142, NBER.

Khundrakpam, J.K. (2007). 'Economic Reforms and Exchange Rate Pass-Through to Domestic Prices in India', BIS Working Paper No. 225, Basle.

Kim, B.J.C. and S. Mo (1995). 'Cointegration and the Long-run Forecast of Exchange Rates', *Economics Letters*, vol. 48, pp. 353–9.

Kim, S. (1999). 'Do Monetary Policy Shocks Matter in the G-7 Countries? Using Common Identifying Assumptions about Monetary Policy Across Countries', *Journal of International Economics*, no. 48, pp. 387–412.

Kleijn, R. and H.K. van Dijk (2001). 'A Bayesian Analysis of the PPP Puzzle using an Unobserved Components Model', Econometric Institute, Report No. EI 2001–35.

Kletzer, K., and R. Kohli (2001). 'Exchange Rate Dynamics with Financial Repression: A Test of Exchange Rate Models for India', ICRIER Working Paper No. 52.

Kohli, R. (2000a). 'Aspects of Exchange Rate Behaviour and Management in India: 1993–98', *Economic and Political Weekly*, vol. 35, pp. 365–71.

_____ (2000b). 'Real Exchange Rate Stabilisation and Managed Floating: Exchange Rate Policy in India, 1993–99', ICRIER Working Paper No. 59, October, ICRIER, New Delhi.

_____ (2001). 'Real Exchange Rate Stabilisation and Managed Floating: Exchange Rate Policy in India', 1993–99, ICRIER Working Paper No. 59, October.

Kong, Q. (2000). 'Predictable Movements in Yen/DM Exchange Rates', IMF Working Paper No. WP/00/143.

Krugman, P. (1998). 'What Happened to Asia?', *mimeo*, MIT.

Kwiatkowski, D., C.B. Peter, P.S. Phillips, and Y. Shin (1992). 'Testing the Null Hypothesis of Stationarity against the Alternative of a Unit Root', *Journal of Econometrics*, vol. 54, pp. 159–78.

Lam, L., L. Fung, and I.W. Yu (2008). 'Comparing Forecast Performance of Exchange Rate Models', Working Paper No. 0808, Hong Kong Monetary Authority.

Larsen, C. and L. Lam (1992). 'Chaos and the Foreign Exchange Market', in Lam, L. and V. Naroditsky (eds). *Modeling Complex Phenomena*, New York: Springer.

Lerner, A.P. (1936). 'The Symmetry Between Export and Import Taxes', *Economica*, New Series, vol. 3, no. 11, pp. 306–13.

Leve-Yeyati, E. and F. Sturzenegger (2000). 'Classifying Exchange Rate Regimes: Deeds vs. Words', *European Economic Review*, vol. 49, pp. 1603–35.

Lewis K.K. (1988). 'Testing the Portfolio Balance Model: A Multi-lateral Approach', *Journal of International Economics*, vol. 24, pp. 109–27.

Lisi, F. and R.A. Schiavo (1999). 'A Comparison between Neural Networks and Chaotic Models for Exchange Rate Prediction', *Computational Statistics & Data Analysis*, vol. 30, pp. 87–102.

Litterman, R.B. (1981). 'A Bayesian Procedure for Forecasting with Vector Autoregressions', Federal Reserve Bank of Minneapolis, Working Paper.

_____ (1982). 'Forecasting and Policy Analysis with Bayesian Vector Auto-regression' Models', *Quarterly Review*, Federal Reserve Bank of Minneapolis, vol. 8, pp. 30–41.

_____ (1986). 'Forecasting with Bayesian Vector Autoregressions—Five Years Experience', *Journal of Business and Economic Statistics*, vol. 4, pp. 25–38.

Lothian, J.R. and C.H. McCarthy (2001). 'Real Exchange-Rate Behaviour under Fixed and Floating Exchange Rate Regimes', *Manchester School*, vol. 70, pp. 229–45.

Love, R. and R. Payne (2003). 'Macroeconomic News, Order Flows and Exchange Rates', *Journal of Financial and Quantitative Analysis*, vol. 43, pp. 467–88.

Luo, J. (2001). 'Market Conditions, Order Flow and Exchange Rate Determination', Financial Market Group, Department of Accounting and Finance, London School of Economics, Second Draft, 29 December 2001.

Lyons, R.K. (1995). Tests of Microstructural Hypotheses in the Foreign Exchange Market', *Journal of Financial Economics*, vol. 39, pp. 321–51.

_____ (2001). *The Microstructure Approach to Exchange Rate*, Cambridge MA: MIT Press.

MacDonald, R. and M.P. Taylor (1991) 'Exchange Rates, Policy Convergence, and the European Monetary System', *Review of Economics and Statistics*, vol. 73, pp. 553–8.

_____ (1993). 'The Monetary Approach to the Exchange Rate: Rational Expectations, Long-run Equilibrium and Forecasting', IMF Working Paper No. 40, WP/92/34, pp. 89–107.

_____ (1994). 'The Monetary Model of the Exchange Rate: Long Run Relationships, Short Run Dynamics and How to Beat a Random Walk', *Journal of International Money and Finance*, vol. 13, pp. 276–90.

McKinnon, R.I. (1999). 'Euroland and Asia in a Dollar-Based International Monetary System: Mundell Revisited'.

Magud, N. and C.M. Reinhart (2004). 'Capital Controls: An Evaluation' presented in NBER's International Capital Flows Conference, Santa Barbara, California, 16–18 December 2004.

Mark, N.C. (1995). 'Exchange Rate and Fundamentals: Evidence of Long Horizon Predictability', *American Economic Review*, vol. 85, pp. 201–18.

Mark, N.C. and D. Sul (2001). 'Nominal Exchange Rates and Monetary Fundamentals: Evidence from a Small Post Bretton Woods Panel', *Journal of International Economics*, vol. 53, pp. 29–52.

Marsh, I.W. and C. O'Rourke (2005). 'Customer Order Flow and Exchange Rate Movements: Is there Really Information Content?' Cass Business School, London, Manuscript.

Marshall, A. (1923). *Money, Credit and Commerce*, London: Macmillan & Co.

Martens, M. (2001). 'Forecasting Daily Exchange Rate Volatility using Intraday Returns', *Journal of International Money and Finance*, vol. 20, pp. 1–23.

Medeiros, O.R. (2005). 'Order Flow and Exchange Rate Dynamics in Brazil', Universidade de Brasília, Brazil (manuscript).

Meese, R.A. and A.K. Rose (1991). 'An Empirical Assessment of Non-Linearities in Models of Exchange Rate Determination', *Review of Economic Studies*, vol. 58, Special Issue: The Econometrics of Financial Markets vol. 58, pp. 603–19.

Meese, R. and K. Rogoff (1983). 'Empirical Exchange Rate Models of the Seventies: Do they Fit Out of Sample?' *Journal of International Economics*, vol. 14, pp. 3–24.

Meese, Richard A. (1990). 'Currency Fluctuations in the Post-Bretton Woods Era.' *Journal of Economic Perspectives*, vol. 4, pp. 117–34.

Menkhoff, L. and M. Schmeling (2006). 'Local Information in Foreign Exchange Markets', Discussion Paper No. 331.

Mihaljek, D. and M. Klau (2008). 'Exchange Rate Pass-through in Emerging Market Economies: What has Changes and Why?', BIS Working Papers No. 35, pp. 103–30.

Mizuno T., M. Takayasu and H. Takayasu (2004). 'Modelling a Foreign Exchange Rate Using Moving Average of Yen-Dollar Market Data', Manuscript, Available at http://arxiv.org/ftp/physics/papers/0508/0508162.pdf

Mohan R. (2005). 'Some Apparent Puzzles for Contemporary Monetary Policy', Paper presented at the Conference on China's and India's Changing Economic Structures: Domestic and Regional Implications, Beijing, China, RBI Bulletin, December.

_____ (2006). 'Monetary Policy and Exchange Rate Frameworks: The Indian Experience', Paper presented at the Second High Level Seminar on Asian Financial Integration organized by IMF and Monetary Authority of Singapore, in Singapore, on 25 May 2006, RBI Bulletin.

_____ (2007). 'Capital Account Liberalization and Conduct of Monetary Policy: The Indian Experience', Paper presented at an International Monetary Seminar organized by Banque de France on Globalisation, Inflation, and Financial Markets in Paris on 14 June.

_____ (2007). 'Monetary Management in Emerging Market Economies: Concerns and Dilemmas', Comments made at Policy Panel at the NBER Conference on International Dimensions of Monetary Policy at S'Agaro, Catalino, Spain, on 12 June 2007.

_____ (2008a). 'Financial Globalisation and Emerging Markets Capital Flows', BIS Working Paper No. 44, December, available at www.bis.org/publ/bppdf/bispap44.html

_____ (2008b). 'The Growth Record of the Indian Economy, 1950–2008: A Story of Sustained Savings and Investment', Keynote Address at the Conference 'Growth and Macroeconomic Issues and Challenges in India' organized by the Institute of Economic Growth, New Delhi on 14 February 2008.

Mohan R. (2009). 'Global Financial Crisis: Causes, Impact, Policy Responses and Lessons', Reserve Bank of India Bulletin, May.

Molodtsova, T. and D.H. Papell (2007). 'Out-of-Sample Exchange Rate Predictability with Taylor Rule Fundamentals', University of Houston, Manuscript, Available at http://www.uh.edu/~dpapell/Taylor%20Rule%20Fundamentals.pdf

Mundell, R. (1961). 'A Theory of Optimum Currency Areas', American Economic Review, vol. 51, pp. 657–65.

_____ (1962). 'The Appropriate Use of Monetary and Fiscal Policy for Internal and External Stability', IMF Staff Papers, vol. 9, pp. 70–9.

_____ (1963). 'Capital Mobility and Stabilisation Policy under Fixed and Flexible Exchange Rates', Canadian Journal of Economics and Political Science, vol. 29, pp. 475–85.

Mussa, M. (1976). 'The Exchange Rate, The Balance of Payments and Monetary and Fiscal Policy Under a Regime of Controlled Floating', Scandinavian Journal of Economics, vol. 78, pp. 229–48.

_____ (1979). 'Empirical Regularities in the Behaviour of Exchange Rates and Theories of the Forward Exchange Market', Carnegie-Rochester Conference Series on Public Policy, vol. 11, pp. 9–57.

Neely, C.J. (1999). 'An Introduction to Capital Control', Federal Reserve Bank of St. Louis Review, November-December.

_____ (2000). 'The Practice of Central Bank Intervention: Looking under the Hood', Central Banking, vol. 11, pp. 24–37.

_____ (2005). 'An Analysis of Recent Studies of the Effect of Foreign Exchange Intervention', Federal Reserve Bank of St. Louis Review, vol. 87, pp. 685–717.

Neely, C.J. and L. Sarno (2002). 'How Well Do Monetary Fundamentals Forecast Exchange Rates?', Federal Reserve Bank of St. Louis Review, vol. 84, pp. 51–74.

Newey, W. and K. West (1987). 'A Simple Positive Semi-Definite, Heteroskedasticity and Autocorrelation Consistent Covariance Matrix', Econometrica, vol. 55, pp. 703–8.

Nijathaworn, B. (2009). 'The Current Financial Crisis, Lessons Learned, and Future Implications', Keynote address at the 11th SEACEN Conference of Directors of Supervision of Asia-Pacific Economies, Bangkok of the Bank of Thailand on 29 July.

Nurkse, R. (1944). International Currency Experience: Lessons of the Interwar Period, Geneva: League of Nations.

Nwafor, F. C. (2006). 'The Naira-Dollar Exchange Rate Determination: A Monetary Perspective', International Research Journal of Finance and Economics, vol. 5, pp. 130–5.

Obstfeld, M. and A.M. Taylor (2004). Global Capital Markets: Integration, Crisis and Growth, Cambridge: Cambridge University Press.

Panda, C. and V. Narsimhan (2007). 'Forecasting Exchange Rate Better with Artificial Neural Network', Journal of Policy Modeling, vol. 29, pp. 227–36.

Pattanaik, S. and S. Sahoo (2001). 'The Effectiveness of Intervention in India: An Empirical Assessment' RBI Occasional Paper, vol. 22, pp. 21–52.

Payne, R. and P. Vitale (2003). 'A Transaction Level study of the Effects of Central Bank Intervention on Exchange Rates', Journal of International Economics, vol. 61, pp. 331–52.

Plasmans, J., W. Verkooijen, and H. Daniels (1998). 'Estimating Structural Exchange Rate Models by Artificial Neural Networks', Applied Financial Economics, vol. 8, pp. 541–51.

Prasad, E.S. and G.R. Rajan (2005). 'Controlled Capital Account Liberalisation—A Proposal', IMF Policy Discussion Paper, No. 05/7.

Prasad, E.S., G.R. Rajan, and A. Subramanian (2007). 'Foreign Capital and Economic Growth', Brookings Papers on Economic Activity, vol. 2007, pp. 153–230.

Prasad, E.S., K. Rogoff, S.J. Wei, and M.A. Kose (2003). 'Effects of Financial Globalization on Developing Countries: Some Empirical Evidence', IMF Occasional Paper No. 220, IMF, Washington.

Putnam, B.H. and J.R. Woodbury (1980). 'Exchange Rate Stability and Monetary Policy', *Review of Business and Economic Research*, vol. 15, pp. 1–10.

Quirk, Peter and Owen Evans (1995). 'Capital Account Convertibility: Review of Experience and Implications for IMF Policies', IMF Occasional Paper No. 131, IMF, Washington.

Rangarajan, C. (1991). *Report of the High Level Committee on Balance of Payments*, New Delhi: Government of India.

Reserve Bank of India [RBI] (1997). *Report of the Committee on Capital Account Convertibility* (Chairman: S.S. Tarapore), New Delhi: RBI.

_____ (2004). *Report of the Working Group on Instruments of Sterilisation* (Chairman: Smt. Usha Thorat), New Delhi: RBI.

_____ (2004). *Report on Currency and Finance, 2003–4*, New Delhi: RBI.

_____ (2006). *Report of the Committee on Fuller Capital Account Convertibility* (Chairman: S.S. Tarapore), New Delhi: RBI.

_____ (2007). *Handbook of Statistics on the Indian Economy, 2006–7*, New Delhi: RBI.

_____ (2007). *Annual Report for 2006–7*, New Delhi: RBI.

_____ (2008). *Annual Policy Statement for the Year 2008–9*, New Delhi: RBI.

_____ (2009). *Report on Currency and Finance, 2008–9*, New Delhi: RBI.

Reddy, Y.V. (2000a). 'Issues in Managing Capital Account Liberalisation', Speech delivered at Commonwealth Secretariat—World Bank Conference on Developing Countries and Global Financial Architecture at London on 23 June.

_____ (2000b). 'Operationalising Capital Account Liberalisation: Indian Experience', Presentation at the Seminar on Capital Account Liberalization: The Developing Country Perspective, at Overseas Development Institute, London, on 21 June.

Reddy, Y.V. (2005). 'Overcoming Challenges in a Globalising Economy: Managing India's External Sector', Lecture delivered at the Indian Programme of The Foreign Policy Centre, London on 23 June.

_____ (2006). Keynote address delivered by Dr Reddy, Governor, Reserve Bank of India at the Regional Seminar on Central Bank Communications sponsored by the International Monetary Fund, held in Mumbai on 23 January.

_____ (2007). 'Monetary Policy Developments in India—an Overview', address made at the Sveriges Riksbank, Stockholm, Sweden on 7 September.

_____ (2008a). 'Financial Globalisation, Growth and Stability: An Indian Perspective', Lecture delivered at the International Symposium of the Banque de France on Globalisation, Inflation, and Monetary Policy, held in Paris on 7 March.

_____ (2008b). 'Management of the Capital Account in India: Some Perspectives', Inaugural address delivered at the Annual Conference of the Indian Econometric Society, Hyderabad, on 3 January.

_____ (2009). 'India's Financial Sector in Current Times', S. Guhan Memorial Lecture on 22 October.

Refenes, A.N., M. Azema-Barac, L. Chen, and S.A. Karoussos (1993). 'Currency Exchange Rate Prediction and Neural Network Design Strategies', *Neural Computing and Applications*, vol. 1, pp. 46–58.

Reinhart, Carmen M. and S. Kenneth Rogoff (2003). 'The Modern History of Exchange Rate Arrangements: A Reinterpretation'. Version: 3 March. www. puaf.umd.edu/faculty/papers/reinhart/papers.htm

Reitz, S. (2002). 'Central Bank Intervention and Exchange Rate Expectations— Evidence from the Daily DM/US-Dollar Exchange Rate', Discussion paper No. 17/02, Economic Research Centre of the Deutsche Bundesbank.

Rodrik, Dani (1998). 'Who Needs Capital Account Convertibility?' Mimeo, Harvard University.

Rogoff, K. (1984). 'On the Effects of Sterilized Intervention: An Analysis of Weekly Data', *Journal of Monetary Economics*, vol. 14, pp. 133–50.

Rogoff, K.S., A.M. Husain, A. Mody, R. Brooks, and N. Oomes (2003). 'Evolution and Performance of Exchange Rate Regimes', IMF Working Paper No. WP/03/243.

Sager, M. and M.P. Taylor (2006). 'Commercially Available Order Flow Data and Exchange Rate Movements: Caveat Emptor', University of Warwick, Manuscript.

Sarno, L. (2003). 'Non-Linear Exchange Rate Models: A Selective Overview', IMF Working Paper No. WP/03/111.

Sarno, L. and M. Taylor (2001). 'Official Intervention in the Foreign Exchange Market: Is it Effective and, if so, How Does it Work?', *Journal of Economic Literature*, vol. 39, pp. 839–68.

_____ (2002). 'The Economics of Exchange Rates', Cambridge: Cambridge University Press.

Scalia, A. (2006). 'Is Foreign Exchange Intervention Effective? Some Micro-Analytical Evidence from the Czech Republic', Bank of Italy, Monetary and Foreign Exchange Policy Department, No. 579, February.

Schmidt, R. (2006). 'The Behavioural Economics of Foreign Exchange Markets', *European University Studies*, Series V, Economics and Management, Peter Lang.

Sharma, Anil Kumar and Anujit Mitra (2006). 'What Drives Forward Premia in Indian Forex Market', RBI Occasional Papers, vol. 27, pp. 119–39.

Sims, C.A. (1980). 'Macroeconomics and Reality', *Econometrica*, vol. 48, pp. 1–48.

Sims, C.A., J. Stock, and M.W. Watson (1990). 'Inference in Linear Time Series Models with Some Unit Roots', *Econometrica*, vol. 58, pp. 113–44.

Smith, P.N. and M.R. Wickens (1986). 'An Empirical Investigation into the Causes of Failure of the Monetary Model of the Exchange Rate', *Journal of Applied Econometrics*, vol. 1, pp. 143–62.

_____ (1990). 'Assessing the Effects of Monetary Shocks on Exchange Rate Variability with a Stylised Econometric Model of the UK', in A.S. Courakis and

N.P. Taylor (eds) *Private Behaviour and Government Policy in Interdependent Economies*, USA: Oxford University Press, pp. 53–72.

Sodhani Committee: 14 Member Expert Group on Foreign Exchange formed in November 1994.

Spencer, D.E. (1993). 'Developing a Bayesian Vector Autoregression Forecasting Model', *International Journal of Forecasting*, vol. 9, pp. 407–21.

Stiglitz, J. (1998). 'The East Asian Crisis and Its Implications for India', Commemorative Lecture for the Golden Jubilee Year Celebration of Industrial Finance Corporation of India Ltd., New Delhi, India, 19 May.

Strauss-Kahn, D. (2009). 'Take-Off or Holding Pattern? Prospects for the Global Economy', An Address to the Confederation of British Industry Annual Conference by Dominique Strauss-Kahn, Managing Director, International Monetary Fund, London, 23 November 2009.

Strozzi, F., J. Zaldivar, and J.P. Zbilut (2002). 'Application of Nonlinear Time Series Analysis Techniques to High-frequency Currency Exchange Data', *Physica A*, vol. 312, pp. 520–38.

Subbarao, D. (2008) *Mitigating Spillovers and Contagion Lessons from the Global Financial Crisis*, New Delhi: RBI.

_____ (2009a). 'The Global Financial Turmoil and Challenges for the Indian Economy', *Reserve Bank of India Bulletin*, January, New Delhi: RBI.

_____ (2009b) 'Impact of the Global Financial Crisis on India: Collateral Damage and Response', *Reserve Bank of India Bulletin*, March, New Delhi: RBI.

Subramanian, Arvind (2011). 'Eclipse: Living in the Shadow of China's Economic Dominance, Peterson Institute for International Economics, Washington DC, September 2011.

Subramanian, Arvind and John Willamson (2009). 'The World Crisis: Reforming the International Financial System', http://www.iie.com/publications/papers/subramanian-williamson0309.pdf

Summers, Lawrence H. (2000). 'International Financial Crises: Causes, Prevention, and Cures', *American Economic Review*, Papers and Proceedings, vol. 90, May, pp. 1–16.

Tarapore, S.S. (1997). 'The 1997 Report of the Committee on Capital Account Convertibility'.

_____ (2006). The 2006 Reports on Capital Account Convertibility.

Taylor, M.P. (1995). 'The Economics of Exchange Rates', *Journal of Economic Literature*, vol. 33, pp. 13–47.

Theil, H. (1966). *Applied Economic Forecasting*, Amsterdam: North Holland Publishing Company.

_____ (1971). *Principles of Econometrics*, New York: John Wiley and Sons, and Amsterdam: North Holland Publishing Company.

Todd, R.M. (1984). 'Improving Economic Forecasting with Bayesian Vector Autoregression', *Quarterly Review*, Federal Reserve Bank of Minneapolis, Fall, pp. 18–29.

Trapletti, A., A. Geyer, and F. Leisch (2002). 'Forecasting Exchange Rates using Cointegration Models and Intra-day Data', *Journal of Forecasting*, vol. 21, pp. 151–66.

Triffin, Robert (1961). 'After the Gold Exchange Standard?' in Herbert G. Grubel (ed.) *World Monetary Reform: Plans and Issues*, Stanford and London: Stanford University Press and Oxford University Press, pp. 422–39.

Verkooijen, W. (1996). 'A Neural Network Approach to Long-Run Exchange Rate Prediction', *Computational Economics*, vol. 9, pp. 51–65.

Vitek, F. (2005). 'The Exchange Rate Forecasting Puzzle', Manuscript, University of British Columbia.

Wang, K.L., C. Fawson, C.B. Barrett, and J.B. McDonald (2001). 'A Flexible Parametric GARCH Model with an Application to Exchange Rates', *Journal of Applied Econometrics*, vol. 16, pp. 521–36.

World Bank (2009). *A Development Emergency*, Global Monitoring Report, Washington, DC: The International Bank for Reconstruction and Development/ The World Bank.

World Economic Outlook (2010). *Rebalancing Growth*, April.

Wu, T. (2006). 'Order Flow in the South: Anatomy of the Brazilian FX Market', Manuscript, University of California.

Yoshitomi, M. and S. Shirai (2000). 'Policy Recommendations for Preventing Another Capital Account Crisis', ADBI and Asian Policy Forum.

Zhang, G. (2003). 'Time Series Forecasting Using a Hybrid ARIMA and Neural Network Model', *Neurocomputing*, vol. 50, pp. 159–75.

Zhang, G. and M.Y. Hu (1998). 'Neural Network Forecasting of the British Pound/ US Dollar Exchange Rate', Omega, *International Journal of Management Science*, vol. 26, no. 4, pp. 495–506.

Zhang, G.P. and V.L. Berardi (2001). 'Time Series Forecasting with Neural Network Ensembles: an Application for Exchange Rate Prediction', *Journal of Operational Research Society*, vol. 52, pp. 652–64.

Zita, S. and R. Gupta (2007). 'Modelling and Forecasting the Metical-Rand Exchange Rate', University of Pretoria Working Paper No. 2007-2.

Zorzi, M., E. Hahn, and M. Sánchez (2007). 'Exchange Rate Pass-Through in Emerging Markets', ECB Working Paper No. 739.

Index